real life

pre-inter...

What teenagers
...ay p. 8

English in real time
...10

...o you have a healthy
...festyle? p. 38

...ow to write good
...nvitations, letters,
messages

...elp with exams

Unique skills support
on the back cover

STUDENTS' BOOK

Make your mark!

SARAH CUNNINGHAM   PETER MOOR

PEARSON
Longman

1 your life

Grammar	Present simple and continuous
	Questions and question words
Vocabulary	Family and social life
Phrases	Meeting and greeting
	Getting to know people

Reading & Listening

1 Complete the information about yourself. Write 'not sure' for information you don't know.

- Your date of birth · *1 May 1992*
- The place you were born · _____
- The time you were born · _____

2 In groups, compare information. Was anyone born on the same date or in the same place as you?

I was born in the same month/place as Tomas.

3 **a** Look at the photos and read the captions. Can you guess what the title, 'time twins', means?

b Now read the text to check your answer.

1.3

Time twins

Do you ever wonder who was born on the same day as you? Many people use the internet to find their time twins — people who were born on the same day. They often find incredible similarities between their lives, their interests and even their personalities!

In this programme, we meet four seventeen-year-olds — Steven, Josh, Amy and Mariam. They were all born on the same morning in the same London hospital! We find out if they really are similar.

JOSH The next time twin is Josh, born just three minutes later. His parents are both teachers but they are divorced now. Josh normally lives with his mother and his older sister in Wales but at the moment his mother is working abroad and Josh is staying with his father for a few weeks. Josh is still at school. He is doing his A-levels and hopes to study Politics at university. So what does Josh do in his free time? 'I'm really lazy,' he says. 'I hate sport and I don't really have any hobbies. I play computer games a lot and I listen to music. Oh, and I'm learning to play the drums but I'm not very good!'

Josh:
born 27 September
07.18 a.m.

STEVEN The first time twin, Steven, is an only child. He still lives near the Royal London Hospital with his parents, Don, an electrician, and Juliana, a nurse. He is doing a Business Studies course at his local college and he also works in a mobile phone shop. Steven doesn't want to go to university. 'It's too expensive,' he explains. And what about his free time? 'I'm a fitness freak*. I never smoke and I don't drink alcohol or coffee. And I go running every morning before college. At the moment, I'm training for the London Marathon.'

Steven:
born 27 September
07.15 a.m.

Amy:
born 27 September
08.37 a.m.

Mariam:
born 27 September
09.59 a.m.

* A person who is crazy about sport

4 Read the text again. Find two sentences below about Steven (S) and three about Josh (J).

1. ☑ is crazy about fitness.
2. ☐ isn't very energetic.
3. ☐ doesn't go to school or college.
4. ☐ plays a musical instrument.
5. ☐ looks after children in a nursery.
6. ☐ goes to a private school.
7. ☐ doesn't have any brothers or sisters.
8. ☐ has parents who are divorced.
9. ☐ sometimes helps his/her father.
10. ☐ wants to become a pharmacist.

5 What other information do you learn about Steven and Josh in the text?

6 (1.2) Listen to the interviews. Mark the sentences in exercise 4 about Amy (A) and Mariam (M).

7 Do you think these time twins are similar? Why? Why not?

I think Steven and Josh are very different because ...

Grammar Focus

Present simple and present continuous

8 Read the sentences 1–4. Which verbs in bold are in the present simple and which are in the present continuous?

1. ☐ I really **love** horror films.
2. ☐ Right now I**'m talking** to Amy.
3. ☐ I**'m working** in a nursery at the moment, just part-time.
4. ☐ I **help** my father in his shop sometimes.

9 **a** Read *Grammar2know* and match the rules a–d with the sentences 1–4 in exercise 8.

b Read about Steven and Josh again and <u>underline</u> more examples of the present simple and present continuous. Find four more examples of rule d.

Grammar 2 know

Present simple

Use the present simple:

a to talk about regular activities in the present:
*I usually **meet** my friends in the evening.*
*What **does** Josh **do** in his free time?*

b to talk about things that are generally true:
*Josh **lives** with his mother.*
*Steven **doesn't drink** coffee.*

Time expressions: *sometimes, often, usually, never, every day, every week, every morning, a lot*

Present continuous

Use the present continuous:

c to talk about actions at the moment of speaking:
*Now I**'m interviewing** Mariam.*

d to talk about actions in the present period but not at the moment of speaking:
*Mariam**'s studying** Maths and Science.*
*Amy **isn't studying** at the moment.*

Time expressions: *at the moment, now, today, this week, this year*

10 Put the verbs in brackets into the correct tense. Use the present simple or present continuous.

1. Josh *plays* (play) computer games nearly every day.
2. Mariam _____ (take) some important exams this week.
3. Steven's parents _____ (not have) any other children.
4. Amy _____ (not look after) her little niece today.
5. Josh's mother _____ (work) in the USA at the moment.
6. Steven _____ (go) to the gym three or four times a week.

11 Use the prompts to tell other students about yourself. Give more information if you can. Use the present simple or present continuous.

1. like horror films
   I don't like horror films, I like comedies.
2. walk to school
3. play a musical instrument
4. read a book at the moment
5. read the newspaper every day
6. study for exams this term
7. save to buy something special

12 WRITING Read about Steven and Josh again. Then write a description of yourself. Write about:
- where you live and who you live with
- your school and other courses
- your interests, free time, friends, etc.

MINI WORKBOOK exercises 1–4 pages 100–101

Vocabulary & Reading

Social life

1 Read the title and introduction to the quiz. Are you 'chilled' or 'hyper'? Do the quiz to find out.

2 Read the quiz key on page 124. Are the conclusions true or not?

3 (1.4) Use the verbs in *Words2know* to complete phrases 1–10 from the quiz. Then listen and check.

> ### Words 2 know
>
> go (x2)   go to   play   do (x2)
> stay   meet   make ✓   have
>
> 1 *make* plans   6 ___ computer games
> 2 ___ a party   7 ___ new people/your friends
> 3 ___ out   8 ___ the cinema/beach
> 4 ___ in   9 ___ nothing
> 5 ___ sport   10 ___ shopping/running

4 Read *Active Study*. Add more phrases to the list.

> **ACTIVE STUDY**
>
> ### Notice collocations
> There are many phrases with verbs like *go*, *have*, *make* and *do*. Notice and remember the correct verb in each phrase:
>
> **have a party** (NOT ~~make~~ a party)
> **make plans** (NOT ~~do~~ plans)
> **go out with friends** (NOT ~~get~~ out with friends)

5 In pairs, talk about what you usually do:
- in the evening   • at the weekend
- in the holidays

" *I normally watch DVDs in the evening. How about you?*
I usually … but I never …

MINI WORKBOOK exercise 7 page 101

(1.7) **Are you Chilled or Hyper?**

Are you the kind of person who never stops or do you take life easy? Do our quiz to find out.

1 It's Saturday morning. What do you think when you open your eyes in the morning?

a What arrangements have I got for today? I must get up and get ready.
b Saturday, great! I'll relax, then call my friends later.
c Good, I can go back to sleep.

2 You're on holiday by the sea! How do you spend your days?

a Do sport, meet new people, go shopping and, of course, go out every evening!
b Go to the beach, meet some nice people and visit some interesting places.
c Sleep until midday, then spend the day by the pool with music and a book.

3 It's your birthday… Happy birthday! What do you do?

a You decide to have a big party but then you worry about what to wear, who to invite, etc.
b You arrange to go out with a group of friends.
c You don't make too many plans – perhaps you'll meet some friends or go to the cinema.

4 It's winter, the weather's terrible and you can't go out. How do you feel?

a You hate doing nothing. You phone all your friends and complain.
b It's nice to stay in but after a while you get bored.
c You can watch DVDs and play computer games all day – what's the problem?

5 How do you feel at bedtime? Is it easy or difficult for you to sleep?

a It's difficult to sleep because you can't stop thinking about your day.
b You read or listen to music and you usually go to sleep easily.
c You aren't tired – you often stay up and watch a film or go on the internet.

Grammar Focus

Questions and question words

6 Look at Zoe's photo from *MyWorld*, a website for meeting friends. Answer the questions.

- Do you like the photo? Why? Why not?
- Do you use websites like *MyWorld*?

7 Read *Grammar2know*. Then complete the *MyWorld* questionnaire with these question words.

> Who (x2) Why What (x3)
> Which How What kind (x2)
> How many How much
> When Where

Question words

Use these words to form questions:

What, Where, When, Which, Who, Why, How, What kind, How much, How many:

What's your favourite CD?
What kind of music do you like?
How much money have you got?

Word order

What is your favourite dessert?
Who do you see at the weekend?
Why are you doing this questionnaire?
How much money have you got?

8 **a** (1.5) Zoe's friend is testing how many questions she can answer in two minutes. Listen and check your answers for exercise 7.

b (1.5) Which of Zoe's answers can you remember? Compare answers in pairs. Listen again and check.

9 (1.6) Close your book and listen to the questions. Write brief answers.

1 Milan

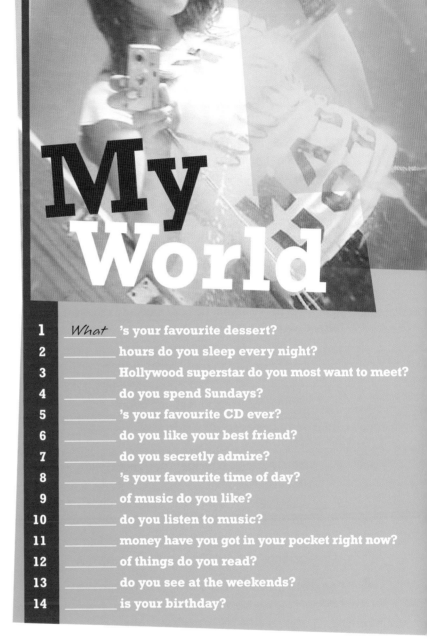

My World

1	*What* 's your favourite dessert?
2	_____ hours do you sleep every night?
3	_____ Hollywood superstar do you most want to meet?
4	_____ do you spend Sundays?
5	_____ 's your favourite CD ever?
6	_____ do you like your best friend?
7	_____ do you secretly admire?
8	_____ 's your favourite time of day?
9	_____ of music do you like?
10	_____ do you listen to music?
11	_____ money have you got in your pocket right now?
12	_____ of things do you read?
13	_____ do you see at the weekends?
14	_____ is your birthday?

10 **a** (1.6) Complete questions 1–7 with *is/are, have* or *do*. Listen again and practise your intonation.

1 Which city ∧ you come from originally? *(do)*
2 How many brothers and sisters you got?
3 What kind of books you like?
4 What you reading at the moment?
5 Which groups you like?
6 Which your favourite day of the week? Why you like it?
7 Which TV programmes you like best?

b Choose five questions above to ask your teacher.

11 In pairs, do the *MyWorld* questionnaire. Take turns to ask and answer as many questions as you can in two minutes.

MINI WORKBOOK exercises 5–6 page 101

your life

7

Reading & Vocabulary

1 a PREDICTING Answer the questions.

- What do you think the people in the photos are talking about?
- How are they feeling?

b Read the introduction to the internet survey. Who is organising the survey and why?

2 Read the survey and complete gaps 1–6 with the questions a–f below.

a Who do you talk to when you have a problem?

b What do you most like about your parents?

c What do you worry about most?

d How could your parents make your life better?

e What's the worst thing about being a teenager?

f What's the best thing about being a teenager? ✓

3 Read the survey again. Tick (✓) true and cross (✗) false. Give reasons for your answers.

1 ☐ Most teenagers think their parents are kind and have a good sense of humour.

2 ☐ Teenagers and parents think that the media is too negative about young people.

3 ☐ Most teenagers think their parents are too strict.

4 ☐ Nearly 30% of teenagers don't like their parents' clothes.

5 ☐ Many parents want their teenage children to do more housework.

6 ☐ Most teenagers say they can talk to their parents about really important problems.

4 Complete the definitions with a word from the text.

Words 2 know (1.8)

1 s _ _ _ _ _ _ : the help you give someone with their problems (paragraph 2)

2 s _ _ _ _ of h _ _ _ _ _ : the ability to laugh about things (paragraph 2)

3 to c _ _ _ _ _ _ _ : to say you are unhappy/angry about something (paragraph 3)

4 the m _ _ _ _ : TV, newspapers, etc. (paragraph 3)

5 exam p _ _ _ _ _ _ _ _ : the worries you have about exams (paragraph 3)

6 your a _ _ _ _ _ _ _ _ _ : how you look (paragraph 6)

5 Answer the questions in exercise 2 about you. Are your answers the same as the English teenagers'?

When I have a problem, I talk to my friends or sometimes my mother.

"TALKING Teenagers" (1.10)

The BBC is doing its biggest ever internet survey* about young people in Britain today to find out about their lives and their worries. They want to help parents
5 and teenagers to talk and understand each other better. Thousands of people are logging on to take part – so far more than 30,000 teenagers and 12,000 parents. This is what they say.

10 *What's the best thing about being a teenager?*
Most teenagers say, 'Going out and having more freedom'. 'Cool music and fashion' and 'the internet' are also popular answers.

2 _____?
15 Young people most like the love and support they get from their parents … and their sense of humour, too. But 40% say that they like their parents because they give them money!

3 _____?
20 Many young people complain about how the media shows teenagers and many parents agree: 'All teenagers have bad publicity … and they are not all bad!' said one parent. Young people also complain about exam pressures,
25 changing moods and boyfriend/girlfriend relationships.

4 _____?

About 20% of teenagers want their parents to give them more freedom. 'Often parents
30 treat you like a child and don't respect your opinions,' writes one. 'Why can't I go to places where my friends go, like nightclubs?' says another. And 29% of young people really hate their parents' clothes! On the other hand,
35 parents want their teenage children to listen to them more and to help more in the house.

5 _____?

One parent said, 'If our kids have a serious problem, they can always talk to us about
40 it.' But teenagers don't always agree. Most feel that they can talk to their parents about everyday things but 60% say they can't talk to their parents about serious personal problems with relationships, drugs and alcohol. They find
45 it easier to talk to friends about these things.

6 _____?

The two big worries for young people are exams and their appearance. In fact, 48% say that their appearance is their biggest worry.
50 Parents worry most about their children's schoolwork.

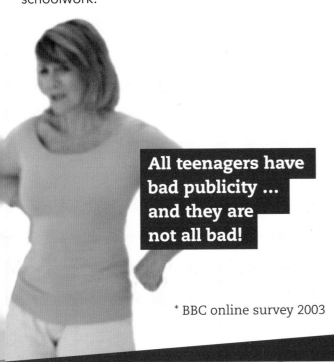

All teenagers have bad publicity ... and they are not all bad!

* BBC online survey 2003

Vocabulary & Speaking

Family and relationships

6 WORD RACE Work in pairs. In two minutes, write down as many family words as you can.

father, brother ...

7 Match the *Words2know* to definitions 1–10.
- Which words are for males and females?
- What are the male forms of the other words?

an older sister – an older brother

Words 2 know ⟨1.9⟩

an only child   a stepmother   an ex-wife   a cousin
a relative   a great-grandmother   an aunt   a niece
a daughter-in-law   a younger/older sister ✓

1 a sister who is younger/older than you
   a younger/older sister
2 your grandmother's mother
3 your mother or father's sister
4 the woman married to a person's son
5 the woman a person divorced
6 your sister or brother's daughter
7 your father's new wife – not your own mother
8 your mother's sister's daughter
9 a member of your family
10 a child with no brothers and sisters

8 Read the questions 1–7 and cross out the ones you can't or don't want to answer. Then swap books with a partner. Ask the questions that your partner did not cross out.

1 Are you an only child or have you got older or younger brothers and sisters?
2 Do you get on well with your brothers and sisters?
3 How many aunts, uncles and cousins have you got?
4 Are your great-grandparents still alive? And your grandparents? How old are they?
5 Do most of your relatives live near you? How often do you see them?
6 Which relations do you like best? Are there any people in your family who don't get on?
7 Is anyone in your family doing anything interesting at the moment? What?

9 WRITING Write a paragraph about yourself. Include answers to the questions in exercise 8.

I've got a younger sister and an older brother. I get on well with my younger sister but ...

MINI WORKBOOK exercise 8 page 101

your life

9

MEETING AND GREETING

1 Look at the photo and read about Zack. Answer the questions.

- Where is Zack from?
- Why is he coming to London?
- Who's meeting him at the airport?

2 (1.11) Listen to the conversation. Tick (✓) true and cross (✗) false.

1 ☐ Zack already knows Fran.
2 ☐ Zack already knows Rosie and Ted.
3 ☐ Fran is driving today.
4 ☐ There were no problems with the flight.
5 ☐ Fran's house is near the airport.

3 (1.11) Read the dialogue and complete the gaps with the correct *Phrases2know*. Then listen again and check.

Phrases

Meeting and greeting
How do you do?
Nice to meet you. ✓
Great to see you again! ✓
Thanks, it's great to be here! ✓
Let me introduce you.
Welcome to London!
This is my brother, Ted.
How was your journey?

---

4 (1.12) Listen to *Phrases2know* and practise the intonation.

5 Rosie introduces Zack to her older sister, Grace. Work in groups:

a Write their conversation using *Phrases2know*.

Rosie: *(calling)* Hi, Grace. Are you in?

Grace: Yeah, I'm here.

Rosie: This is Zack, Mum's friend Rebecca's son. Zack …

b Act out the dialogue.

ZACK is from California and is coming to London to study. He is staying with Fran, a friend of his mother's, and her daughters, Rosie and Grace. Fran, Rosie and Fran's brother, Ted, are meeting Zack at Heathrow Airport. It's Sunday morning.

F: Zack … hi!

Z: Hi, Fran!

F: ¹ *Great to see you again!* ² _____

Z: ³ *Thanks, it's great to be here,* … finally!

F: ⁴ _____ . This is my younger daughter, Rosie. She's twelve.

Z: Hi, Rosie.

R: Hi.

F: And, ⁵ _____ . He's driving us today because my car's at the garage.

Z: ⁶ *Nice to meet you,* sir.

T: ⁷ _____ ? Welcome to England!

F: So, how are you? ⁸ _____ ?

Z: Well, the flight was forty-five minutes late but after that, it was fine. The in-flight movies were really cool but there wasn't much food, so I'm kind of hungry!

F: Oh, you poor thing! Well, it's a long drive home so why don't we get some breakfast first? Look, there's a place over there …

FILLING IN A FORM

Zack is doing a summer course for overseas students at a London university. A receptionist asks him questions to complete his enrolment form.

6 (1.13) Use *Phrases2know* to complete Zack's enrolment form. Then listen and check.

Phrases 2 know

Forms

full name	email address
place of birth	UK address
date of birth	mobile number
home address	postcode ✓
emergency contact details ✓	nationality ✓
passport number ✓	

University Enrolment

Name of course European History
Dates of course 2 July – 9 September

1	_____	Zachery James Garber
2	_____	21.10.92
3	_____	Santa Barbara, CA, USA
4	*nationality*	American
	passport number	....
5	_____	2356 Washington Drive, Santa Barbara, CA, USA
6	_____	25 Manorgate Rd, London.
7	*postcode*	NW10 2PQ
8	_____	07654 8878960
9	_____	zackjg192@hotmail.com
10	*emergency contact details:*	

NAME: Mrs Frances Connor

ADDRESS: 25 Manorgate Rd, London NW10 2PQ

TELEPHONE: 0208 654 9768

7 Work in pairs. Look at the enrolment form on page 124.

a Write questions for 1–11.
What's the name of your course?

b Choose a course and the date. Then ask and answer the questions. Complete the form with your partner's details.

There is a party at Zack's university for new students to get to know each other. Zack is chatting to Monika, a Polish girl.

GETTING TO KNOW PEOPLE

8 Look at the photo and answer the questions.
- Where is Zack and who is he talking to?
- Do you think he's enjoying himself? Why? Why not?

9 (1.14) Read *Phrases2know*. Which three questions sound too formal for a party? Listen and check.

Phrases 2 know

Getting to know people
What's your nationality? ✓ *Where are you from?*
Which part of (Poland) are you from?
What's your full name?
Which course are you doing?
How about you?
Where are you staying?
Are you enjoying London?
What's your date of birth?
Do you like London/this music?

10 In pairs, take turns to act out the dialogue below. Follow the prompts and use the *Phrases2know* in this lesson.

- You are new students at the same party as Zack and Monika. One of you is Zack.
- Introduce yourself. Then find out as much as you can about each other.
- You can invent information.

2 the greats

Grammar	Past simple and past continuous
Vocabulary	Life events
	Personal characteristics
Phrases	Narrating past events

icons

Audrey Hepburn

For many people, Audrey Hepburn was 'the most beautiful woman of all time'. She was born in Belgium in 1929 into a rich family. But she **¹** _____ and life wasn't easy for her. After the war, she moved to London and **²** _____ and an actress. In 1953, she made her first big movie, *Roman Holiday*. Many films followed, including the most famous, *Breakfast at Tiffany's* in 1961 and *My Fair Lady* three years later. Hepburn was popular with other actors — they say she always thought of others before herself. After 1967, she didn't act much; she **³** _____ for the United Nations. She died in 1993.

Kurt Cobain

After his death in 1994, Nirvana singer Kurt Cobain quickly became a legend … but did he really kill himself or was it murder? Cobain was born on 20 February 1967. He **⁴** _____ but his life changed in 1975 when his parents divorced. His teenage years were miserable and he **⁵** _____ . He got his first guitar when he was fourteen and played with different teenage bands.

Then he formed Nirvana with Krist Novoselic, and they **⁶** _____ with songs like *Smells like Teen Spirit* in 1991. But Cobain didn't enjoy fame – he once said, 'famous is the last thing I wanted to be'. He married singer Courtney Love in 1992 and they had a daughter. But his depression got worse. He had serious drug problems and he **⁷** _____ at the age of just 27.

Reading & Vocabulary

1 In pairs, discuss these questions.

- Do you know any of the people in the photos? Which person is:
  a famous sportsman?
  a famous actress?
  a famous musician?
- Can you think of three famous people who are 'icons'? Do you admire them, or not?

2 Words 2 know (1.15) Check the words in blue. Guess which person in the photos:

a worked as a model   *Audrey Hepburn*
b came from a very poor family
c grew up in the Second World War
d had a happy childhood
e became world champion
f quickly became very successful
g refused to fight in the Vietnam War
h was often depressed
i worked with children in Africa and Asia
j shot himself.

3 (1.16) Read the texts and match phrases a–j in exercise 2 with gaps 1–10 in the texts. Then listen and check your answers.

MINI WORKBOOK exercise 7 page 103

Grammar Focus

Past simple

4 Read *Grammar2know*. <u>Underline</u> all the examples of the past simple in the text about Kurt Cobain. Which verbs are regular and which are irregular?

Grammar 2know

Past simple

Use the past simple to talk about actions and events that started and finished in the past.

Form

+ He **played** with different teenage bands. (regular)
  He **became** very successful. (irregular)

– He **didn't play** with different bands. (regular)
  He **didn't become** very successful. (irregular)

? **Did** he **play** with different bands? (regular)	Yes, he **did**. No, he **didn't**.
Did he **become** very successful? (irregular)	

Why did he **become** very successful?

to be

+ Life **was** easy for him.
  His teenage years **were** happy.

– Life **wasn't** easy for him.
  His teenage years **weren't** happy.

? **Was** life easy for him?	Yes, it **was**. No, it **wasn't**.
Were his teenage years happy?	Yes, they **were**. No, they **weren't**.

Time expressions: *in 1967, yesterday, last week, last year, ten years ago, when he was fourteen*

Muhammad Ali

To his fans, he was 'The Greatest' but his real name wasn't Muhammad Ali. He was born Cassius Marcellus Clay in Kentucky in 1942. He **8** _____ and started boxing when he was just twelve years old. As a boxer, he was incredibly fast on his feet – he almost 'danced'. He won the world championship for the first time in 1964 but he lost his title a few years later because he **9** _____ . After that, he became a Muslim and changed his name to Muhammad Ali. In the 1970s, he **10** _____ again. Ali got Parkinson's disease in the 1980s and stopped fighting. He began to raise money for poor people around the world. In 2000, the United Nations named him a 'Messenger of Peace'.

---

5 (1.17) **PRONUNCIATION** Listen to the regular past simple forms from the texts and put them in the correct column. Then listen again and repeat.

/t/	/d/	/ɪd/
worked	*moved*	*started*

6 a Use the past simple to complete the sentences about yourself. Make two sentences false.

1 I (be) born on … *1 January 1995*
2 My family (move) to our present house when I …
3 I (start) primary school … ago.
4 I (learn) to read when I …
5 I (start) to learn English … ago.
6 I (come) to this school in …

b Read your sentences to a partner. Can he/she spot the false information?

7 a Find out why these people are 'icons'. Write the questions, 1–6, below.

Che Guevara

Marilyn Monroe

1 Why (he/she be) famous?
   Why was she famous?
2 When and where (he/she be) born?
3 (he/she have) a happy childhood?
4 What (he/she achieve)?
5 (he/she get) married?
6 When and where (he/she die)?

b Work in pairs. Student A, look at page 124. Student B, look at page 135.

c Take turns to ask and answer the questions about the famous people.

" *Why was Marilyn Monroe famous?*
  She was famous because …
  When was she …?

8 Discuss these questions with the class.
* Which of the five people on pages 12–13 do/don't you admire? Why?
* Do you feel sorry for any of them? Why?

MINI WORKBOOK exercises 1–4 page 102

the greats

Vocabulary & Writing

Life events

1 Read about the life of 'Joe Average'. In pairs, put the events in each section in the best order 1–8. Compare answers with another pair.

- ☐ He went to secondary school.
- ☐ Kate met someone else.
- ☑ Joe was born.
- ☐ His family moved house and Joe changed primary schools.
- ☐ They had an argument and Kate dumped him.
- ☐ They started going out together.
- ☐ He started school.
- ☐ He met his first girlfriend, Kate, at secondary school.

- ☐ He met his future wife, Meg, at a party.
- ☐ He got a job.
- ☐ They rented a flat together.
- ☑ He left school and went to university.
- ☐ He passed his final exams and got a degree.
- ☐ They fell in love and got engaged.
- ☐ They got married.
- ☐ They lived happily ever after …

2 (1.18) Match the words from A and B to make collocations without looking at exercise 1. Then listen and check.

get married

Words 2 know

A

get (x4)   start   leave   have   pass   fall
rent   move

B

school (x2)   an argument   married   house
engaged   a job   in love   a flat   a degree
your exams

3 (1.19) Listen and complete the first part of Joe's story with the *Phrases2know*. What else do you learn about Joe's life?

Joe was born [1] *in 1985* and was very happy as a small child. He started school when he was five. [2] _____ , his family moved house and Joe changed primary schools but he hated the new one. [3] _____ , he moved to secondary school.

[4] _____ , he met Kate, his first girlfriend, and they started going out. Joe really liked Kate but [5] _____ , they had an argument and [6] _____ , Kate dumped him. [7] _____ Kate met someone else and Joe was really miserable again …

Phrases 2 know

Narrating past events

after a few months   When he was fourteen

in 1985 ✓   after that   Then   A few years later

After a couple of years

4 Use the *Phrases2know* to tell the second part of Joe's life story. Add three more pieces of information to the story.

" *When he was eighteen, Joe left school and went to university …*

5 Write the life story of one of these people:

- a typical 'Joe Average' from your town
- a relative or friend with an interesting life story
- yourself!

Use the *Words2know* and the *Phrases2know* in this lesson.

MINI WORKBOOK exercise 8 page 103

Grammar Focus

Past simple and past continuous

6 Look at the photos and captions on page 15. What is the connection between the two people in each photo? What other famous pairs do you know?

7 (1.20) Listen and read text A on page 15. Find five mistakes in the text and correct them.

8 Read *Grammar2know*. Then read text B about how the other pair met and complete the gaps.

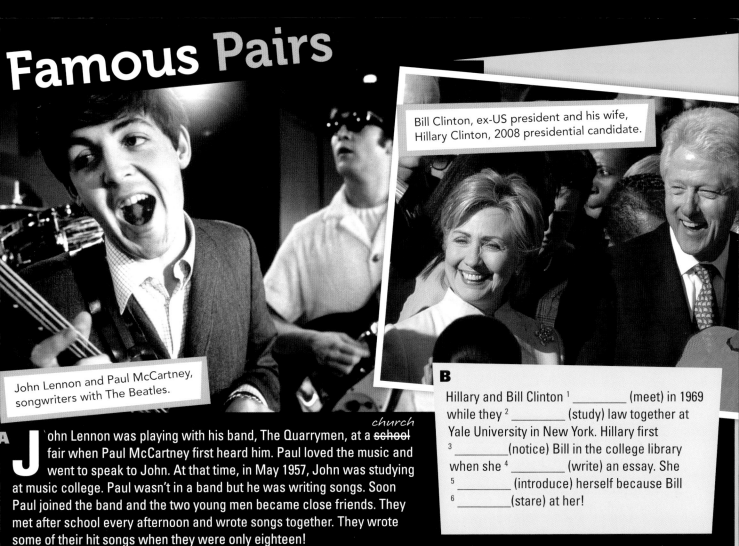

Famous Pairs

John Lennon and Paul McCartney, songwriters with The Beatles.

Bill Clinton, ex-US president and his wife, Hillary Clinton, 2008 presidential candidate.

A

church

John Lennon was playing with his band, The Quarrymen, at a ~~school~~ fair when Paul McCartney first heard him. Paul loved the music and went to speak to John. At that time, in May 1957, John was studying at music college. Paul wasn't in a band but he was writing songs. Soon Paul joined the band and the two young men became close friends. They met after school every afternoon and wrote songs together. They wrote some of their hit songs when they were only eighteen!

B

Hillary and Bill Clinton [1] _____ (meet) in 1969 while they [2] _____ (study) law together at Yale University in New York. Hillary first [3] _____ (notice) Bill in the college library when she [4] _____ (write) an essay. She [5] _____ (introduce) herself because Bill [6] _____ (stare) at her!

Grammar 2 know

Past continuous

Use the past continuous to describe actions in progress at a time in the past. The action started before that time and continued after that time:

*At that time, in July 1957, John **was studying** at art college.*

Past simple and past continuous

We sometimes use the past simple and past continuous together:

*John **was playing** with his band at a church fair* (= action in progress) *when Paul first **heard** him.* (= event)

```
                        Paul heard him
                             ↓
  John was playing          ×
~~~~~~~~~~~~~~~~~~~~~~~~~~~~~~~~~~~~~~~~~~~~~~→
        PAST                            now
```

+ *I/He/She **was** playing the guitar.*
*You/We/They **were** playing the guitar.*

− *I/He/She **wasn't** playing the guitar.*
*You/We/They **weren't** playing the guitar.*

? ***Was** I/he/she playing the guitar?*	*Yes, I/he/she **was**.*
	*No, I/he/she **wasn't**.*
***Were** you/we/they playing the guitar?*	*Yes, you/we/they **were**.*
	*No, you/we/they **weren't**.*
***What was** he doing?*	

9 **a** Complete the questions in the past continuous.

What were you doing at eight o'clock last night?

1 What (you do) at eight o'clock last night?
2 What (you wear) last Friday?
3 When (you come) to school this morning (the sun shine)?
4 (it rain) when (you get) home last night?
5 What (the other students do) when you (arrive) at this lesson?
6 What (everyone in your family do) at four o'clock last Saturday afternoon?
7 What (your teacher wear) last English lesson?

b In pairs, ask and answer the questions. How good is your partner's memory?

What were you doing at eight o'clock last night?
I was watching TV. And you?

MINI WORKBOOK exercises 5–6 pages 102–103

the greats

15

Reading & Listening

1 SCANNING Quickly read about the BBC poll on the Greatest Britons. Find the names of:
- a military leader • a writer • a scientist
- an engineer • a political leader • royalty

2 **a** Words 2 know Check the words in blue below. You have two minutes to read and match the descriptions, 1–8, to the people in the text. Who finished first?

1 _Darwin_ developed the theory of Evolution.
2 _____ led the British army against the king.
3 _____ died in a car crash.
4 _____ killed his/her cousin.
5 _____ designed important bridges.
6 _____ wrote plays and poetry.
7 _____ discovered the law of gravity.
8 _____ wanted peace.

b (1.21) Listen and check your answers.

3 Read about the winner of the BBC poll. Do you know who it is? Check your answer on page 124.

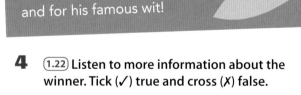

1 **??? (1874–1965)**
BRITISH PRIME MINISTER
He came from a famous aristocratic family and became a Member of Parliament at the age of twenty-six. He led Britain through the difficult years of the Second World War and inspired ordinary people with his great speeches. British people today remember him for this – and for his famous wit!

4 (1.22) Listen to more information about the winner. Tick (✓) true and cross (✗) false.

1 ☐ He was a very good pupil at school.
2 ☐ He stayed with the same political party all his life.
3 ☐ Not everyone was happy when he became Prime Minister.
4 ☐ He won a Nobel Prize for peace after the war.
5 ☐ He didn't have very healthy habits.
6 ☐ He retired at the age of sixty-one.
7 ☐ His funeral was quiet and private.

MINI WORKBOOK exercise 9 page 103

Vocabulary & Speaking

Personal characteristics

5 Look at the *Words2know* from the text that describe people. Write them in the correct column in the table.

Positive characteristics	Negative characteristics
successful	brutal

Words 2 know (1.23)

successful brutal talented violent intelligent
determined brave cruel weak glamorous
popular friendly sympathetic brilliant

6 WORD RACE How many adjectives can you add to the lists in exercise 5 in two minutes?

7 Choose three adjectives in exercises 5 and 6 to describe:
- a famous person you like (e.g. a musician)
- someone in your family
- yourself

My mother is very friendly and sympathetic.
I'm talented, popular and modest!

8 **a** Imagine there is a poll to find the greatest men/women in your country's history. In pairs, think of four people from the list below. Explain why they were great, using the *Phrases2know*.

CAN YOU DO IT IN ENGLISH?

actor sports person king/queen
scientist writer/artist musician composer
president philosopher prime minister

Phrases 2 know (1.24)

Talking about famous people

a brilliant (artist)
the best (footballer) in the world
wrote/composed …
the greatest (scientist) in our history
was the first person to …
invented/discovered …
won …
led the country when …

How about Bartok? He was a brilliant …
I think Galileo was a great Italian because he …

b With the class, make a list of the ten best candidates. Vote for the winner.

MINI WORKBOOK exercise 10 page 103

GREATEST *Britons*

The BBC recently did a poll to find the 'Greatest Britons'. There were TV programmes about the candidates and over a million people voted. These were the top ten.

10 OLIVER CROMWELL (1599–1658)
A successful but brutal military leader. Cromwell led the British parliament and army against King Charles I and executed the king in 1649. Britain was a republic until 1659.

9 HORATIO NELSON (1758–1805)
Defeated Napoleon in the battle of Trafalgar and died in the battle. A famous statue of Nelson stands in Trafalgar Square in London.

8 JOHN LENNON (1940–1980)
Talented songwriter, peace campaigner and member of The Beatles. His music and ideas inspired millions of people. A violent fan, Mark Chapman, shot him in New York.

7 ELIZABETH I (1533–1603)
Queen of England for forty-five years. She was extremely intelligent, determined and brave but she was also cruel (she executed her cousin, Mary Queen of Scots). In a famous speech she said: 'I may have the body of a weak and feeble woman but I have the heart and mind of a king.' Elizabeth never married.

6 SIR ISAAC NEWTON (1643–1727)
One of the greatest scientists and mathematicians in history. People say he discovered the law of gravity when an apple fell on his head!

5 WILLIAM SHAKESPEARE (1564–1616)
The greatest writer in the English language. He wrote about thirty-eight plays, including *Hamlet* and *Macbeth*, and hundreds of poems. But some people say Shakespeare didn't write the plays himself.

4 CHARLES DARWIN (1809–1882)
Naturalist. He developed the theory of Evolution, and in 1859 he wrote his famous work, *On the Origin of Species*. In his lifetime, many people were unhappy about his ideas and even now, some people do not believe them.

3 DIANA, PRINCESS OF WALES (1961–1997)
Glamorous mother of Princes William and Harry. Diana was very popular in her lifetime because she was friendly and sympathetic to ordinary people, especially the sick and the poor. She died in a car crash aged just thirty-six.

2 ISAMBARD KINGDOM BRUNEL (1806–1859)
A brilliant engineer. He designed and built many important railways, ships and bridges. He was a surprising Number 2, as he was not very famous before the BBC programme!

1 ???

activestudy1

Vocabulary

1 Complete the categories with these words.
Write two more words for each category.

> aunt ✓   cruel   engineer   friendly
> nephew   receptionist   niece   talented
> scientist

Personality	Family	Jobs
	aunt	

2 Match the words to make collocations.

A

1	do	**a**	school
2	fall	**b**	married
3	go	**c**	nothing
4	leave	**d**	running
5	get	**e**	in love

B

1	get	**a**	your friends
2	make	**b**	house
3	meet	**c**	plans
4	move	**d**	a flat
5	rent	**e**	engaged

3 PRONUNCIATION (1.26) Listen and <u>underline</u> the
stressed syllable. Then listen again and repeat.

1	<u>po</u>pular	4	relationship	7	discover
2	address	5	exam	8	develop
3	journey	6	emergency	9	talented

Grammar

4 Complete the sentences with the correct form
of the verbs in brackets. Use the present simple,
present continuous, past simple or past continuous.

1 Stephanie usually _____ (wear) black but
today she _____ (wear) a white dress.

2 I (not go) _____ to the cinema on
weekdays.

3 What (you/do) _____ when I (phone)
_____ you at 7 o'clock last night?

4 Which sport (Tom/like) _____ best?

5 Choose the correct verb form to complete the
magazine article about Johnny Depp.

HOLLYWOOD'S FAVOURITE SON?

Johnny Depp is probably the
most popular and best-paid
actor in the world. He is appearing in
several big films this year. *Pirates of the
Caribbean 3* [1] _____ in cinemas across the world right
now and he [2] _____ a new film at the moment.

Johnny Depp [3] _____ in Kentucky in 1963 and
he [4] _____ in Florida. He dropped out of school
at sixteen because he [5] _____ to be a rock star.
His first movie role was a small part in the 1984 film
Nightmare on Elm Street.

He [6] _____ his current partner, French pop
singer Vanessa Paradis, while he [7] _____ a film
in France in 1998. Apparently, he [8] _____ her when
she was coming out of a Paris hotel and he immediately
[9] _____ in love with her! The couple have two
children and [10] _____ in a small village in France.

1	**a** shows	**b** is showing	**c** showed
2	**a** make	**b** makes	**c** is making
3	**a** is born	**b** was born	**c** born
4	**a** grew up	**b** grow up	**c** was growing up
5	**a** was wanting	**b** wanted	**c** wants
6	**a** met	**b** meet	**c** meets
7	**a** made	**b** was making	**c** makes
8	**a** see	**b** was seeing	**c** saw
9	**a** fell	**b** fall	**c** was falling
10	**a** live	**b** lives	**c** is living

6 Put these jumbled questions in order. Then read
the text about Johnny Depp again and write the
answers.

1 Johnny Depp/where/born/was
Where was Johnny Depp born?
In Kentucky.

2 did/why/he/out of school/drop

3 the name/his first film/was/of/what

4 partner/is/who/Johnny Depp's

5 meet/did/when/her/he

6 do/children/they/how many/have

Reading Skills

7 a Scan the UCL webpage and find:
- the number of international students at UCL
- the name of the office that helps foreign students
- the name of the online newsletter for foreign students.

b Read the webpage again. Tick (✓) true and cross (✗) false.

1 ☐ UCL offers courses in many subjects.
2 ☐ Half the students at UCL are not from the UK.
3 ☐ The International Office is open on Sundays.
4 ☐ The International Office does not close for the summer holidays.
5 ☐ It costs £10 to join the UCL Students' Union.
6 ☐ The ULC Students' Union is a sports club.

University College London welcomes you! (1.28)

UCL

- University College London (UCL) is in the heart of London, close to the British Museum and the British Library. We are a large university – 20,200 students. We offer a variety of courses each year so you can study any subject you wish.

- University College London is truly an international university. We now have 6600 foreign students from more than 140 countries – that's almost one-third of the total number of our students.

- If you have any questions, please contact us at The International Office. We're here to help. The office is open from 10 a.m. to 4 p.m., Monday to Friday (closed weekends and public holidays). We are open all summer. The International Office can help you with visa and immigration problems. There is also an online newsletter, International Student News.

- All students can join the UCL Students' Union. Membership is free. The Union represents students' interests, organises sports events and concerts.

Listening Skills

8 (1.27) Listen to three conversations in the International Office. Match students 1, 2 and 3 to the statements a–g. There is one extra statement.

a ☐ He/She can't find Room 101.
b ☐ He/She lost something.
c ☐ He/She has a question about accommodation.
d ☐ He/She wants to pay for a course.
e ☐ He/She found a mobile phone.
f ☐ He/She was at the office this morning.
g ☐ He/She says he/she'll come back tomorrow.

Speaking Skills

9 What do you say in these situations?
- You want to introduce your friend Thomas to your teacher.
- Someone just came to your town and you want to greet them.
- You meet someone at the airport and want to ask about their journey.
- You meet a friend at a party. The last time you saw him/her was three years ago.

10 Write down four events from your life. Tell another student when they happened using the *Phrases2know* on page 14.

I learned to play football when I was five. A few years/months/weeks later, I ...

SKILLS STRATEGIES back cover

Grammar	Comparatives and superlatives *too* and *enough*
Vocabulary	Places and people; money
Phrases	Describing a place Expressing opinions Polite requests

Vocabulary & Reading

Describing a place

1 In pairs, discuss the questions.
- Do you have your own bedroom or do you share with someone else?
- Which *Words2know* describe your room?

Words 2 know (1.29)

modern   well-organised   comfortable   stylish
dark   tidy   messy   noisy   quiet   bright

2 Use the *Words2know* and the captions to describe the bedrooms in the photos.

Will's room is very messy.

3 PREDICTING Read the heading and the introduction to the text. Who is Ben Yee and what is the article about?

4 Read the article. Match the descriptions (1–4) to the photos. What does Ben say about the four people who live in these rooms? Do you agree?

Through the (1.32) keyhole

What does your bedroom say about you? Ben Yee, our style expert, takes a secret look at four very different teenagers' rooms. Ben says:

Kieron's room

Will's room

Holly's room

1 'I think this is a boy's room but it's hard to say. It's very tidy but it's the most boring of the four rooms … nothing interesting on the walls … no decorations. I think he's probably like his room – well-organised but difficult to get to know.'

2 'Ah, that's better! This room's much nicer. It isn't as tidy as the first room but for me it's probably the most interesting because I can imagine the kind of person who lives here. I think she has a strong personality. She likes music, art, fashion and reading. She's a very creative person, I think.'

3 'This is an interesting room, too. It's the smallest of the four rooms but I think it's the most stylish. The colours are brighter and more modern than the other rooms and the decorations are really attractive. It's also tidier than the last room. It's a very feminine room – she's definitely a 'girly' girl. I think the owner is like her room … bright and stylish.'

4 'Ugh! This is the messiest of all the rooms. I can't stand this kind of mess, so for me this is the worst of the four! It's quite dirty, too, and I don't like that either. The person who lives here has lots of interests – football, travelling – but he doesn't care about his bedroom!'

Grammar Focus

Comparatives and superlatives

5 Read *Grammar2know* and complete the table with comparative and superlative adjectives from the article.

Grammar 2 know

Comparative and superlative adjectives

	adjective	comparative	superlative
one syllable	*small*	*smaller*	_____
	nice	_____	*the nicest*
two syllables ending in -y	*tidy*	_____	*the tidiest*
	messy	*messier*	_____
two or more syllables	*modern*	_____	*the most modern*
	interesting	*more interesting*	_____
irregular	*good*	_____	*the best*
	bad	*worse*	_____

Other forms for comparison

*The colours are more modern **than** the other rooms.*
*It isn't **as** tidy **as** the first room.*

6 Write three true and three false sentences comparing the bedrooms. Then work in pairs. Say if your partner's sentences are true or false.

Olivia's room is tidier than Holly's room.   False!

7 Complete the questions with the correct superlative form.

1 Which is _____ (messy) room in your house?
2 What is _____ (important) thing in your bedroom?
3 Which is _____ (comfortable) room in your house?
4 What is _____ (good) place to study in your house?
5 What is _____ (bad) place to study?

Then ask and answer the questions in pairs.

Which is the messiest room in your house?
My brother's bedroom!

MINI WORKBOOK exercises 1–4 page 104

Olivia's room

Listening Speaking

My favourite place

8 (1.30) Olivia is telling Holly about her favourite coffee shop. Listen and tick the things that she mentions.

> a coffee table   rugs   cushions
> tables and chairs   armchairs
> a cupboard   a sofa
> a coffee bar ✓   a picture   a stool
> a mirror   plants   a poster

9 (1.30) Listen again and look at the pictures on page 135. Which one is Olivia describing? Give at least two reasons.

10 How much do you remember about Café Rosso? Complete the sentences with the *Phrases2know*. Then listen and check.

1 *It looks* really modern.
2 _____ , there's a coffee bar.
3 _____ , there are tables and chairs.
4 _____ , there are some armchairs and a coffee table.
5 _____ bright, colourful rugs _____ .
6 _____ a big mirror _____ the bar.

Phrases 2 know (1.31)

In the centre/middle of the room …
On the left/right of the picture, there is/are …
On the wall/floor/table …
Behind/near/next to the sofa …
There is/are a sofa/some armchairs …
It looks friendly/busy/modern.

11 Now use *Phrases2know* to describe the other picture on page 135. Find seven differences between the two pictures. Use the *Phrases2know* to talk about them.

In picture A, the … is on the right but in picture B it's on the left.

12 What's your favourite place to hang out? Describe it to your partner, using the *Phrases2know* and *Words2know* in this lesson.

MINI WORKBOOK exercise 7 page 105

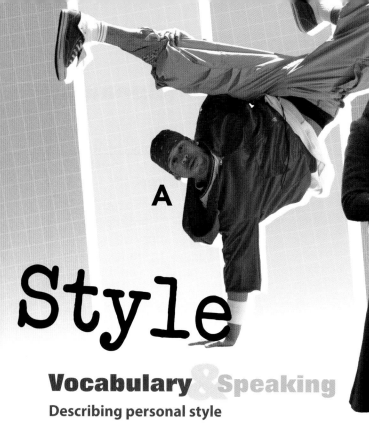

Style

Vocabulary & Speaking

Describing personal style

1 WORD RACE Write down twelve items of clothing. The first person to finish shouts 'stop'. Compare answers with the class.

2 Check the words in blue in *Words2know*. Find a person in the photos who …

Words 2 know (1.33)

1 is wearing smart clothes.   *B, E*
2 is wearing casual clothes.
3 is wearing make-up or jewellery.
4 has long, wavy hair.
5 has a tattoo.
6 has dyed hair.
7 has piercings.
8 is wearing something tight.
9 is wearing something baggy.
10 is well-dressed.

3 Put the *Words2know* in the correct column. How many more words can you add to each group.

hair	clothes and appearance	'decorations'
long	*smart*	*tattoo*

4 Choose one person in the photos. Give three clues about their appearance. Other students guess who it is.

This person looks smart, isn't wearing jeans and has got long hair. Who is it?

MINI WORKBOOK exercise 8 page 105

Grammar Focus

too and *enough*

5 **a** Read the comments about the people in the photos. Who do you think they are about?

1 To me, she isn't young enough to dress like that.   *D*

2 She's wearing too much make-up – it looks weird.

3 She's got too many tattoos.

4 I don't think his trousers are too baggy.

5 Personally, I think she's too young to wear clothes like that.

b Are the comments positive or negative? Do you agree or not?

E

9 Use the ideas in A and B to make five true sentences.

It's too cold to wear sandals.

A

> It's too hot/cold …
> I'm too young/old/shy …
> I'm not old/brave enough …

B

> wear a business suit   wear sandals
> wear school uniform   wear short trousers
> wear ribbons in my hair dye my hair
> wear a winter coat   have a piercing
> have a tattoo

MINI WORKBOOK exercises 5–6 page 105

6 Read the comments in exercise 5 again and complete *Grammar2know* with *too* or *enough*.

too and enough

Use *too* + adjective and *not* + adjective + *enough* to say that something is not right.
*His trousers are **too long**.* (=He needs shorter trousers.)
*His trousers are **not long enough**.* (=He needs longer trousers.)

too and enough with infinitive
*She's _____ young **to wear** clothes like that.*
*She isn't young _____ **to dress** like that.*

too much and **too many** + noun:
too many (countable)   *_____ **many** tattoos*
too much (uncountable)   *_____ **much** make-up*

Notice the word order with *not enough*:
*I haven't got **enough** smart clothes.*
*My clothes aren't smart **enough**.*

7 Rewrite the sentences using *too* or *enough* and the adjectives in brackets.

1 His hair's too long. (short)
   His hair's not short enough.
2 His clothes are too casual. (smart)
3 These shoes aren't big enough. (small)
4 Her dress is too small. (big)
5 Her top isn't big enough. (tight)
6 Her skirt is too short. (long)

8 Complete the gaps with *much* or *many*.

1 She's wearing too _____ make-up.
2 He's got too _____ piercings.
3 She's got too _____ pairs of shoes.
4 She always wears too _____ perfume.
5 I don't like wearing too _____ jewellery.

Listening & Speaking

10 a (1.34) Listen to a street survey about fashion. Match the speakers and their opinions.

1 _C_ worries that young people spend too much money on clothes.
2 ____ really enjoys fashion.
3 ____ thinks the clothes in fashion shows are too strange to wear.
4 ____ thinks designer clothes are too expensive.
5 ____ thinks people can show their personality through their clothes.
6 ____ isn't interested in fashion.

b (1.34) Listen again. Which people do you agree with?

11 (1.35) Listen to the *Phrases2know* and practise the intonation.

Phrases 2 know

Expressing opinions

I think fashion's cool.
To me, fashion's fun.
I love fashion.
I really like clothes.
I don't know much about fashion/clothes.
I don't really care.
I don't think it's a good thing.
Personally, I think people care too much about clothes.

12 In groups, tell other people what you think of the people in the photos. Use the *Phrases2know*.

" *Personally, I really like tattoos but I think C's got too many.*
I think she looks weird/good.

your style

23

Vocabulary & Speaking

Money and spending

1 **Words 2 know** (1.36) **Check the words in blue and then do the quiz. Choose T (true), S (sometimes true) or N (not true).**

Quiz

What's your spending style? £

Do you put your money in the bank or spend, spend, spend? Do our quiz and find out.
(T = true, S = sometimes, N = never)

1 I often buy things that I didn't plan to buy.
T=2 S=1 N=0

2 I always look for bargains when I go shopping.
T=0 S=1 N=2

3 If I lend money, I make sure the person pays me back soon.
T=0 S=1 N=2

4 I enjoy giving presents to other people.
T=2 S=1 N=0

5 If I can't afford something that I want, I borrow it.
T=2 S=1 N=0

6 I don't usually owe money.
T= 0 S=1 N=2

7 When I finish with games, CDs, etc. I often sell them.
T=0 S=1 N=2

8 If I earn money or get money for my birthday, I usually save it.
T=0 S=1 N=2

9 I usually spend money when I get it.
T=2 S=1 N=0

Conclusions

1–4 You're a natural saver and you never owe money. Of course, some people might say you're mean …
6–12 You're generally sensible with money but you like giving and know how to enjoy yourself. Just stop and think before you spend.
14–18 Oh dear, you're a natural spender! You're generous and have a good time. But try to pay back what you owe, before you spend more!

2 **Read the quiz conclusions. Do you agree? In pairs, talk about your spending habits. Use the *Words2know*.**

" *I often borrow money but I never …*
If I can't afford something, I …

MINI WORKBOOK exercise 9 page 105

Reading & Vocabulary

3 **Look at the three texts, A–C. Which is:**
- an internet blog?
- a magazine interview?
- a newspaper article?

4 **SKIMMING Match the titles to the texts, A–C. There is one extra title.**
1 Big Spender Not Sorry
2 The Meanest Man in the World
3 Teenage Business Tycoon
4 Help! I can't stop shopping!

A

(1.37)

Help! My name is Lori and I am … a bargain-aholic (is that a word?????)

My problem is … every time I walk into a clothes shop and I see something really cheap, I buy it. And I walk into a lot of clothes shops …

Do you know the worst thing? When I get home and try them on again, I think, 'That's horrible! Why did I buy it?' My wardrobe's full of clothes that don't suit me. I'm sure they're laughing at me.

Sometimes I try to give them to my friends but they smile kindly and say things like, 'Thanks Lori, but … no, thanks!!!'

My latest bargain is a pair of jeans. They only cost £10 and they looked okay in the shop … but now I see they are the wrong size, the wrong colour, they are just … the wrong trousers!

I think you can see my problem … but can anyone help me?? PLEEEAASSSSE!!!

Posted by LoriH @ 08.55 a.m.BST

A teenager who spent thousands of pounds using his father's credit card returned home yesterday. Ben Jones, seventeen, 'borrowed' the credit card while his father was out jogging. First, he flew to Rome, where he checked into a luxury hotel. The next day, he spent thousands of pounds on designer clothes, including a £500 coat, three pairs of designer jeans and a £500 bag that he later gave to his sister as a present. After his shopping trip, he hired a limousine to go sightseeing. Finally, Jones returned to London, where his parents were waiting …

'I am not sorry I spent the money,' Jones told journalists, 'because I have lots of lovely things.'

4 ● + CM K

C Daniel Harding started a successful business at the age of sixteen ... in his bedroom.

Q So how did you get the idea to start your own airline?
A I knew university wasn't for me. At first, I wanted to be a pilot. Then I had the idea for an airline and I wrote a business plan for a school project.

Q How did you get the money to start the business?
A A family friend lent me £10,000. That was enough to hire our first plane. In the first week, we sold 20,000 tickets and after a few months, I paid the money back. It continued from there …

Q What do your school friends think?
A Most of them think I'm crazy … I work sixteen hours a day!

Q But I imagine you have a lot more money than your friends?
A Yes and no. I save everything I earn and invest it in the business – I only pay myself pocket money, like my friends. Right now, spending money isn't important to me. I'm not interested in sports cars or designer clothes! I see myself as a successful businessman in the future.

5 Read the texts again and choose the correct answers.

1 Lori spends all her money on
   a clothes she doesn't really want.
   b expensive clothes.
   c clothes for her friends.

2 Lori doesn't like her new jeans because
   a her friends don't like them.
   b they were too expensive.
   c they don't look good on her.

3 Ben Jones
   a bought expensive presents for all his family.
   b used his father's money to buy lots of expensive things.
   c went on holiday with his parents and spent a lot of money.

4 Ben feels
   a sorry about spending so much money.
   b sorry that he behaved badly to his parents.
   c pleased that he's got lots of nice clothes.

5 Daniel Harding had the idea for the airline
   a while he was at university.
   b while he was doing a school project.
   c because a family friend gave him some money.

6 Daniel
   a likes spending more money than his friends.
   b isn't interested in spending money.
   c doesn't want to be a successful businessman.

6 a Match the questions with the people in the texts.

1 'Why did you take your father's credit card?'
   Ben

2 'Do your parents help you with the business?'

3 'What did your parents say when you got back from Italy?'

4 'Do you have enough money to buy all those clothes?'

5 'Do you still have time to study?'

b Think of two more questions to ask Lori, Ben or Daniel.

7 a Read *Active Study*. Then copy the word map into your notebook. Add the other words in blue from the quiz on page 24 to the correct section.

b Find more money words in the texts in this lesson and add them to the word map.

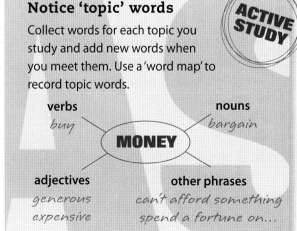

Notice 'topic' words

ACTIVE STUDY

Collect words for each topic you study and add new words when you meet them. Use a 'word map' to record topic words.

verbs — buy
nouns — bargain
MONEY
adjectives — generous, expensive
other phrases — can't afford something, spend a fortune on…

GOING SHOPPING

1 (1.38) **Listen and choose all the correct answers.**

1 Zack is reading emails from
   a Grace. b his mother.
   c his girlfriend.

2 He needs to buy
   a shampoo and toothpaste.
   b paper and files.
   c a sweater.

3 In the end, he decides to go to
   a the corner shop.
   b the local supermarket.
   c the high street.

4 He decides to go
   a with Rosie. b with Grace.
   c alone.

5 Before Zack goes shopping, he wants to
   a have breakfast.
   b make a phone call.
   c find his passport.

2 (1.39) **Listen and complete the conversations with these words.**

> PIN bag the fitting room
> try it on a medium
> a large size receipt size ✓

3 (1.40) **Listen to the *Phrases2know* and practise the intonation.**

Phrases **2** know

Polite requests
Can you enter your PIN, please?
Could you put it in a bag?
Can I try it on?
Could I have a bigger size?
Is it okay if I pay by card?

Responding
Sure, no problem.
Yes, of course.
I'm sorry but …

ZACK forgot to pack several things when he came to London and needs to go shopping.

a

Assistant:	Can I help you?
Grace:	We're just looking, thanks.
Zack:	Actually, I like this one – what do you think?
Grace:	I like it, yeah.
Assistant:	What ¹ *size* are you looking for?
Zack:	I'm not sure, medium?
Grace:	Yeah, I think medium. Look, here's ² _____ .
Zack:	Can I ³ _____ ?
Assistant:	Yes, of course, ⁴ _____ is over there, can you see?

b

Assistant:	Is everything okay there?
Zack:	Could I have a bigger size? This one's too small, I think.
Assistant:	I'm sorry but we've only got purple in ⁵ _____ . Do you want to try that?
Zack:	Yes, I like the purple colour. It's good.
Assistant:	Is that size better?
Zack:	Yes, thanks, it's fine.

c

Assistant:	That's fifteen seventy-five, please.
Zack:	Is it okay if I pay by card?
Assistant:	Sure, no problem. Can you enter your ⁶ _____ , please? Okay, that's all fine and here's your ⁷ _____ .
Zack:	Thanks, could you put it in a ⁸ _____ ?
Assistant:	Of course, thank you very much.

4 Rewrite the conversations politely. Use the *Phrases2know* on page 26. Then practise in pairs.

1 **A:** I want to use your mobile for a quick call.

B: Yes.

> *Is it okay if I use your mobile for a quick call? Sure, no problem.*

2 **A:** I want to borrow your pen.

B: No, it doesn't work.

3 **A:** Help me with my Maths homework.

B: Yes.

4 **A:** I want to open the window.

B: No, I'm really cold.

AN EMAIL LETTER HOME

6 Read the email from Zack's mother and answer the questions.

1 Why is she worried?

2 Which three pieces of news does she mention?

3 Who do you think Hannah is?

7 Read Zack's reply and put the sections in the correct order.

8 Look at the *Phrases2know* from Zack's email. Match the underlined phrases in his mother's email to the headings 1–4 in *Phrases2know*.

Phrases 2 know

Informal emails/letters

1 Opening emails/letters
Hi Mom

2 Saying/Asking how things are
I hope you are all well.
Everything's going really well here.

3 Ending emails/letters
Take care,
Give my love to Dad and Hannah.

4 Signing off
Love, Zack

9 Write an email to a foreign friend.
- Ask how he/she is.
- Apologise for not emailing before.
- Ask about his/her news.
- Give news about your friends and family.

5 In pairs, take turns to act out the dialogue below. Follow the chart and use the *Phrases2know* on page 26.

Customer

You want to try a T-shirt/jacket on. Ask politely.

Say what size you need.

Say 'thank you'.

You need a bigger/smaller size. Ask politely.

Shop Assistant

Say 'yes' and ask what size the customer wants.

Explain where the fitting room is.

Ask if everything is okay.

Explain that there isn't a bigger/smaller size at the moment. Say 'sorry'.

mailbox   Today | Mail | Calendar | Contacts

Reply | Reply All | Forward | Delete

Dear Zack,

How are things with you? How was your journey? Dad and I are a little worried because you didn't email to say you arrived! How's college going? Are you happy at Fran's? We're really interested to hear all your news!

Everything's fine here. Hannah finished her exams and Dad's new job is going well. I met Lily in the street yesterday but I guess you already know her news. She's coming to London next month! She's so excited about seeing you!

Well, I think that's everything. I really hope everything's okay with you. Write soon, we all miss you!

All my love,

Mom

Zack's reply

I hope you are all well. Sorry I didn't email you before – things here are pretty busy! ☐

Lily told me about her visit. She arrives in about three weeks, I think. I'm really looking forward to seeing her! Take care and give my love to Dad and Hannah. ☐

Hi Mom, [7]

Love, Zack XXX ☐

Everything's going really well here. Fran, Grace and Rosie are really nice people and they're helping me a lot. My course is really interesting but I travel two hours every day by train, so it's a long day. ☐

4 your goals

Grammar	Wishes and intentions
	Gerunds and infinitives
Vocabulary	Education, training and work
Phrases	Discussing opinions

Listening & Vocabulary

Education

1 Look at the photos and discuss the questions in pairs.

- What subjects are the people in the pictures studying?
- Do you find these subjects interesting? Why? Why not?

2 **Words 2 know** (2.2) Check the words in blue in the fact file. Then read the fact file and discuss the questions in groups.

1 Are foreign languages compulsory in English and American schools? Is this the same in your country?

2 Which other subjects do English and American pupils study? Do you study them at your school?

3 What are the most popular subjects in English universities? Which university courses are most popular in your country?

3 (2.3) Listen to Part 1 of an interview with Jess about her school life and <u>underline</u> the correct answer.

1 Jess goes to a *private/state* school.

2 It's a *mixed/single-sex* school.

3 She is studying *ten/eleven* subjects for GCSE.

4 Students normally take *three/five* A-levels.

5 There *are/aren't* any compulsory subjects for A-level.

4 (2.4) Listen to Part 2 and match the subjects, 1–5, with the statements, a–e.

1 ☐ English language, English literature, Maths, three sciences and ICT

2 ☐ Drama and Art

3 ☐ Latin

4 ☐ Design and Technology

5 ☐ Cookery

Jess

a Jess was terrible at this.

b Her brother dropped this after an accident.

c These subjects are compulsory for GCSE.

d Jess really likes these subjects.

e She doesn't think this subject is useful.

5 Work in groups and discuss the questions.

- Are you 'terrible at' any subjects? Which subjects would you like to drop?
- Do you study any subjects that are not very useful, in your opinion?
- What would you like to study instead?

" *I'd like to drop Music because I'm terrible at it!*

MINI WORKBOOK exercise 6 page 107

→ FactFile (2.6)

Which courses are English and American students choosing?

→ In English secondary schools, it's compulsory for 11–14-year-olds to study one foreign language. But at 14, many pupils drop foreign languages when they choose the subjects they want to study for their GCSE exams. In the USA, foreign languages are not compulsory in most states.

→ Some English pupils go to mixed schools and some to single-sex schools but all pupils, boys and girls study Design and Technology (DT) which includes cookery, sewing and woodwork. Many American high school students also learn accounting, car mechanics and even how to drive!

→ Drama, media and film studies are becoming popular subjects in English and American schools. In England, many pupils choose these courses for their A-levels**. Perhaps that's because 22% of English 16- to 19-year-olds want to be actors, pop stars or models! Only 8% are planning to become doctors, engineers or lawyers. But ... the most popular courses at English universities are: 1 Law 2 Design Studies 3 Psychology 4 Medicine 5 Management Studies

* General Certificate of Secondary Education. Pupils take these exams at 16.
** They need to pass these exams to go to university.

Grammar Focus

Wishes and intentions

6 (2.5) Read and listen to Part 3 of the interview with Jess. Answer the questions.

- What does Jess want to study for her A-levels?
- Which careers is she interested in?
- What does she want to do before she goes to university?

Interviewer: So, next year you're going to start your A-levels. Tell me about that. Which subjects are you going to choose?

Jess: I'm definitely going to do English and Spanish because they're my favourite subjects and then I'm not really sure … I'd like to do Art but I don't know if it's very useful for my career …

Interviewer: What do you want to do? Do you know?

Jess: I think I'd like to be a journalist or a lawyer but I don't know for sure. So, I guess History or something is more useful … or I'd like to try Psychology. It sounds really interesting.

Interviewer: Do you want to go to university?

Jess: Yeah, but I'm not going to start university straight after I leave school. I'm planning to have a gap year, you know, a break from studying for a while …

Interviewer: And what would you like to do in your gap year? Any ideas?

Jess: I want to travel … I'd like to go to Italy and learn Italian. I don't know if it's really practical but that's my dream!

7 Read the interview again. Which verbs does Jess use to talk about her intentions and wishes for the future? Read *Grammar2know* to check.

Grammar 2 know

Intentions and wishes

going to and *planning to*
Use *going to* and *planning to* to talk about intentions:
She*'s going to study* Spanish.
She *isn't going to start* university straight after school.
She*'s planning to have* a gap year.

want to and *would like to*
Use *want to* and *would like to* to talk about wishes:
She *wants to travel*.
She*'d like to be* a lawyer. (*'d = would*)

Notice the auxiliaries in the question forms:
Which subjects *are* you *going* to choose?
What *do* you *want* to do?
What *would* you *like* to do in your gap year?

8 Use the prompts to complete the questions. Then ask and answer in pairs.

1 going/take any exams this year?
   Are you going to take any exams this year?
2 plan/go to university? what/like/study?
3 like/learn any other languages in the future?
4 like/learn any other skills?
5 plan/travel before you settle down? where/like/go?

9 Use the verbs in *Grammar2know* and the ideas below to talk about your future plans.

> work with computers   be a teacher
> study Psychology   learn how to cook
> do the same job as my father/mother
> use English in my job

" *I'd like to work with computers. I'm going to …*

10 WRITING Write about your future plans and ambitions. Use ideas from exercises 8 and 9 to help you.

MINI WORKBOOK exercises 1–2 page 106

Vocabulary & Listening

Getting a job

1 (2.7) Look at the photo and read the caption. In pairs, check the *Words2know* and put Adam's story in order. Then listen and check.

Words 2 know

- ☐1 Adam needed to **earn** some **money**.
- ☐ So he **wrote his CV** and took it to the supermarket.
- ☐ They took his CV and gave him **an application form**.
- ☐ He saw **an advert** for **vacancies** at his local supermarket.
- ☐10 He **started work**.
- ☐ So he decided to look for **a part-time job**.
- ☐ They phoned him to arrange **an interview**.
- ☐ He **filled in** the **application form** at home.
- ☐ He put on smart clothes and went for the interview.
- ☐ They **offered** him **a job**.

2 In pairs, answer the market research questionnaire below.

Part-time jobs for young people
....

1 Is it easy to find part-time work in your area?
   ☐ Yes ☐ No
2 Do many of your friends have part-time jobs?
   ☐ Yes ☐ No
3 Which of these jobs do they do?
   ☐ part-time work in shops or cafés
   ☐ babysitting
   ☐ delivering newspapers or leaflets
   ☐ other _____
4 How do young people in your area find jobs?
   ☐ through adverts
   ☐ by sending their CV to companies
   ☐ through friends or family
   ☐ other _____
5 Do you have any experience of part-time work?
   ☐ Yes ☐ No
6 What did you do? _____

Thank you for your time!

---

3 (2.8) Listen to Adam's answers. Are they the same or different from yours?

MINI WORKBOOK exercise 7 page 107

Adam is in his last year at school and is looking for a part-time job.

Grammar Focus

Gerunds and infinitives

4 Read the internet postings a–d on page 31 and match them to the people 1–4. Are their experiences positive or negative?

1 ☐ a successful businessman
2 ☐ a school leaver who is worried about unemployment
3 ☐ someone who is remembering his first job
4 ☐ a graduate who is looking for a job

5 Find these verbs in postings a–d and <u>underline</u> them. Are they followed by an infinitive (*to* + verb) or a gerund (verb + *-ing*)?

> start   'd (would) like   expect   not mind
> spend time   plan   want   learn   love
> decide   need

6 Read and complete *Grammar2know* with verbs from exercise 5.

Grammar 2 know

Gerunds and infinitives

Verbs + gerund: *like*, *enjoy*, *hate*, *can't stand*, *miss*, _____, _____, _____, _____ .
The assistant started laughing at me.

Verbs + infinitive: *hope*, *intend*, *try*, *agree*, *would love*, _____, _____, _____, _____, _____, _____, _____ .
I learnt to use a computer.

Notice that modal verbs take an infinitive without *to*:
You can't get a job without experience.
(NOT ~~You can't to get a job~~.)

Discussion Board

Getting your first job ...
a piece of cake or a nightmare?

➤ Click here and join the conversation!

Comments

a On my first day at work, my boss sent me to the shop and told me to buy a tin of striped paint. When I got there the assistant started laughing at me and I realised it was a joke. I felt really stupid!

Posted by:
Iain from EDINBURGH
27 May 23.11

b Hi there, job hunters! I'd like to tell you about my experiences here in Australia. After seven years of university, I expected to find a good job pretty easily. But you can't get a job without experience ... and you can't get experience without a job! I don't mind starting on a low salary but I don't get the chance. Right now I'm spending all my time filling in application forms and I'm getting pretty depressed. Does this happen in other countries?

Posted by: Craig from AUSTRALIA 28 May 08.05

c Unemployment is a real big problem where I live, too ... I'd like to find a job here in my home town but it's really difficult ... A lot of people from school are planning to move or go abroad and find a job ... but I don't want to leave my friends and family! What can I do??!!

Posted by: Melanie 1 June 18.37

d I didn't pass any exams at school but in my first job (this was the 1980s!!) I learnt to use a computer. I soon found that I loved working with computers and so I saved up and bought one. After a few years, I decided to start my own computer company and today I am a multi-millionaire with homes in London and California. Success is all in your head ... you need to know exactly what you want to do in life, then nothing can stop you.

Posted by: Sandy
1 June 21.35

page 1 of 2

7 Read postings e–f from the same site and put the verbs in the correct form.

Discussion Board

e My dream is to be on TV. I'd love [1] _to be_ (be) a presenter but my parents say this is silly – they expect me [2] _____ (study) something practical like accountancy. But I don't want [3] _____ (spend) my life in an office. I hate [4] _____ (sit) in front of a computer all day!!! Somebody help me, please!!

Posted by: Erica 25 May 05.12

f I'm still at school. I really enjoy [5] _____ (work) with animals. I spend all my time [6] _____ (help) on a local farm. This summer, I'm planning [7] _____ (travel) to the USA and I hope [8] _____ (find) a job there ... with animals, if possible!! Has anyone got any ideas?

Posted by: KS 3 June 02.00

page 2 of 2

8 Use the ideas in A and B to write five true sentences about yourself. Then compare answers in pairs.

A

In my future career, I'd like to/ I don't want to/I hope to ...
I love/enjoy/don't mind/don't like/ hate ...

B

take exams   help people
be outdoors/indoors
work in an office
earn a lot of money
meet new people
work with children/animals/ computers/cars

I love being outdoors. What about you? In my future career, I'd like to work with computers.

MINI-WORKBOOK exercises 3–5 pages 106–107

your goals

31

Vocabulary & Speaking

Describing jobs

1 WORD RACE Write down the letters of the alphabet. In five minutes, try to think of a job for each letter. Compare answers.

A – actor   *B – bus driver*   *C ...*

2 Complete the definitions 1–6 with these words.

> an accountant   a social worker
> a graphic designer   a nanny ✓
> a sales representative   an IT consultant

1   <u>*A nanny*</u> looks after children in their own home.

2   _____ sells a company's products.

3   _____ looks after a company's money.

4   _____ gives advice about computer systems.

5   _____ helps families with problems.

6   _____ designs magazines, adverts, etc.

3 Check the *Words2know*. Think of two jobs to match each description.

stressful – doctor, social worker

Words 2 know (2.10)

stressful   rewarding   secure   glamorous
well-paid   good with numbers   creative
good with your hands   good with people

4 **a** Think of a job you:

- would like to do
- wouldn't mind doing
- don't want to do.

b Discuss your answers in pairs, using ideas from exercise 3 and your own ideas.

❝ *I'd like to be an accountant because I'm good with numbers.*
I wouldn't. It's too boring.

MINI WORKBOOK exercise 8 page 107

Reading & Vocabulary

5 SCANNING Find Claire and Lukas in the photos and guess the job they did. Then read the text and check.

6 **Words 2 know** (2.11) Check the words in blue. Then read the text again and tick (✓) true and cross (✗) false.

1 ☐ Claire earned a proper salary when she was teaching.

2 ☐ Claire's experience with the monks was very positive.

3 ☐ There are 600,000 foreign workers in the UK doing temporary jobs.

4 ☐ It is impossible for foreigners to have good careers in the UK.

5 ☐ Lukas had experience with children before he came to the UK.

6 ☐ Lukas's employers think he's as good as a female au pair.

(2.13) Doing something different

Would you like to take a break from your education for a year or two? Do you want to earn money, help other people or just see the world? You might find yourself in a place you never dreamt of ...

The volunteer teacher

A quarter of British sixteen–eighteen-year-olds want to take a 'gap year', according to a recent survey. Many, like nineteen-year-old Claire Fuller from Manchester, volunteer through special gap-year organisations. She applied to Projects Abroad and they sent her to teach English at Molligoda Monastery in Sri Lanka. Her pupils were teenage Buddhist monks.

'Before I started, I was worried about teaching monks but the classes were really fun! The younger monks don't concentrate very well and, at first, they were throwing paper aeroplanes in lessons! But we learnt to respect each other and I got to know them quickly because they are not at all shy! The older monks are great fun, too – they have a great sense of humour and love jokes! I loved every minute of my time at Molligoda and I totally loved all the monks – they were so kind. It was such a rewarding experience.'

Claire hopes to return to Sri Lanka after she finishes university.

The 'Manny'

No one knows exactly how many young people come to work in the UK from abroad but there are around 300,000 young French people, about 600,000 from Eastern Europe, and many others. Some do temporary jobs in shops and hotels but many follow careers in management or banking. However, if you want to meet British people and learn the language, au pairing is the perfect job, and many young men are now trying it. Twenty-three-year-old Lukas Zeman from Prague is one of the new 'mannies'.

'I needed a change and there were no interesting jobs at home, so I decided to come to Britain. I have a younger sister and I am good with children, so au pairing seemed like a good idea. I get on very well with the family. Every day I have breakfast with the three children (Gemma, twelve, Rosie, ten and Max eight) and then I do the housework. I don't mind cleaning and cooking but I hate ironing! I play with the children a lot – we play games in the garden and they love playing cards! I don't know when I'm going to return home, right now I'm happy here.'

Susie and Ian Harrison, his employers, are happy, too. 'We had three au pairs before Lukas, all girls, but Lukas is one of the best. He's very calm and good with the children. They spend a lot of time doing sport and play-fighting – he's like a big brother.' ∎

*'Manny' is a new word for 'male au pair' made from man + nanny.

7 Mark the descriptions: C (Claire), L (Lukas), M (the monks) and HC (the Harrison children).

1 _M_ like(s) throwing paper aeroplanes.
2 ___ enjoy(s) playing cards.
3 ___ want(s) to work in the same place again.
4 ___ have/has a good sense of humour.
5 ___ doesn't/don't like ironing.

8 Work in groups and discuss the questions.
- Would you like to work abroad? Why? Why not?
- Would you like to try Lukas or Claire's jobs?

9 **a** Read the Harrisons' ad for a new au pair. Complete the first column in the table.

CAN YOU DO IT IN ENGLISH?

> Friendly family need au pair to look after three children. If you are aged nineteen to twenty-four, speak good English, can cook and clean, have experience with children, enjoy sport and have a good sense of humour, please email harrisons@wizzmail.com

Qualifications	Katrina	Martin
Age: 19 to 24	✓	
speaks good English		✓
can cook and clean		

b Work in pairs. Student A, read the notes about Katrina on page 124. Student B, read about Martin on page 135. Complete the correct column in the table with a tick (✓) or cross (✗).

c Think of questions to ask about the other candidate and complete the table.

“ *How old is Katrina?*
She's twenty. And how old is Martin?

d In groups, decide who is the best au pair and why. Use the *Phrases2know*. Compare your answers with the rest of the class.

 2.12

Discussing opinions

I think Katrina is best because she's older.

I don't think Katrina is suitable because …

I agree …

Yes, but Martin speaks better English.

I don't agree because …

MINI WORKBOOK exercise 9 page 107

your goals

activestudy2 EXAMS

<table>
<tr><td>ACTIVE STUDY</td><td>Notice words with opposite meaning</td></tr>
</table>

Vocabulary

1 For each word or phrase, 1–8, find the word below which is opposite in meaning. There are three extra words.

> bright   smart   tight   the worst   worse
> love   tidy   modern   generous ✓
> well-paid   sell

1 mean _generous_   5 casual _____
2 better _____   6 baggy _____
3 buy _____   7 messy _____
4 can't stand _____   8 dark _____

<table>
<tr><td>ACTIVE STUDY</td><td>Learn words in groups</td></tr>
</table>

2 Complete the sentences with the verbs below.

> afford   invest   lend ✓   owe   save

1 I need to borrow some money. Could you _lend_ me £10?

2 Sally always plans to _____ her pocket money but, in the end, she usually spends it all very quickly.

3 I _____ Jack £15. I have to pay him back next week.

4 I can't _____ to buy a new bike now. I've spent too much on my holidays.

5 He decided to _____ all his money in his friend's business.

<table>
<tr><td>ACTIVE STUDY</td><td>Learn collocations</td></tr>
</table>

3 **a** Match words a–i with the words below.

> consultant   your exams   form   hours
> job   languages ✓   representative
> worker   school

a foreign _languages_   f a social _____
b an IT _____   g a part-time _____
c an application _____   h a private _____
d to work long _____   i a sales _____
e to pass _____

b Which of the collocations are names of jobs? Which of them would you like/not like to do? Why?

I would/wouldn't like to be a … because …

<table>
<tr><td>ACTIVE STUDY</td><td>Notice the pronunciation of 'o': /ɒ/ or /əʊ/</td></tr>
</table>

4 **a** PRONUNCIATION (2.14) Listen to the pairs of words. Is the pronunciation of the letter 'o' the same (S) or different (D)?

1 f<u>o</u>reign   dr<u>o</u>p   3 m<u>o</u>dern   s<u>o</u>fa
2 l<u>o</u>cal   sh<u>o</u>pping   4 p<u>o</u>ster   wardr<u>o</u>be

b (2.14) Put the words in the right column in the table. Listen and check.

/ɒ/	/əʊ/
foreign	local

Grammar

5 Complete the second sentence so that it means the same as the first sentence.

1 Amy's bedroom is smaller than Veronica's.
Veronica's bedroom is _bigger than_ Amy's.

2 This suit is cheaper than other suits in the shop.
This suit is _____ one in the shop.

3 The blue sofa is more expensive than the green one or the black one.
The blue sofa is _____ of the three.

4 I think Physics is more difficult than Maths.
I think Maths is _____ Physics.

5 My school bag is too small.
My school bag is _____ enough.

6 Choose the correct words to complete the text.

Help! I've got the summertime blues!

Summer is holiday time. Of course I enjoy [1] *go/going/to go* on holiday with my family but this year I'd like [2] *do/doing/to do* something different. Some of my friends are planning [3] *to go/go/going* camping in the mountains and I want to go with them … but there's one problem … Well, two problems, actually.

Problem one is my father. He says I'm not [4] *enough old/old enough/too young* to go on holiday without them. But my brother is only two years older [5] *as/like/than* me and he [6] *goes/is going/to go* to have a holiday with his friends! Is that fair?

And problem two is … even if my father decides [7] *say/saying/to say* 'yes', holidays cost a lot of money. So I need [8] *to find/find/finding* a part-time job and that's not easy! I like [9] *look/looking/to look* after children but people say I'm [10] *too/too many/too much* young and I haven't got [11] *enough/many/too many* experience!

Reading Skills

ACTIVE STUDY Read for specific information

7 Three students are looking for summer jobs in the UK. Choose the best summer job, A–D, for each of them. There is one extra job.

1 Anna is studying modern languages. She speaks good English, Italian and French. She is very well-organised. She worked in her mother's office last summer and all the customers liked her. She'd like to get a night job so she can do other, interesting things during the day.

2 Peter is twenty-two and is studying literature at university. He speaks good English and some Spanish. In his free time, he does a lot of sport. Peter has got two younger brothers and a sister. He is good with children and sometimes babysits for his neighbours. He hates housework.

3 Karel is hardworking, tidy and good with his hands. At home, he always helps with housework. He would like a job where he can relax outdoors after work. But he is worried because he can't speak English.

Listening Skills

ACTIVE STUDY Listen for general understanding

8 (2.15) Listen to the interview with Imran and choose the correct answer.

1 Digital Superstore
 a always opens at 9 a.m.
 b is closed on Sundays.
 c is open seven days a week.

2 Imran works
 a at the weekend.
 b five days a week.
 c in the evening.

3 Most of his work is
 a helping customers.
 b on the telephone.
 c taking money.

4 The difficult thing about Imran's job is that
 a he's busy all the time.
 b too many people ask him for advice.
 c he needs to know about all the products.

5 He really likes
 a repairing things.
 b learning about the latest gadgets.
 c talking to people.

(2.16) Summer Jobs in the UK

A Family in Kent needs a nanny to look after four children aged three to ten during the summer. You should speak English well, have a friendly personality, get on well with children and enjoy outdoor games. Housework is not part of the job.

B Pink Cactus Café offers part-time jobs for waiters and waitresses in cafés around London. We need friendly, energetic young people with experience. You should speak some English.

C The Hanover Hotel in London has a temporary vacancy for a receptionist. You must be well-organised and good with people, speak English well and be prepared to work at night. Another European language (French, German, Spanish) a plus.

D The Kings Hotel in the seaside town of Brighton is looking for extra cleaners to work during the busy summer season. Hard work, long hours, good pay – and you can have fun on the beach in your free time! English not necessary.

Speaking Skills

9 **a** Choose one of the photos and describe it. Use the *Phrases2know* from page 21.

b Compare the photos. Use the *Phrases2know* below and your own ideas.

Phrases 2 know

In both photos the people are …

The shop on the left/on the right/in the first picture is … than the other one.

This shop looks … while this one is rather …

The couple in this picture are … than the couple in the other one.

c Talk about the kinds of shops you like.

SKILLS STRATEGIES back cover

Grammar	*should* and *must* articles
Vocabulary	Health and food
Phrases	Discussing customs Making arrangements

Vocabulary & Listening

Healthy lifestyle

1 Which of these things are good or bad for you?

> exercise   sweets   cake   soft drinks
> sleep   water   fresh fruit   vegetables
> smoking   fast food   ready meals   milk

2 **Words 2 know** (2.17) Check the words in blue. In pairs, discuss which things in exercise 1:

1 help you to lose weight?
2 make you put on weight?
3 give you energy?
4 are good for your skin?
5 are bad for your heart?
6 contain a lot of sugar?
7 contain a lot of salt?
8 are low fat?
9 are important for a healthy diet?

❝ *Exercise helps you to lose weight.*

3 How much do you know about a healthy lifestyle? Do the quiz to find out.

4 (2.18) LISTENING FOR SPECIFIC INFORMATION
Listen to Julie Maitland, a fitness expert, answering the quiz questions on a radio programme. Are your answers the same as Julie's?

5 (2.18) Listen again and tick (✓) true and cross (✗) false.

1 ☐ People who eat a good breakfast are often slimmer than people who don't.
2 ☐ Danny eats the right kind of breakfast.
3 ☐ Danny drinks eight glasses of water a day.
4 ☐ Experts say that teenagers need more exercise than adults.
5 ☐ People who sleep well live longer than people who don't.
6 ☐ Teenagers need more sleep than adults.

6 Does DJ Danny Bailey have a healthy lifestyle? Why? Why not?

MINI WORKBOOK exercise 8 page 109

LOOK GOOD, LIVE LONGER!

1 Which breakfast is best to give you energy?
a a sweet pastry
b fresh fruit
c bread or toast with an egg

2 Why is it a good idea to drink eight glasses of water a day?
a It's good for your skin.
b It helps you to stay slim.
c It's good for your digestion.

3 What's the recommended amount of exercise every day for a teenager?
a 15 minutes
b 30 minutes
c one hour

4 What's the recommended number of hours sleep for a teenager?
a 6–8 hours
b 7–9 hours
c 8–10 hours

Grammar Focus

should/shouldn't and *must/mustn't*

7 a Read Julie's advice to Danny. Match the advice in bold in 1–4 with the explanations a–d.

1 'Breakfast is the most important meal of the day. You **mustn't miss breakfast** … people who have a good breakfast live longer!'

2 'The government recommends that adults should get thirty minutes of exercise a day … So, perhaps you **should leave the car at home**, Danny?'

3 'Sleep is really important, Danny. You **must get a good night's sleep**. People who sleep well live longer than people who don't.'

4 'You **shouldn't stay in bed too late** in the morning, Danny, because it's more difficult to sleep at night when you get up late.'

a ☑ Julie thinks it's very important to do this.

b ☐ Julie thinks it's very important not to do this.

c ☐ Julie thinks this is a good idea.

d ☐ Julie thinks this isn't a good idea.

b Read *Grammar2know* and check your ideas.

Grammar 2 know

should, shouldn't

Use *should/shouldn't* to say something is/isn't a good idea or to give advice:
*You **should drink** two litres of water every day.* (it's good for your skin)
*You **shouldn't drive** everywhere.* (you don't get enough exercise)

Notice the question form of ***should***: *What **should** I eat?*

must, mustn't

Use *must/mustn't* to say that something is very important or to give rules:
*You **must** get a good night's sleep.* (you will live longer)
*You **mustn't** eat too much salt.* (it's bad for your heart)

8 (2.19) Match 1–6 with a–f to make rules about running. Then choose the right word, *must* or *mustn't*. Listen and check.

The Golden Rules of Running

Running is great exercise and doesn't cost anything … but you *must* be careful!

1 You must/mustn't warm up
2 You must/mustn't eat a big meal
3 You must/mustn't check with a doctor
4 You must/mustn't wear
5 You must/mustn't run late at night
6 You must/mustn't drink plenty of liquid

a because it can be dangerous.
b immediately after you run.
c good running shoes.
d that you are healthy enough to run.
e after you finish.
f before you start running.

9 Complete the advice for Freddie. Use *should* and *shouldn't*.

Freddie has no energy. He can't get to sleep at night and he can't get up in the morning, so he's always late for college.

1 You _____ get up when the alarm clock goes off.

2 You _____ have a shower when you wake up.

3 You _____ leave the house without having breakfast.

4 You _____ take more exercise.

5 You _____ play computer games all evening.

6 You _____ listen to heavy metal music in bed!

10 Read the situations 1–2. Use the prompts and your own ideas to give advice with *should, shouldn't, must* or *mustn't*.

1 George is a sixty-year-old man with a bad heart. He smokes, takes no exercise and puts a lot of salt on his food.

• stop smoking
• eat so much salt
• try to walk more

2 Jack has his A-levels in six months and wants to go to university. But he goes out every night, sometimes misses lessons and is getting very bad marks.

• miss any more lessons
• have a good time at weekends but stay in during the week

MINI WORKBOOK exercises 1–4 page 108

Vocabulary & Speaking

Food and drink

1 Find the odd word out and put it in the correct group.

Words 2 know

a potatoes	~~bananas~~	onions	lettuce	_____
b orange juice	sausages	mineral water	milkshake	_____
c steak	bacon	cabbage	chicken	_____
d pasta	rice	cream	cornflakes	_____
e yoghurt	lemonade	margarine	cheese	_____
f lemons	bread	grapes	strawberries	*bananas*

2 (2.20) Match groups a–f in exercise 1 with categories 1–6 below. Listen and check.

1 ☐ Meat   4 ☐ Vegetables

2 ☐ Dairy products   5 ☐ Fruit

3 ☐ Cereals   6 ☐ Drinks

3 WORD RACE How many words can you add to each category in exercise 2 in two minutes?

4 Find these things in the pictures. What other food goes with the words in blue?

Words 2 know (2.21)

a box of pastries   a loaf of bread

a packet of biscuits   a carton of yoghurt

a bottle of mineral water   a bar of chocolate

a can of lemonade   a bowl of salad

a piece of cheese   a glass of milk

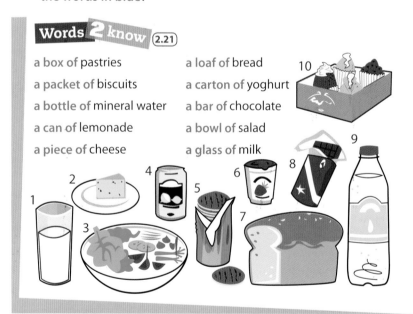

5 In pairs, answer the questions. Use the *Words2know*.

Which food/drink do you choose if you:

- need a quick breakfast?
  a piece of cheese, a glass of milk
- want a healthy snack?
- are preparing a picnic?
- are really, really thirsty?
- are starving and in a hurry?

MINI WORKBOOK exercise 9 page 109

Grammar Focus

a/an, the, zero article (ø)

6 **a** PREDICTING Look at the photos and answer the questions about the people.

- What are their jobs? Do you think their diet is important for their work?
- Guess what they eat before a match or performance.

b Read the three texts quickly and check.

7 Read about Sonny. <u>Underline</u>:

- five examples of *a/an*
- five examples of *the*.

Then read *Grammar2know*.

SONNY ALABA, 19, is a young footballer from Nigeria. He plays for a club in the English Premier League, called Portsmouth. 'Diet is really important for footballers. Pasta and potatoes are the best kinds of food if you want to play well – they give you energy. I've got an important match this afternoon. The match starts at three so I'm having lunch now, about four hours before the match starts. I always have a bowl of pasta with tomato sauce and then fruit but I can't eat meat because it's difficult to digest. Oh, and I drink a lot of water, because during the match, we lose two or three litres!'

Grammar 2 know

Articles: *a/an* and *the*

Use *a/an* to talk about one of many:
*He plays for **a** football club …* (there are many football clubs)

Use *the* for things that are unique:
*… in **the** English Premier League.* (there is only one)

Use *a/an* to talk about things for the first time. After that, use *the*:
*I've got **an** important match this afternoon.*
***The** match starts at three o'clock.*

No article (ø)

Don't use an article when you talk about generalisations:
ø Diet is important for ø footballers.
ø Pasta gives you ø energy.

Remember!

Use *a/an* with:
- jobs: *Sonny is **a** professional footballer.*
- expressions of quantity: ***a** plate of pasta, **a** lot of water*

Use *the* with:
- superlative adjectives: *Pasta is **the** best thing.*
- parts of the day: *in **the** morning/afternoon*

Don't use an article with meals and mealtimes:
I have ø lunch at half past eleven.

8 Complete the texts about Marina and Katsuko with *a/an*, *the* or ø.

9 (2.22) Use the words in A and B below to make generalisations. Then listen and compare your ideas to the recording.

A
> fish coffee tea salt olive oil chocolate

> … is/are good/bad for your …

B
> heart skin teeth brain hair waistline concentration

Chocolate and coffee are bad for your skin.

MINI WORKBOOK exercises 5–7 page 109

EAT RIGHT (2.23)

MARINA SCHNEIDER, 19, is ¹ ___ professional ballet dancer with ² ___ Royal Ballet, ³ ___ most famous ballet company in Britain. 'Usually, ⁴ ___ ballet dancers only weigh about 45 kg so we are very careful about ⁵ ___ food. Three or four hours before ⁶ ___ performance, I have ⁷ ___ baked potato or ⁸ ___ bowl of pasta. Then, just before ⁹ ___ performance starts, I eat ¹⁰ ___ orange and ¹¹ ___ bar of chocolate. ¹² ___ orange gives me liquid and ¹³ ___ chocolate gives me energy.'

KATSUKO SASAKI, 18, wants to become ¹⁴ ___ professional sumo wrestler. ¹⁵ ___ Sumo wrestlers need to be fat, so their diet is very unusual. They don't have ¹⁶ ___ breakfast before they train in ¹⁷ ___ morning, so they're very hungry at ¹⁸ ___ lunchtime. They start lunch with five or six bowls of special soup, called chankonabe. Then, they eat ¹⁹ ___ big bowl of rice and ²⁰ ___ lot of meat – maybe fifteen or twenty pieces! They also drink ²¹ ___ lot of beer and then they go to sleep in ²² ___ afternoon for about four hours!

Reading & Speaking

1 In pairs, put these meals in the correct order. Then answer the questions.

- [ ] lunch [ ] late snack [ ] elevenses
- [ ] dinner [ ] breakfast [ ] tea

- Do you normally eat these meals?
- What time and where do you usually have them?

2 SCANNING Read the text and find two things that the British eat or drink at the meals in exercise 1.

breakfast – a cup of coffee or a bowl of cereal

3 Read the text again and choose the correct answer.

1 Somerset Maugham
  a ate three breakfasts every day.
  b thought breakfast was the best meal in England.
  c ate a very big breakfast every day.

2 Most people in Britain
  a have breakfast in a hotel.
  b don't have time for a 'full' breakfast.
  c don't eat breakfast.

3 At around 11.00 in the UK,
  a schools and offices close.
  b people eat eleven kilos of biscuits.
  c people often have a snack.

4 At lunchtime, people do not usually
  a have a packed lunch.
  b have lunch with their family.
  c have a sandwich.

5 At 5.00, younger children often
  a eat sandwiches and cakes.
  b eat without their parents.
  c have tea in a hotel.

6 Many British families
  a don't eat together very often.
  b eat a takeaway once a month.
  c don't eat ready meals from the supermarket.

7 Many people say that
  a curry is more 'typical' than fish and chips in Britain.
  b curry is nicer than fish and chips.
  c there are too many Chinese and Indian takeaways.

2.25

EATING AROUND THE CLOCK

What do British people really eat?

7–9 a.m. Breakfast

'To eat well in England,' wrote the novelist Somerset Maugham, 'you should eat breakfast three times a day.' A traditional British breakfast includes cereal, bacon, sausages, eggs, tomatoes … and if that's not enough,
5 there's toast and marmalade and tea or coffee to drink. Of course, it all takes a long time, so people normally only eat a 'full' breakfast when they are staying in a hotel or on special occasions. Most people just have a quick cup of coffee, a glass of fruit juice or a bowl of cereal
10 as they hurry to school or work … and 22% of people don't eat breakfast at all!

11 a.m. Elevenses

Getting hungry? Many schools and offices in Britain stop for a coffee break around 11 o'clock and people have 'elevenses': maybe a bar of chocolate, a piece of fruit, a
15 biscuit or two … or three! Actually, the British eat more biscuits than any other nation in the world, eleven kilos per person every year!

12–2 p.m. Lunch

Sunday lunch is a popular time for a family meal but during the week, most people eat lunch at work or
20 school. Generally, people don't have time for a hot meal at lunchtime, so sandwiches (a British invention, of course!) are very popular; in fact, we eat two billion of them every year. Did you know that the London department store, Selfridges, sells the world's most
25 expensive sandwich? It costs £85! Children often take a packed lunch to school and healthy school lunches are a 'hot topic' right now.

5 p.m. Tea

Because parents work late, younger children often eat separately, at around five o'clock. We call this meal 'tea',
30 although in reality, children probably have pizza, pasta or sausages (and ice-cream)! In hotels and teashops, however, you can still get a traditional English tea. This is much more than just a cup of tea – it comes with sandwiches, toast, tasty cream cakes and scones!
35 Plenty to fill you up until it's time for …

6–9 p.m. Dinner

Usually this is the main meal of the day but as people get busier, it is becoming less common for families to eat together. One survey found that the average British family only eats together once a month! Instead,
40 different members of the family eat different meals at different times: often ready meals from the supermarket or takeaways. Traditional 'fish and chips' are still popular but there are now more Chinese and Indian takeaway restaurants. Many people believe that curry is the
45 national dish, not fish and chips!

10–11 p.m. … and a little late snack

Many people enjoy a late night snack, often with a hot drink: tea or hot chocolate are popular at bedtime. Then there is time for a few hours sleep before it all starts again!

---

4 Read *Active Study*. Then match the words in A and B to make compound nouns from the text. Read and check.

Notice compound nouns

We often put two words together to make a new word:

| noun + noun: | *fruit juice, ice-cream* |
| adjective + noun: | *hot chocolate* |

We call these words compound nouns.

bedtime

A	B
bed	break
coffee	time
lunch	lunch
packed	dish
cream	meal
ready	time
national	cake

5 Discuss these questions with the class.
- Do families in your country normally eat together or not?
- Are takeaways popular? What kind?

6 Work in pairs. One of you is a British visitor. Ask and answer questions about food in your country, using the *Phrases2know*.

- What do you normally eat for breakfast?
- How is the evening meal different from lunch?
- What's your favourite snack?

Phrases 2 know (2.24)

Discussing customs

Most people have cereal and milk.

Generally, people have lunch at home.

We don't usually eat takeaways.

Chicken is traditional/very popular.

Responding

Really?

Yes, it's the same in my country.

It's similar/different in my country because people work very late.

What do you normally eat for breakfast?
Most people have toast and cereal.
Really? In my country, people generally …

REAL TIME

AN INVITATION

1 Look at the photo. Where do you think Zack and Grace are going?

> Grace and friend
> <u>Please come to</u>
> Ellie's 18th birthday party!
> On Saturday 7 August
> <u>from 8 till very late!</u>
> At 17 Clifton Gardens.
> <u>With drinks, food and dancing</u>!
> Casual dress
> <u>Contact</u> EllieM@tikit.com

2 Look at the invitation and put the information below in order.

a the date ☐
b how to reply ☐
c short description of the party ☐
d the time ☐
e whose party it is and the reason ☐
f the address ☐
g who the invitation is for ☐

3 Which *Phrases2know* are similar to the <u>underlined</u> phrases in the invitation?

Phrases 2 know (2.26)

Invitations
RSVP   *contact*
From 8.00 p.m. until midnight
Please come in fancy dress
You are invited to
Live band and dancing
Please bring drinks or nibbles

4 In pairs, write an invitation to one of the parties below. Include all the information in exercise 2. Use the *Phrases2know*.

- End of exams party
- Fancy dress party
- Birthday party
- Farewell party

5 Grace decides to invite Zack as her guest. Read the text messages they exchange below.

a Find the text abbreviations for these words.

[you   are   later   see   birthday
Saturday   great   and   night]

you = u

b Rewrite the messages in full. Does Zack accept or refuse?

> 16:57
> **Grace**
> 04-Aug 16:55
>
> It's my friend's bday party this sat nite. r u free? can u come?
>
> Reply

> 17:00
> **Grace**
> 04-Aug 16:59
>
> 8pm her place. c u l8r xxx
>
> More

> **Zack**
> 04-Aug   16:58
>
> ▮ sounds gr8.
> ▮ when n where?
> ▮ z
>
> Options   Back

MAKING ARRANGEMENTS

6 (2.27) **Look at the photo and read the caption. Then listen and answer the questions.**

1 Who's calling Zack?
2 How is Zack feeling? How do we know?
3 Why is Pat calling?
4 Why does Zack refuse?
5 What reason does Zack give?
6 What arrangements do they make in the end?

It's the morning after Ellie's party. There's a phone call for Zack.

7 (2.28) **Listen and complete the *Phrases2know*. Listen again and practise the intonation.**

Phrases 2 know

Making arrangements
Would you like to ¹_____ ?
Are you free ²_____ ?
How about ³_____ instead?
Why don't you ⁴_____ ?
Shall we ⁵_____?

Accepting
That would be lovely, ⁶_____ .
That sounds ⁷_____ !
That's a good idea.

Refusing
I'm sorry, ⁸_____ .
I'm afraid I've got ⁹_____ .

Grace and Zack go for lunch with Zack's aunt and uncle.

8 (2.29) **Listen to the conversation at lunch and put these events in order.**

a ☐ Ken offers Zack and Grace drinks.
b ☐ Pat asks Zack about his girlfriend in California.
c ☑ 1 Zack and Grace arrive.
d ☐ Ken asks Zack about his university course.
e ☐ They all sit down to eat.
f ☐ Zack says his girlfriend is coming to Europe.
g ☐ Pat offers Grace more pudding.

9 **Use the prompts and the *Phrases2know* in exercise 7 to write the dialogues below. Then act out the dialogues in pairs.**

1 **A:** have a coffee together after class
Why don't we have a coffee together after class?
B: no/I've got a dentist's appointment
I'm sorry, I can't …
A: tomorrow instead?
B: yes/go to Gino's café
A: yes

2 **A:** go swimming together one day?
B: yes/Saturday morning?
A: no/go shopping on Saturday
B: Sunday morning?
A: yes/10.30?
B: meet at my house?
A: yes

10 **In groups of three, take turns to act out the dialogue below. Follow the chart and use the *Phrases2know* in exercise 7.**

CAN YOU DO IT IN ENGLISH?

A: Invite B and C to your place to watch a movie and have a pizza. → **B and C:** Accept.

A: Suggest next Friday night. → **B:** Refuse politely. It's your brother's birthday.

A: Suggest Saturday night instead. → **B and C:** Accept.

A: Suggest a film to watch. → **B:** Agree and suggest the time.

A and C: Agree.

6 the rules

Grammar	Obligation and permission in the present and past
Vocabulary	Rules and behaviour *make* and *do*
Phrases	Discussing opinions

Reading & Listening

1 Look at the photo of Ed, an 'out-of-control' teenager. Read Part 1 of the text. <u>Underline</u> Ed's problems.

2 Use the verbs to complete the phrases. Read Part 1 again and check.

Words 2 know (2.30)

do   go   have   get   not get ✓   not take

1 <u>*not get*</u> on with someone
2 _____ an argument with someone
3 _____ badly at school
4 _____ into trouble
5 _____ wrong
6 _____ any notice

3 Read various opinions about Ed. Which do you agree with?

1 'Ed's only young. He'll be okay in a couple of years.'
2 'He needs to get a job and do some hard work.'
3 'We need to understand teenagers like Ed and help them with their problems.'
4 'He needs something like prison or the army.'
5 'Ed needs more love from his parents.'

4 Read Part 2. Answer the questions about what Ed's parents did.

- Where did Ed's parents send him? Do you think it's a good idea?
- Which camp rules do you think are good/bad?
- Do you think Ed changed or not?

(2.32)

BRAT CAMP

Part 1

Ed, sixteen, is an out-of-control teenager. He lives in a comfortable home in North London with his parents and younger sister but something in Ed's life is going wrong. He is doing badly at school and often misses lessons. His teachers say he needs professional help but Ed refuses to see anyone. He uses drugs and alcohol regularly and he often has arguments with his parents. He also gets into trouble for stealing.

His parents cannot understand him. His mother, Sheila says, 'We try to discipline him but he doesn't take any notice. Every day's a battle. We just don't know what to do.'

According to Ed, 'I try not to spend too much time with my parents because we always have arguments. I don't get on with them, end of story.'

Part 2

Ed's parents heard about 'Brat Camps' in the USA. These are camps where difficult teenagers live far away from other people, in an atmosphere of strict discipline and hard work. They decided to send Ed to 'Turnaround Camp' in the Arizona desert. Here are some of the rules:

- There is no contact with friends or family. Parents can phone and check on their children but teenagers aren't allowed to phone their parents.
- Students do all the housework, as well as normal schoolwork. They have to prepare their own meals and eat together.
- Students can't have mobile phones, TV, MP3 players or computer games.
- Students have to wear camp uniform. They aren't allowed to wear make-up, hair products or jewellery.

5 **(2.31)** LISTENING FOR GIST Listen to Ed and his mother talking about their experiences. Tick (✓) the true statements.

1 ☐ At the camp, Ed realised that he was very unhappy with himself.

2 ☐ Ed's mother stopped worrying about him after he returned from the camp.

3 ☐ Brat Camp was a success for Ed and his life is better now.

4 ☐ Ed is still angry with his parents.

MINI WORKBOOK exercise 5 page 111

Grammar Focus

Obligation and permission in the present

6 **a** Read Part 2 of the text and <u>underline</u> the rules about these things.

> parents phoning camp   using mobile phones
> wearing camp uniform   wearing make-up
> watching TV if students behave well
> working on Sunday

b Now mark the <u>underlined</u> rules:

1 = it's necessary to do this
2 = it isn't necessary to do this
3 = it's permitted
4 = it's not permitted.

- There is strictly no bad language, smoking, alcohol or drugs.
- There are no beds – students sleep outside in tents. Wake-up time is 6.30 a.m.
- If students break the rules, they have to move to a special tent and are not allowed to speak to anyone.
- If they behave well, they get small rewards – they are allowed to eat cakes or watch a little TV.
- Sunday is a rest-day – students don't have to work and they can talk about their problems with camp counsellors.
- Camp counsellors are with the students twenty-four hours a day, as teachers, friends and helpers.

7 Read *Grammar2know* and find more examples of the camp rules in exercise 6.

Permission in the present

- Use *can* and *is/are allowed to* to talk about things that are permitted:
  Students **are allowed to** watch TV if they behave well.
  _Parents can ..._____

- Use *can't* and *is/are not allowed to* to talk about things that are not permitted:
  Students **can't** have TV.

  _____

Obligation in the present

- Use *have to* to talk about things that are necessary to do:
  They **have to** cook their own meals.

- Use *don't have to* to talk about things that are not necessary to do:

  _____

8 Read Part 2 of the text again and find rules about 1–8. Write sentences, using the verbs in *Grammar2know*.

1 use bad language
  Students are not allowed to use bad language.

2 wear jewellery

3 do all the housework

4 get up at 6.30

5 eat cake if they're good

6 listen to MP3 players

7 do schoolwork on Sunday

8 discuss their problems with counsellors

9 Imagine you are going on a weekend camping trip with your class. Make a set of rules for the class and teachers to follow. Think about:

- mobile phones/games consoles/MP3 players
- food/drink/cooking
- bed time/getting up time
- clothing and equipment.

❝ *We can bring mobile phones but we aren't allowed to bring games consoles.*

MINI WORKBOOK exercise 1 page 110

the rules

Listening & Speaking

Rules and behaviour

1 Work in pairs and discuss these questions.

- Does your family have a lot of rules?
- What rules are there about these things?

  ☐ watching TV ☐ tidying your room
  ☐ going on the computer ☐ clothes
  ☐ make-up ☐ staying out late
  ☐ mobile phone ☐ homework

> *I'm allowed to watch TV when I want. What about you?*
>
> *I can watch TV after I do my homework.*

2 Look at the photos of Ivy, Sally and Katie. How old are they? When were Sally and Ivy teenagers?

I think Sally was a teenager in the 70s.

3 (2.33) Listen to Katie, Sally and Ivy talking about their parents' rules. Which topics in exercise 1 does each person mention? Mark the topics K, S or I.

4 Words 2 know (2.33) Check the words in blue. Then listen again and tick (✓) true and cross (✗) false.

1 ☐ Katie's parents are strict about everything.
2 ☐ Katie's mum punished her when she got bad marks in her exams.
3 ☐ Sally's parents were very easy-going.
4 ☐ Sally thinks parents should guide their children but not control them.
5 ☐ Ivy doesn't agree with the way Sally is bringing her daughter up.
6 ☐ The rules in Ivy's family weren't very fair for the girls.
7 ☐ Ivy didn't have any freedom about things like clothes and make-up.

5 Do you think parents should be easy-going or strict?

MINI WORKBOOK exercise 6 page 111

Ivy

Sally

THREE GENERATIONS

Katie

Grammar Focus

Obligation and permission in the past

6 Read what Ivy and Sally said 1–8 and <u>underline</u> the past forms of *can*, *have to* and *be allowed to*. Then complete *Grammar2know*.

1 'I wasn't allowed to stay out after a certain time.'

2 'All the girls had to help my mother with the housework.'

3 'My brothers didn't have to do the washing-up.'

4 'I couldn't wear clothes if my mother didn't like them.'

5 'We weren't allowed to wear make-up.'

6 'After I was sixteen, I was allowed to wear a little bit of lipstick.'

7 'We were allowed to play out in the streets.'

8 'We could walk around after dark.'

Grammar 2know

Obligation and permission

in the present	in the past
is allowed to	*was allowed to*
are allowed to	_____
isn't allowed to	_____
aren't allowed to	_____
can	_____
can't	_____
have to	_____
don't have to	_____

7 a (2.34) Listen to Ivy saying more about when she was young. Write the verbs that she uses to talk about topics 1–8.

1 Taking a lot of exams *didn't have to*

2 Staying at school _____

3 Taking the school leaving exam _____

4 Leaving school at fourteen to get a job _____

5 Giving her wages to her mother _____

6 Spending her pocket money on herself _____

7 Boys going in the army _____

8 Her brother going to university _____

b Write about Ivy in full sentences.

1 Ivy didn't have to take a lot of exams at school.

8 a Make the sentences below true for you. Then compare your answers with a partner.

" When I was little, I couldn't play out in the street. What about you?

1 When I was little, I …
   a … (can) play out in the street.
   b … (be allowed to) watch a lot of TV.
   c … (have to) go to bed early on school nights.
   d … (have to) help with the housework.

2 At primary school, I …
   a … (have to) wear school uniform.
   b … (allowed to) walk home by myself.
   c … (have to) do lots of homework every night.
   d … (can) play ball games at playtime.

b What other important rules can you remember from your childhood? Tell the class.

MINI-WORKBOOK exercises 2–4 page 110

Vocabulary & Speaking

make and *do*

9 a Do you share domestic tasks in your family? Answer the questions in the *Words2know*.

Words 2know (2.35)

In your family, who …

• makes breakfast? *everyone makes their own*

• does the cooking? _____

• does the most housework? _____

• makes the most phone calls? _____

• does the hoovering? _____

• makes the beds? _____

• does the washing-up? _____

• does the ironing? _____

• makes the best sandwiches? _____

• makes the most mess? _____

• does nothing in the house? _____

b Compare answers in pairs.

10 Look at the *Words2know* and make two lists.

Phrases with *make*: *make phone calls*

Phrases with *do*: *do housework*

11 Write six sentences about what people in your family do/don't do. Then compare and discuss them, in pairs.

" I make the most phone calls. My father never does the ironing.

MINI WORKBOOK exercise 7 page 111

the rules

47

Reading & Vocabulary

Society and the law

1 Look at the photos on page 49 and answer these questions.

- What are the people in each photo doing?
- How old do you think they are?

2 Read the paragraph headings on page 49. Which paragraph(s) do you think these words come from?

Words 2 know (2.36)

- ☐ to join the army   ☐ to go to prison
- ☐ to steal   ☐ to commit a crime/a murder
- ☐ to vote   ☐ ID   ☐ to be banned
- ☐ to take a driving test   ☐ to be illegal
- ☐ the death penalty

3 SCANNING Read the text on page 49 and complete the sentences with a correct number or date.

1 In Iran, you are allowed to vote from the age of _____ .

2 Women started voting in New Zealand in _____ .

3 In China, no one can get married until they are _____ .

4 Swiss men have to do military service every year for _____ weeks.

5 In Australia, the age of criminal responsibility is from _____ .

6 The minimum age you can buy alcohol in the USA is _____ .

7 In parts of the USA, you can drive from the age of _____ .

8 British people didn't have to take a driving test before _____ .

4 Read the text again. Complete the sentences with the *Words2know* from exercise 2. Put one word in each gap.

a In England, it's _____ to get married at the age of sixteen without your parents' permission.

b In Britain, children under ten aren't responsible if they _____ _____ _____ , even if they kill someone!

c In Britain, young men don't have to do military service but if they want to, they can _____ the army at sixteen.

d If you don't vote in Argentina, you can go to _____ .

e If young people want to buy alcohol in the USA, they have to show _____ .

f In Britain, you can _____ your _____ test at seventeen.

5 Now match sentences a–f in exercise 4 with paragraphs 1–6 in the text.

6 **a** Work in pairs. Find three laws in the text that are the same in your country, and three that are different.

CAN YOU DO IT IN ENGLISH?

b In pairs, use the ideas below and your own ideas to invent six new laws for your country. Write out your laws.

People can vote from the age of fourteen. Smoking is banned in all public places.

- People can vote/drive a car/get married/ go to nightclubs/leave school from the age of …
- All young men/women have to do military/voluntary service for … months/ years.
- Smoking/drinking is banned in all public places/in the street/everywhere.
- School students don't have to study… / do homework any more.
- Parents have to …/Teenagers aren't allowed to …

c Work with a new partner. Read out your laws and find out what he/she thinks of them. Use the *Phrases2know*.

Phrases 2 know (2.37)

Discussing opinions

Personally, I think that's a really good idea!

I completely agree with that.

I'm not sure about that.

I don't really agree with that.

Sorry, but I don't think that's a very good idea!

" *People can vote from the age of fourteen. Sorry, but I don't think that's a very good idea!*

d Choose the best two laws from both lists and present them to the class.

" *I think it's good that it's illegal to buy alcohol …*

MINI WORKBOOK exercise 8 page 111

10...14...16...18...21
How does the law affect you? (2.38)

1 Voting

In most countries around the world, including Britain, you can vote from the age of eighteen. In some countries, like Argentina, you have to vote – if you don't, you can go to prison! The youngest voters in the world are in Iran. You can vote there from the age of fifteen. Some politicians in Britain want to change the voting age to sixteen, to involve young people more in politics.

FACT! New Zealand was the first country to give women the vote – in 1893.

2 Marriage

In most of Europe, you are allowed to marry at eighteen (sixteen with your parents' permission). In China, couples need to be more patient – men can't marry before the age of twenty-two and women before twenty.

FACT! In Scotland, young people can marry at sixteen without their parents' permission. That's why, traditionally, young couples run away to Gretna Green (on the English/Scottish border) for 'quickie' weddings.

3 Military Service

In many European countries, young men have to do military service, usually for between three and eighteen months. In Switzerland, men have to go back into the army every year for three weeks. In Britain, there is only a professional army. You can join the army from the age of sixteen.

FACT! If you drop out of high school in Egypt, you have to do four years military service instead!

4 Criminal responsibility

In Britain, you become responsible for crimes you commit from the age of ten. Before that, the law says that you are too young to understand your actions, whether you spray graffiti on a wall, steal sweets or commit murder! In parts of the USA and Australia, this age is just six, while in most European countries, it is fifteen or sixteen.

FACT! Until recently, many US states used the death penalty for criminals under eighteen. Between 1990 and 2005, nineteen young people died in this way.

5 Smoking and drinking

In the UK, it's illegal to buy alcohol until you are eighteen years old (although you're allowed to drink alcohol at home from the age of five!). In the USA, you're not allowed to buy alcohol until you're twenty-one and they are very strict about ID.

FACT! In most US states and in the UK, smoking is banned inside bars and nightclubs and you're not allowed to drink alcohol outside them!

6 Driving

According to UK law, you are not allowed to drive until you are seventeen, while in most of Europe it is eighteen. In the USA, you can drive much younger, in some states from the age of just fourteen!

FACT! Until 1935, you didn't have to take a driving test in the UK – you could just buy a car and drive away!

DRIVING LICEN

49

activestudy3

Vocabulary

1 Choose the words a–c that can complete each phrase 1–6. There are two correct answers for each.

1 a healthy _diet_
   a diet   **b** energy   **c** lifestyle

2 to _____ weight
   a put on   **b** lose   **c** get

3 a bowl of _____
   a cheese   **b** cereal   **c** soup

4 a _____ lunch
   a school   **b** ready   **c** packed

5 a can of _____
   a lemonade   **b** bread   **c** cola

6 to commit _____
   a a murder   **b** a crime   **c** a law

2 Match the beginnings and endings to make sentences.

1 **Strict** parents …

2 **Easy-going** parents …

3 **Fair** parents …

4 To **bring up** children, parents often have to …

a … **guide** them in difficult situations.

b … often **punish** their children.

c … don't **control** their children much and give them a lot of **freedom**.

d … **treat** all their children in the **same way**.

3 Underline the correct verb: *do, have* or *make*.

1 My sister and I never *do/have/make* any arguments.

2 My father always *does/has/makes* our holiday arrangements.

3 My brother is so lazy! He never *does/has/makes* any housework at all.

4 You can use the kitchen – but please don't *do/have/make* a mess!

5 I'm worried about Lukas – he is *doing/having/making* badly at school right now.

6 You have to *do/have/make* your homework before you go out.

7 My mum says I should *do/have/make* my bed before going to school.

8 In Spain, people often *do/have/make* dinner at 9 p.m.

4 PRONUNCIATION (2.39) Listen to the words and put them in the right column. Then listen again and check.

> fizzy   involve   tidy   slim   skin
> diet   rice   crime   prison   drive

/ɪ/	/aɪ/
fizzy	tidy

Grammar

5 Choose the best alternative for each sentence.

> don't have to ✓   can   should   mustn't

English teachers [1] _don't have to_ speak English perfectly but they [2] _____ be able to explain things clearly. It usually helps if they [3] _____ speak their students' language, too. They certainly [4] _____ get angry if students make mistakes!

> mustn't   are allowed to   have to   should

Most students of English [5] _____ do exams at some time in their life. If you want to do well, you [6] _____ study hard before the exam. In some exams, you [7] _____ use dictionaries but you [8] _____ copy from your neighbours or you will fail the exam.

> could   didn't have to   had to
> weren't allowed to

I didn't enjoy learning French when I was at school. Our teacher was very strict. Every lesson we [9] _____ listen to him reading from the textbook. We [10] _____ speak even when we didn't understand and we [11] _____ only ask questions at the end of the lesson. I was happy I [12] _____ take an exam at the end because my French was terrible!

6 Complete the sentences with *a, an, the* or ø.

1 Let's go to _a_ restaurant today! How about ___ new Greek restaurant on the corner?

2 My neighbours have ___ cat and ___ dog. ___ cat is quiet but ___ dog makes a lot of noise.

3 ___ children shouldn't be allowed to drink fizzy soft drinks with lots of sugar.

4 ___ love is the most important thing in life.

5 My father is ___ engineer.

6 Let's buy her ___ box of chocolates.

7 I usually have ___ breakfast at 8 a.m.

Reading Skills

ACTIVE STUDY | Read for gist

7 **a** Read the text quickly. What problem is the British government trying to solve? How?

b Read the text again. Choose the best answer a–d for questions 1–5.

Cooking at School (2.41)

According to experts, nearly 25% of Britons, including children, are overweight. The government is worried and it is looking for ways to solve the problem.

Many 11-14-year olds already do cookery at school but from 2011, the government is making this compulsory. They hope that this will encourage people to cook instead of eating ready meals, fast food and snacks.

All secondary school students will have cooking lessons for one hour a week for one term. They will learn to use simple, fresh ingredients and simple recipes to prepare healthy, tasty meals, for example a good tomato sauce for pasta.

And schools are setting up cookery clubs called 'Let's Get Cooking' throughout the country. The clubs will give more children the chance to learn to cook after school.

Head Teachers worry about the equipment they will need for the lessons. About 15% of schools do not have kitchens and there are not enough cookery teachers.

The government is promising to train 800 cookery teachers and to give schools £2.5 million a year to help children from poorer families to pay for ingredients.

1 The British government is worried because
   a the number of people in Britain is growing.
   b many people in Britain are overweight.
   c 25% of British children are overweight.
   d it does not know how to solve the problem.

2 All pupils are going to learn to cook
   a in primary school.
   b for one hour a week for a year.
   c for two hours a week for one term.
   d using simple ingredients and recipes.

3 Schools are setting up 'Let's Get Cooking' clubs to
   a train cookery teachers.
   b teach children cooking skills.
   c help poorer children.
   d give parents cooking lessons.

4 One problem mentioned in the article is that
   a head teachers do not know how to cook.
   b some schools do not have enough equipment.
   c students prefer to eat snacks and ready meals.
   d students forget to buy ingredients.

5 The government is promising to
   a buy the equipment.
   b pay the teachers.
   c pay for ingredients for poorer students.
   d pay for school lunches for poorer students.

Listening Skills

ACTIVE STUDY | Listen for specific information

8 (2.40) Jenny and David are discussing the food they want to have at a party. Listen to their conversation and complete sentences 1–6 with one word in each gap.

1 David offers to buy _eight_ bottles of fizzy drinks.
2 Jenny wants to put a bowl of _____ fruit on the table.
3 David's mother cooks a lot of rice and _____ .
4 David would like to order _____ .
5 Jenny wants to buy six cartons of _____ .
6 They also plan to buy _____ loaves of bread.

Speaking Skills

9 In pairs, act out the dialogue below. Use the *Phrases2know* on page 43. Student A begins the conversation.

A	B
You want to go out on Friday evening. Ask if B is free. ⟶	You are busy on Friday (say why). Suggest Saturday.
Accept Saturday. ⟵	
Suggest an activity (e.g. going to a film). ⟶	You don't like A's suggestion. Suggest a different activity (e.g. going bowling).
Accept. Suggest a time and place to meet. ⟶ ⟵	Agree the time and place.

SKILLS STRATEGIES back cover

7 time out

Grammar	Future arrangements *will, may, might*
Vocabulary	Holidays and travel
Phrases	Describing holidays / Showing interest / Giving and asking for advice

Vocabulary & Reading

Holidays

1 What do you like doing on holiday? Divide the activities in *Words2know* into three categories. Add your own ideas and compare answers in pairs.

Things I love	Things I quite like	Things I don't enjoy
shopping		

Words 2 know (3.2)

shopping   sightseeing   sunbathing
visiting galleries   looking at scenery   relaxing
going to clubs   going to the beach   eating out
camping   hanging out with friends

I love shopping on holiday but I hate sunbathing. And you?

2 **Words 2 know** (3.3) Check the words in blue below and discuss these questions in pairs.

- Do you agree that family holidays can be 'heaven or hell'?
- Who are these tips for, parents or teenagers? Are they good ideas?

Family holidays can be heaven or hell! Follow these tips for a stress-free holiday with your teenagers.

- Try not to spend too long travelling to and from your holiday destination. Long journeys can be boring.
- Don't ask your teenagers to get up at 8 o'clock every day! Most young people hate getting up early … especially during the holidays!
- Plan your excursions together, so there is something for everyone.
- Make sure your hotel has internet access so that they can keep in touch with friends at home.
- Make sure you go somewhere with a bit of nightlife or late-night shopping, so that your teenagers have something to do in the evening.

3 Read the holiday brochure. Match the destinations 1–3 with the holidays A–C.

1 London – one of the world's great cities
2 The beautiful Greek island of Rhodes
3 Two-centre holiday in unforgettable Florida

4 Read about the holidays again. Make a list of places to go and things to do on each holiday.

Rhodes	London	Florida
windsurfing		

5 Choose your favourite holiday. Compare and explain your choices in pairs.

I like the holiday in London best because there's lots of nightlife.
Personally, I don't like dancing, I like …

MINI WORKBOOK exercise 5 page 113

Families2gether (3.5)

Why not try one of our top three family holidays?

A • Comfortable family accommodation with private pool near the beach.
- Try windsurfing or even paragliding!
- Close to the lively resort of Faliraki with nightclubs, restaurants and shopping.

B **Week one: Orlando**
- Visit world-class theme parks, like Wet'n'Wild and Disney World.
- Exciting restaurants and nightlife.

Week two: Everglades Nature Reserve
- World-famous wildlife including fish, birds and alligators.
- Free cycling, fishing and camping.

Grammar Focus

Future arrangements

6 (3.4) Listen to Sophie (S) talking to her friend, Laura (L) about her holiday plans. Answer the questions.

- Where is Sophie going?
- Who is she going with?

7 (3.4) Put the dialogue in the correct order. Listen again and check.

L: Cool … who's going? ☐
S: Mum and Dad, obviously … but my big sister's not coming this year, just my little brother.

L: So, are you going on holiday with your family this summer? ☐ 1
S: Yeah, we're flying to Florida two days after the end of term.

L: What's that? ☐
S: It's a kind of nature reserve, with alligators and birds and stuff. We're going camping!

L: It sounds really cool! You are so lucky! ☐
S: I know. I can't wait!

L: Oh well, nothing's perfect! What are you doing there? ☐
S: We're spending a week in Orlando, you know, visiting all the theme parks and stuff. Then we're staying in this place called the Everglades.

C • Top city centre hotel, minutes from Big Ben and other famous sights.
  • Close to world-famous theatres, restaurants, shops, markets, parks, galleries and museums.
  • Includes half-day boat trip along the River Thames.

Familie2gether

8 Read *Grammar2know*. Then underline three more verbs in the dialogue that describe the arrangements for Sophie's holiday.

Grammar 2 know

Future arrangements

Use the present continuous to describe definite arrangements in the future:
We're flying to Florida **two days after the end of term**.
My sister**'s not coming this year**.
Are you **going** on holiday **this summer**?

Notice that we often use a time expression to show that it is in the future.
Time expressions: *this evening/year, at the weekend, after lunch, next Friday/week, in the next few days/weeks,* etc.

9 Read the notes in Sophie's diary and write sentences about her arrangements. Use the present continuous.

Sophie's having a guitar lesson at 11.00 on Monday.

Monday	guitar lesson 11.00
Tuesday	babysit 7.30
Wednesday	no school! meet Laura and Isabel – Market café 2.30
Thursday	holiday shopping with Mum – 4.00
Friday	Laura's end of term party – 7.30
Saturday	morning – pack!!!
Sunday	fly from Heathrow at 4.30 a.m.!!!

10 Use the prompts to make questions. Then ask and answer in pairs.

1 do anything/later today?
2 go out/this evening?
3 meet any friends/at the weekend?
4 make any trips/in the next few weeks?
5 go on holiday/next summer?

" *Are you doing anything later today? I'm going to town with my friends./ Not really.*

MINI WORKBOOK exercises 1–2 page 112

Listening & Vocabulary

Flying

1 Read about the things you do at an airport and check the words in blue. Which sentences are illustrated in the pictures?

a

b

c

MADRID	delayed
WARSAW	11.10
LONDON	delayed
ISTANBUL	delayed
NEW YORK	12.30

d

Words 2 know

1 You arrive at the airport.
2 You find the check-in desk for your airline.
3 _____
4 You go through passport control.
5 You go through security with your hand luggage.
6 You do some shopping in the duty-free shop.
7 You check the departures board to see if your flight is delayed.
8 _____
9 You board the plane.
10 _____
11 The plane takes off.
12 The plane lands at your destination.
13 _____
14 You go through the arrivals gate. You're there!

2 (3.6) In pairs, put the activities a–d in the correct place in *Words2know*. Then listen and check.

a You sit down and fasten your seat belt.
b You check in your luggage and get your boarding card.
c You find the departure gate.
d You get off the plane and collect your luggage.

3 Close your book. How many of the fourteen activities can you remember?

4 (3.7) Listen to five announcements at an airport. Underline the correct words.

1 Passengers travelling on flight *AA32/AA23* to Milan must go to gate *23/32*.
2 The flight *to/from* Moscow is delayed.
3 The flight to Barcelona *is/is not* ready to board.
4 Flight AA211 will land at *London, Heathrow at 9.15/in Orlando, Florida at 8.55*.
5 Passengers must wear their seat belts *at all times/when the plane takes off and lands*.

MINI WORKBOOK exercise 6 page 113

Grammar Focus

may, might and will

5 Read the article about cheap travel. Tick (✓) true and cross (✗) false.

1 ☐ Flights from Warsaw to London are cheaper than they were twenty years ago.
2 ☐ Most people travel on business these days.
3 ☐ Travel helps people from different countries to understand each other better.
4 ☐ It is good for historic places to have more tourists.

(3.9)

Cheap travel – a good or a bad thing?

→ Twenty years ago the price of a one-way plane ticket from Warsaw to London was around $300. Now a return flight can cost just $90 … cheaper than the train! More and more people are flying – on business, to visit friends or just to enjoy a weekend break. Travel experts say that in a few years, Europeans will be able to fly to destinations like China and Australia for less than $100! But are cheap flights a good thing for our future? Here are the arguments for and against.

6 Read *Grammar2know*. Then find examples in the text for the rules, a–f.

Grammar 2 know

may, might and will

a Use *will* (*'ll*) to show that we think something is sure to happen:
Europeans will be …

b Use *will not* (*won't*) to show that we think something is sure not to happen:

c Use *might* or *may* to show that we think something is possible in the future:
This **might** create a more peaceful world in the future.

will + definitely or probably

d Use *will + definitely* or *probably* to show how sure we feel:
definitely (= very sure)   **probably** (= quite sure)
People **will definitely work** abroad more in the future.

Word order in negative sentences:
People **definitely won't work** abroad.

Future forms of can and have to

e The future of *can* is **will be able to**:

f The future of *have to* is **will have to**:

7 (3.8) Listen and complete the predictions. Do you agree with the speakers?

'I think travelling ¹ _will be_ more and more miserable in the future. More people ² _____ , we ³ _____ to have more security everywhere and there ⁴ _____ more delays.'

'In a few years, some people ⁵ _____ to the moon or other planets for their holidays – but I think it ⁶ _____ rich people because it ⁷ _____ very expensive.'

'Governments ⁸ _____ something about global warming, so air travel ⁹ _____ more expensive again. People ¹⁰ _____ abroad so much in the future. I think they ¹¹ _____ their holidays closer to home, like they did in the past.'

8 Make predictions. Use *will* (*definitely/probably*), *won't* or *may/might*. Discuss your ideas with the class.

1 It _might_ snow tomorrow.
2 It _____ be dark at 6.00 this evening.
3 Traffic and pollution _____ get worse in my city.
4 Global warming _____ be a big problem in the future.
5 My country _____ win the next football world cup.
6 Our teacher _____ give us a lot of homework today.

9 **a** How will your life be different when you are twenty-one? Write sentences about these things using *will/won't have to* and *will/won't be able to*.

I'll be able to vote.

> go on holiday with your parents
> vote   buy a car   go in the army
> go to school   earn money
> have a credit card

b Compare answers with other students.

MINI WORKBOOK exercises 3–4 pages 112–113

For
• Young people and other people on low incomes will be able to travel more.
• People will definitely work abroad more in the future. They will have to go home to visit relatives, fly to meetings, etc.
• People will probably learn more about other cultures as they travel more. This might create a more peaceful world in the future.

Against
• There are too many tourists already. In a few years' time, there will be many more visitors to interesting cities like Prague, Seville and Florence. Many historic places won't be special any more.
• More flights will mean more pollution and noise.
• Pollution from planes may increase global warming.

time out

55

Vocabulary Speaking

Describing holidays

1 Discuss these questions.
- Where does your family usually go on holiday?
- What was the best holiday of your life? Why?

2 Check the words in blue. Tick (✓) the good things about a holiday and cross (✗) the bad things.

Words 2 know (3.10)

1. ☐ You stay in really nice accommodation.
2. ☐ You get sunburnt.
3. ☐ You eat delicious food.
4. ☐ Your flight is delayed.
5. ☐ There are lots of traffic jams during the journey.
6. ☐ The airline loses your luggage.
7. ☐ The hotel food is disgusting.
8. ☐ You have time to relax.
9. ☐ You visit some really interesting places.
10. ☐ The weather's awful.
11. ☐ You get food poisoning.
12. ☐ You have lots of fun.

3 In pairs, discuss which things in exercise 2 are important for you. Which don't matter?

Having lots of fun is really important for me but the accommodation doesn't matter.

4 (3.11) Listen to a dialogue about a holiday in Scotland. Why was the holiday terrible? <u>Underline</u> the correct information in *Phrases2know*.

Phrases 2 know

Describing your holiday

Our holiday in Scotland was *terrible/boring/exciting*!
We had a *fantastic/horrible* time!
First, we had a really *bad/long/scary* journey.
After that, we lost our *luggage/passports*.
And then it *rained/snowed* every day.
In the end, we *came home early/changed hotels*.

Showing interest

How was your holiday?
Cool!
Really?
What happened?
Oh no!
You're joking!
So what did you do?

5 **a** Imagine that you are just back from a fantastic holiday. Make notes about:
- where you went
- what you did
- why it was good.

b Work in pairs. Take turns to talk about your holidays, using the *Phrases2know* in exercise 4.

So how was your holiday?
Well, we had a fantastic time!

MINI WORKBOOK exercise 7 page 113

Reading Vocabulary

6 Look at the cartoons 1–3. Guess which complaint, a or b, matches each cartoon. Read the article and check.

1. a 'The fish bit us.'
   b 'There are fish in the sea.'
2. a 'There was no air-conditioning outside.'
   b 'It was very hot.'
3. a 'She didn't understand Spanish.'
   b 'People speak Spanish in Spain.'

(3.12)

The sea is full of fish!

Travel companies often have to deal with people who are unhappy about bad accommodation and food, or lost luggage. But according to Britain's leading tour operators, holidaymakers also try to get
5 compensation for some very strange reasons …

One company received a complaint from a parent who was unhappy about the fish in the sea. 'No one told us there were fish in the sea,' he wrote. 'My children were startled!' Another customer wrote, 'A mosquito bit me.
10 No one told us they bite!'

7 There are four more complaints in the text. Choose the best description for each.

1 One customer was unhappy because
   a a mosquito bit him.
   b the company did not tell him that mosquitoes bite.
   c there wasn't any wildlife in the area.

2 Another customer complained because
   a the sand was yellow.
   b there was no beach.
   c the sand looked different in the brochure.

3 A British tourist complained because
   a American tourists had a shorter journey than him.
   b he was angry about the number of American tourists in Jamaica.
   c his journey to Jamaica took three hours.

4 A woman complained because the hotel gave her and her husband a room with
   a an uncomfortable bed.
   b twin beds.
   c a double bed.

8 GUESSING MEANING FROM CONTEXT Find these words, 1–5, in the text and then choose the right definition, a or b.

1 **to deal with** (line 1)
   a buy or sell something
   b find the answer to a problem

2 **compensation** (line 5)
   a money you pay for a holiday
   b money you get if something goes wrong

3 **startled** (line 9)
   a surprised and frightened
   b sad and lonely

4 **genuine** (line 32)
   a strange   b real

5 **to blame someone** (line 36)
   a to say someone is responsible for a problem
   b to make a mistake

9 In pairs, discuss these questions.
   • Are any of the complaints in the text fair?
   • Which complaint do you think is the most ridiculous?

MINI WORKBOOK exercise 8 page 113

It isn't just the local wildlife that causes problems. One holidaymaker complained about the beach: 'The sand in the brochure looked yellow but when we got there, we found it was white.' Another unhappy customer wrote, 'We had to
15 queue and there was no air-conditioning outside.'

A travel agent spokesman said, 'In the past, going abroad was a real treat. But people are travelling abroad much more nowadays and they don't accept anything that they are not happy with.'
20 Even geography, it seems, can be a problem. One customer complained angrily because British tourists had to travel nine hours to reach their holiday destination (Jamaica) and American tourists got there in just three hours.

Another British holidaymaker wrote, 'There were too many Spanish people. The hotel staff spoke Spanish and the food was Spanish.' And where did the woman choose to book her holiday? Spain, of course!

Airtours deal with 17,000 customer complaints every year. They use complaints like this to help their staff
30 deal with the problems they may meet in the summer. A spokesman for the company said they always take genuine complaints seriously even if they are sometimes strange. 'We give holidaymakers as much information as we can about their trip but sometimes there are
35 still problems. When things go wrong, people feel they need to blame someone. They always think the travel company is responsible.'

Perhaps the most extreme example was the woman who wrote, 'My husband and I asked for a twin-bedded
40 room but the hotel put us in a room with a double bed. I am now pregnant and in my opinion your company is responsible.'

Buenos dias

Zack, Grace, Rosie and Fran are discussing Zack's trip to Paris.

A TRIP TO PARIS

1 (3.13) **Listen to Part 1 of the conversation and circle the correct answers.**

1 Fran recommends travelling
a by coach.
b by plane.
c by train.

2 Zack isn't meeting Lily in Paris because
a Lily doesn't like Paris.
b she isn't his girlfriend any more.
c she's going to Germany.

3 Zack is going
a with Grace and her family.
b with some friends from college.
c by himself.

4 Grace recommends the 'Lucky Hostel' because
a it's good for young people.
b it's very pretty.
c it's near the train station.

2 (3.14) **Listen to the *Phrases2know* from the dialogue and practise the intonation.**

Phrases 2 know

Asking for advice

Can you recommend anything?
Where should we stay?
Do you think we should book?
What's the best way to do it?

Giving advice

Go by train.
You must go to Montmartre.
You should definitely stay there.
I don't think you should take the coach.
Don't fly.

3 (3.15) **Read and listen to Part 2 of the conversation and <u>underline</u> the phrases for giving and asking for advice.**

Zack: So, where should we go and what should we see?
Grace: Oh, there's loads to do! Obviously there's Notre Dame – the cathedral – and the Eiffel Tower and all those things, and there are loads of art galleries and gardens and stuff like that.
Zack: Yeah, I definitely want to see some art galleries – which is the best one?
Fran: Well, of course, there's the Louvre – you should go to the Louvre and see the Mona Lisa but the gallery's huge, so it's best to take a guided tour.
Grace: And if you like modern art, I think you should go to the Pompidou Centre – it's amazing!
Zack: And what about nightlife?
Grace: We went to this area called Le Marais – there are loads of bars and cafés and clubs, you'll love it! Don't go to the Champs-Élysées area because it's really, really expensive! I'll go and get all my maps and guidebooks and I can show you everything.

4 (3.16) **Listen to five people who are visiting your country. What does each person want? Give advice using the *Phrases2know*.**

I think you should go to …
Don't go to …!

5 **Zack is visiting your town or a famous town in your area. In pairs, take turns to act out a dialogue with Zack, using the *Phrases2know*.**

Give Zack advice about:

- a cheap and nice place to stay
- interesting places to visit
- a good place to eat.

CAN YOU DO IT IN ENGLISH?

Zack and his friends meet at St Pancras train station in London before their trip to Paris.

A POSTCARD AND A LETTER

6 Read Zack's postcard and letter. Answer the questions.

- Which did he write first?
- Who is each one to?
- Does he say the same things about Paris in each one?

8 Write a letter or postcard from holiday to an English friend. Write:

- where you are
- what you did yesterday/today
- what you like/don't like
- plans for the rest of the holiday.

   Use *Phrases2know* in exercise 8 on page 27.

Hi Everyone!

Having a fantastic time – I love Paris!
We went for a long walk by the River
Seine yesterday and saw Notre Dame
and the Eiffel Tower. We had a great
Vietnamese meal in the evening – it
was really cheap!! The cafés and bars
here are so cool!! We're going clubbing
tonight. Having great weather, too!
Hope all is well with you!

Love, Zack XXX

Fran, Grace and Rosie
25 Manorgate Road,
London
NW10 2PQ
ANGLETERRE

25 Manorgate Road,
London NW10 2PQ
16 August 2010

Dear Grandma,

How are you? I hope you are well, and that your bad
knee is better now.

Sorry I didn't write before. Life is pretty busy here
and there are so many interesting things to do – the
museums and parks in London are really wonderful.

Thank you very much for the cheque you sent me.
I used the money to pay for my train ticket to Paris.

I went last weekend with two guys from my course.
It was fantastic! We saw all the famous sights like the
Eiffel Tower and, of course, we spent a lot of time in the
art galleries.

Well, I think that's all the news. I'm looking forward to
seeing you in September, when I get home.

Lots of love,

Zack   XXX

7 Read the postcard and letter again and mark the statements P (for postcard), L (for letter) or B (for both).

1. ☐ It opens with *Hi* or *Dear* and ends with *love, lots of love*, etc.
2. ☐ It uses short forms like *I'm, didn't, that's*.
3. ☐ It doesn't give detailed information and often leaves out pronouns and auxiliary verbs in sentences.
4. ☐ It gives more details about news.

8 just do it!

Grammar Present perfect with *ever*, *never*, *just*, *already* and *yet*
Vocabulary Sports and equipment
Phrases Describing sports and achievements

Vocabulary & Listening

Sports

1 (3.17) WORD RACE Look at the list of the ten most popular sports. How many can you complete in two minutes? Listen and check.

Words 2 know

1 f _ _ _ _ _ l   6 t _ b l _ t _ _ _ _ s
2 c r _ _ k _ t   7 b _ s _ b _ _ l
3 h _ _ k _ _   8 g _ _ f
4 t _ _ _ _ s   9 b _ _ k _ _ b _ _ _
5 v _ l _ _ _ b _ _ _   10 c y _ _ _ _ g

2 Work in pairs and answer the questions.

Which of the sports and activities in exercise 1 and the photos:

- are most popular in your country?
- do you do?
- do you like watching on TV?

3 **a** Read the questions from a TV quiz. Which questions can you answer?

b (3.18) Listen to the quiz. Your teacher will pause the recording before each answer. Were the contestants right or wrong?

A QUESTION OF SPORT

1 Which country did the tennis player Martina Navratilova come from originally?
a Russia   b Bulgaria   c Czech Republic

2 Where did the first Winter Olympics take place?
a France   b the USA   c Switzerland

3 Which team won the 2002 football world cup?
a Germany   b Brazil   c Turkey

4 Which sport does Tiger Woods play?
a football   b basketball   c golf

5 How many players are there in a basketball team?
a five   b eleven   c ten

4 Work in pairs. Write two more questions about sport for the quiz in exercise 3. Take turns to ask the class your questions.

Grammar Focus

Present perfect with *ever* and *never*

5 Read about the Champions Tomorrow awards and answer the questions.

- How do the awards help young people?
- Who is this year's young sports person of the year?
- Which sport does she play?

6 (3.19) Read and listen to an interview with Jo-Anne. Correct three more mistakes in the dialogue.

Champions Tomorrow

The Champions Tomorrow awards help Britain's young people to become future champions by giving them money for training and travel. Every year, one young person receives a prize of £1000. This year's winner, eighteen-year-old Jo-Anne Parry, is a volleyball player from Stevenage.

INTERVIEWER: Congratulations, Jo!
JO: Thanks!
INTERVIEWER: Now, Jo, you're only ~~seventeen~~ *eighteen*. Tell us something about your career up to now.
JO: Well, I've played for the England Schools team and last year, I was captain of the England Under-25 team.
INTERVIEWER: Well done! So what are your ambitions now?
JO: Well, I haven't travelled outside Europe much. I want to play in the Olympics next year and I'd love to visit Australia. I've never been there.
INTERVIEWER: Well, good luck with that. One more thing … who is your sporting hero?
JO: That's easy … Lewis Hamilton, the footballer! He's from Stevenage, the same as me!
INTERVIEWER: Really? Have you ever met him?
JO: No, I haven't but I've seen him on TV hundreds of times … so, maybe one day. That's my dream!

rock climbing

snowboarding

yoga

7 Read *Grammar2know*. Complete the lists of regular and irregular past participles with examples from the interview with Jo-Anne.

Grammar 2 know

Present perfect

Use the present perfect:

- to describe actions that happened in the past but are still important now. We do not say when they happened:
  I've played for the England Schools team.
  I haven't travelled outside Europe much.

- with *ever* and *never* to talk about past experience:
  Have you *ever met* Lewis Hamilton?
  I've never been to the United States.

Use the past simple to say when something happened:
Last year, I *was* captain of the Under-21 team.

Form: *have/has* + past participle

+ *I/You/We/They* **have ('ve) seen** him on TV.
  He/She **has ('s) seen** him on TV.

− *I/You/We/They* **have not (haven't) met** him.
  He/She **has not (hasn't) met** him.

? **Have** I/you/we/they	Yes, I/you/we/they **have**.
met him?	No, I/you/we/they **haven't**.
Has he/she **met** him?	Yes, he/she **has**.
	No, he/she **hasn't**.

regular past participles: *played,* _____

irregular past participles: *seen,* _____

8 (3.20) <u>Underline</u> the correct words. Listen and check.

A: ¹ *Have you ever been/Did you ever go* surfing?

B: No, I ² *haven't/didn't* but ³ *I've done/I did* some windsurfing.

A: Really?

B: Yes, I ⁴ *have had/had* lessons last year when I ⁵ *have been/was* on holiday.

C: ⁶ *Have you ever broken/Did you ever break* an arm or a leg?

D: Yes, I ⁷ *have/did*, actually. I ⁸ *have broken/broke* my arm last year.

C: Oh no! How ⁹ *has it happened/did it happen*?

D: I ¹⁰ *have gone/went* riding last summer and I ¹¹ *have fallen/fell* off my horse!

9 Complete the past participles of these verbs. Use the irregular verb list (back cover).

1 run _____ 2 win _____ 3 do _____

4 ride _____ 5 meet _____ 6 try _____

10 a Use the prompts 1–8 to make questions. Then ask and answer in pairs. Mark your partner's answers with a tick (✓) or a cross (✗).

" *Have you ever done rock climbing?*
Yes, I have, lots of times.

Have you ever ... ?

1 (do) rock climbing?
2 (run) a long distance?
3 (score) a goal in a match?
4 (play) for a school or a local team?
5 (meet) a famous sports person?
6 (ride) a horse?
7 (win) a sporting competition?
8 (try) yoga?

b Tell the class one thing that your partner has done and one thing he/she hasn't done.

" *Jan has scored a goal in a football match but he's never met a famous sports person.*

MINI WORKBOOK exercises 1–4 page 114

just do it!

Vocabulary & Writing

Sports equipment

1 Check the meaning of the *Words2know*. Which items are missing in the pictures? Which can you see?

> **Words 2 know** (3.21)
>
> ball   boots   gloves   goggles
> net   racket   shorts   skates

2 a **Words 2 know** (3.22) Check the words in blue. Which sports is the speaker describing?

1 'You don't need any special equipment for this sport except a pair of trainers … and a nice park! But if you want to win races, you need to train hard.'

2 'It's an indoor game – each team has six players plus fourteen substitutes. You play on a special ice rink and you need a stick, of course. It's a really exciting sport!'

3 'It's a very popular sport all over the world. To play, you need a bat, a ball, a table and a net! You beat your opponent if you score 11 points. You have to be fast to win but it's really good fun.'

b Add the words in blue to the correct column below.

People	Places	Equipment	Adjectives/phrases	Verbs/phrases
			good fun	to win a race

3 a Write a description of a sport. Use the *Phrases2know* and the texts in exercise 2 to help you.

>  **Phrases 2 know** (3.23)
>
> **Describing sports**
>
> It's a very popular sport in Italy/all over the world.
>
> People play in summer/in winter/all year round.
>
> It's an indoor/outdoor game.
>
> Each team has six players.
>
> To play the game, you need a ball.
>
> It's very exciting.

b Read your description to other students. They guess which sport it is.

MINI WORKBOOK exercises 7–8 page 115

Grammar Focus

Present perfect with *just*, *already* and *yet*

4 In pairs, answer the questions.
* What are the most popular leisure activities for young people in your country?
* Do you and your friends do enough sport? What do you do to keep fit?

5 Read the website about Ian Wright's *Unfit Kids* TV series. Tick (✓) true and cross (✗) false.

1 ☐ Ian Wright is a retired footballer.

2 ☐ All the teenagers spend too much time on computer games.

3 ☐ Ian wants to get money for his sports clubs.

4 ☐ Ian gets some money for the clubs, in the end.

5 ☐ At the end of programme 3, all the kids are playing sport.

www1.ia

(3.25) **Ian Wright's**

In this series of three TV programmes, ex-England footballer Ian Wright tries to help unfit teenagers.

6 Read the sentences with *just*, *already* and *yet* in the text. Complete *Grammar2know* with these sentences.

Present perfect with *just*, *already* and *yet*

Use *just* to say that something has happened recently:
*Ian has **just** had some good news.*

Use *already* to say that something happened before the expected time.
He has already become ...

Use *yet* if something didn't happen in the past but might happen in the future.

• In negative sentences:

_____

• In questions:

_____

7 Write *just*, *already* or *yet* in the correct place in the sentences. Tania wants to get fit, so:

1 She's joined a gym. (just)   *She's just joined a gym.*
2 She's stopped buying fizzy drinks and unhealthy food … (already)
3 … but she hasn't given up chocolate! (yet)
4 She only started her fitness programme two weeks ago, but she's lost some weight. (already)
5 She's started swimming at the weekends. (just)
6 She's decided to learn yoga but she hasn't started her lessons. (yet)

8 (3.24) Cross out the words in brackets which can't be used. Listen and check.

1 A: Where's Annie?
  B: She's (just) gone home (~~yet~~).
2 A: Can I have your homework, Alex?
  B: Sorry, I haven't (already) done it (yet).
3 A: Have you seen Ben today?
  B: Yes, I've (just/already) seen him – he's in the coffee bar!
4 A: What time is your train?
  B: Three o'clock. I've (just/already) told you three times!
5 A: Have you (just) tidied your room (yet), Annie?
  B: I'm doing it now, Mum.

MINI WORKBOOK exercises 5–6 pages 114–115

Unfit Kids

IN PROGRAMME 1: Over a million British schoolchildren are unfit and Ian Wright wants to do something about it. He has chosen eight North London teenagers to take part in his special fitness programme. Robert, for example, spends over thirty hours a week on his PlayStation®. Jerome has four TVs in his room and Gabby needs to lose weight. But can Ian persuade them to change their habits? Ian also wants to start after-school sports clubs for teenagers in the area and is looking for companies to sponsor them.

IN PROGRAMME 2: Six weeks later. Some of the teenagers are making progress but Ian is having problems with some of the kids. Robert hasn't changed his PlayStation® habits **yet** but Gabby is now playing badminton. Jerome is boxing and he has **already** become a lot fitter. But has Ian found any sponsors **yet**?

IN PROGRAMME 3: After six months, the fitness programme is at an end and Ian has **just** had some good news. The computer company Microsoft has offered some money for his after-school clubs. All eight teenagers have started exercising regularly. Even Ian's most difficult student, Robert, has joined a gym. But can he give up his PlayStation®?

just do it!

63

Reading & Vocabulary

1 Look at the photos and read the title of the text. Answer the questions.
- Which sports and games can you see?
- Are any of the players or athletes unusual? Why?
- Which is the best explanation of the title, a or b?
- **a** These people are unusual champions.
- **b** These people are champions in unusual sports.

2 **Words 2 know** (3.26) Read the text and check the words in blue. Which person:
1 had a terrible accident when he/she was a teenager? *Natalie du Toit*
2 refuses to play in some competitions?
3 often surprises other players?
4 inspires children who have the same problem as him/her?
5 continued training at a very difficult time in his/her life?
6 was taught to play by his/her father?

(3.28)

Champions against the odds

Earl Boykins is only 1.65 m tall and he weighs just 60 kg … small by most standards but especially small in the world of professional basketball, where most players are around 2 m tall! Born in Cleveland, Ohio, Boykins is the smallest player in the NBA League. But his strength and speed often surprise his opponents and he has led the US team at the World University Games.   5

These days, Boykins gets hundreds of letters from parents of children of below average height, thanking him for inspiring them. 'I don't see my height as a problem,' says Boykins. 'I'm unique.'

It is very unusual for a woman to be a top international chess player but Hungarian Judit Polgár is no ordinary woman. She has always refused to play in women-only tournaments. Her father educated Judit at home with one special subject: chess. At the age of only fifteen, Judit became a chess grandmaster and she has now beaten nearly all the world's top players. In 2005, she became the first woman to play for the world chess title and in 2006 she became number 16 in the world – the only woman in the top 100. 'Of course, I'd love to become world champion but I'm just happy to play a nice game,' says Judit.   10   15

Born in Cape Town in 1984, Natalie du Toit was a talented swimmer from childhood: at fourteen she was already competing internationally. Then, when she was seventeen, there was a tragedy. Natalie was riding her scooter to school when a car drove into her. She was badly hurt and lost part of her left leg. But the young swimmer was determined and three months later, before she could walk again, Natalie started training.   20   25

Her career has been incredibly successful. She has won many gold medals in competitions for disabled athletes, including five at the Athens Paralympics. Natalie has also competed successfully against able-bodied swimmers. She represented South Africa in the 2002 Commonwealth Games and has won medals in the All-African and African–Asian Games.   30

3 Read the text again and make notes about each person's difficulties and achievements.

> Earl Boykins:
> Difficulties: He is only 1.65 m tall (most basketball players are 2 m)
> Achievements: He has led the US team

4 Which of the people in the texts do you most admire? Use your notes in exercise 3 to explain why.

> " *I admire Earl Boykins because he's very short for a basketball player. However, he has led the US team.*

5 Read *Active Study* and complete the table with the irregular forms in the text.

ACTIVE STUDY

Notice irregular verbs

Make a note of new irregular verbs.
For example: *He has led the US team.*

Use the irregular verb list (back cover) to check the different forms.

Infinitive	Past simple	Past participle
to lead	*led*	*(has) led*
to drive	_____	_____
to lose	_____	_____
to become	_____	_____
to beat	_____	_____
to win	_____	_____

MINI WORKBOOK exercise 9 page 115

Writing Speaking

6 In groups, answer the questions.
- Who are the most famous sports people in your country?
- Do you have a sporting hero? Why do you like him/her?

7 **Phrases 2 know** (3.27) Check you understand the phrases in blue in the student's composition about a sporting hero. Read the composition and complete the first column of the table below.

Kelly Holmes

My sporting hero is Kelly Holmes, an athlete. She won two gold medals at the 2004 summer Olympics – the first British woman who has ever done this.

Kelly was born in 1970 near London and she started running when she was twelve. Her early career wasn't easy. She had bad luck with injuries and she often felt depressed. But at the age of thirty-four, Kelly won her first gold medal at the Athens Olympics. Everyone was amazed – especially Kelly! A few days later, she won another gold medal. She suddenly became a national hero.

I like her because she is always very friendly to her fans and she has inspired a lot of young people.

	Kelly Holmes	Your sporting hero
Name and sport		
Where he/she's from		
Early life/career		
Greatest achievements		
Other information		
Why you like him/her		

8 **a** Make notes about a sporting hero you really admire in the table in exercise 7.

b Write about your sporting hero. Use your notes and the *Phrases2know* in blue above to help you.

9 Give a short presentation about your sporting hero to the class. Use the *Phrases2know*. Answer any questions that the other students have.

> " *My sporting hero is …*
> *He/She's a …*

just do it!

65

activestudy4

Vocabulary

ACTIVE STUDY | Learn collocations

1 Find three words below for each verb.

> basketball   a competition   gloves
> a medal   shopping ✓   shorts   skiing
> swimming   table tennis   volleyball
> a race   goggles

go	play	wear	win
shopping			

ACTIVE STUDY | Notice collocations

2 Read Kitty's email to her friend, Julie. Complete the gaps 1–8 with the words a–i. There is one extra word.

---

mailbox   Today | Mail | Calendar | Contacts

Hi Julie!

So far, this is the worst holiday I've ever had in my life! The problems started at the airport. I ¹ _____ my luggage OK. But when I was going through security, they took my perfume away. Did you know that you aren't allowed to take perfume in your ² _____ ? Then our flight was ³ _____ for an hour. When the plane ⁴ _____, I felt sick. And when we finally arrived, I went to collect my luggage and it wasn't there.

On the way to the hotel, there was a terrible ⁵ _____ and then I didn't have time to ⁶ _____ because I had to go and buy the basic things. As for the food. I was really looking forward to dinner but I got food ⁷ _____ on the first night! Oh well, perhaps it'll get better now. It certainly can't get any worse! Perhaps I'll have ⁸ _____ on the beach. I'll let you know.

Love,

Kitty

(a) checked in	d hand luggage	g sunburnt
b delayed	e poisoning	h took off
c fun	f relax	i traffic jam

ACTIVE STUDY | Notice silent letters

3 PRONUNCIATION (3.29) Listen and <u>underline</u> the silent letters. Then listen again and check.

1 mi<u>gh</u>t   4 flight   7 fasten

2 island   5 psychology   8 scenery

3 knee   6 weight

Grammar

4 Put the verbs in brackets into the present perfect or present continuous.

1 _____ you _____ (go) to a rock concert tonight?

2 My sister _____ just _____ (buy) a new car.

3 Where _____ you _____ (go) this weekend?

4 I _____ never _____ (eat) Japanese food.

5 We _____ already _____ (seen) this film.

6 My friend _____ (have) an eighteenth birthday party next week.

5 Read the interview and choose the best answer a, b or c for each gap.

Journalist (J): Hannah, you're only seventeen and you ¹ _____ five novels! When ² _____ writing?

Hannah Darby (HD): I wrote my first story when I was about eight years old. The title was *Looking For Maisy*. I ³ _____ it difficult to get ideas. I read the papers and watch TV like everyone else.

J: Who inspires you?

HD: ⁴ _____ anything by Jacqueline Wilson? I ⁵ _____ all her books. She's my hero!

J: Tell us about your next novel.

HD: I've just finished writing another novel but I ⁶ _____ it a title yet. I ⁷ _____ it *Big Chance 2*.

J: ⁸ _____ what to do with the money yet?

HD: I ⁹ _____ on holiday with my parents next week so the money ¹⁰ _____ be very useful!

---

1 (a) have already written   **b** are already writing
   c will already write

2 **a** you started   **b** have you started
   c did you start

3 **a** have never found   **b** will never find
   c never finding

4 **a** You read   **b** Have you read
   c Will you read

5 **a** reading   **b** did read   **c** have read

6 **a** have given   **b** haven't given
   c not given

7 **a** probably called   **b** probably call
   c will probably call

8 **a** Have you decided   **b** Will you decide
   c You have decided

9 **a** will go   **b** 'm going   **c** have been

10 **a** has definitely   **b** is definitely
    c will definitely

Reading Skills

ACTIVE STUDY | Read for specific information

6 **a** **Read the text about sightseeing in Paris. Find five different forms of transport.**

(3.30)

Getting around Paris

(INTRODUCTION | GETTING AROUND |)

The cheapest way to see Paris is on foot. It's the best way to enjoy the street life of areas like Montmartre, the Latin Quarter or the Bois de Boulogne. But, as in any big city, you should be careful at night in certain areas.

The Metro – Paris's underground system, the second largest in Europe – is the quickest way to get around. It's open from 5.30 a.m.–12.45 a.m. Tickets cost €1.40 or you can buy a book of ten tickets for €10.50.

Everyone should take a River Seine boat trip on the famous Bateaux-Mouches (for reservations and information call 01 42 25 96 10). A recorded commentary describes sights along the river in six different languages. The boats leave from the Pont de l'Alma in the 8th district. The trips last between 60 and 75 minutes and depart between 10.15 a.m. and 11 p.m. (9 p.m. in winter).

You can also go on a helicopter ride over all the sights (contact Héli-France). But be careful! A 30-minute trip will cost you around €150! And if you prefer a slower way to see Paris from the air, Paris Atmosphère organises balloon trips over the city. Telephone: (01) 46 09 44 22.

For more information in English, look for the weekly magazine, *Pariscope*, available from newspaper kiosks.

b **Read the text again and complete each of the sentences below with one or two words.**

1 Obviously, walking is _____ than other ways of seeing the city.

2 You should be careful when walking in certain parts of the city _____ .

3 The fastest way to get around Paris is by _____ .

4 A book of ten tickets _____ €10.50.

5 _____ on the famous Bateaux-Mouches are also popular.

6 On the Bateaux-Mouches, you can hear a recorded commentary in _____ .

7 The first boat trip departs at 10.15 in the _____ .

8 The most expensive way to see Paris is by _____ .

9 If you want to see the city from a balloon, contact the company called _____ .

10 There is an English-language _____ which gives more information.

Speaking Skills

7 **a** **Choose one of the photos and describe it. Use the *Phrases2know* and your own ideas.**

In the photo I can see …

The man/woman is … /The people are …

I think they/he/she will probably … later.

b **Compare the photos. Use these ideas.**

What is similar? What is different?	people scenery activities

c **In pairs, ask and answer these questions:**

· Do you think the people are having a good time? Why? Why not?

· What problems could they have on a holiday like this?

· Which of the two holidays would you prefer? Why?

SKILLS STRATEGIES back cover

cool tech

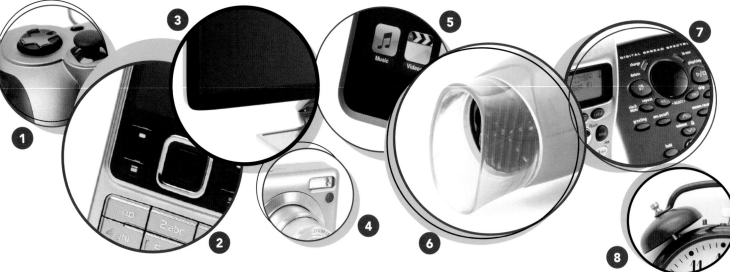

Grammar	Defining relative clauses
	First conditional and future time clauses
Vocabulary	Machines and how they work
Phrases	Giving instructions
	Complaining

Vocabulary & Listening

Operating machines

1 Check you understand the *Words2know*. Match the gadgets with the photos.

> **Words 2 know** (3.31)
>
> an MP3 player   an answering machine   a games console
> an alarm clock   a hairdryer   a digital camera   a mobile phone
> a flat screen TV

2 WORD RACE Work in pairs. How many more gadgets can you add to the list in exercise 1 in two minutes?

3 **Words 2 know** (3.32) Check the meaning of the words in blue. Match the gadgets in exercise 1 to the descriptions, 1–8.

1 You have to put batteries in. *alarm clock, mobile phone*
2 You have to plug it in.
3 You charge the battery using a charger.
4 You switch it on and off with a remote control.
5 You press a button to turn the volume up or down.
6 You select from the menu.
7 It can record messages.
8 You have to set the time.

4 Read *Active Study*. Then find other two-word verbs in exercise 3. Learn the verbs and test your partner.

> ### Notice two-word verbs
> Notice the prepositions in two-word verbs:
> ***switch** the TV **on*****   ***switch** it **on***
> ***plug** the phone **in*****   ***plug** it **in***

ACTIVE STUDY

5 (3.33) Use the *Words2know* in exercise 3 to complete the explanations of how two gadgets work. What are they? Listen and check.

First of all, you need to plug it ¹ __in__ and press this button to switch it ² _____ . Then you need to ³ _____ the time. If you have any messages, you ⁴ _____ this button to listen to them.

Before you use it for the first time, ⁵ _____ the battery for about twelve hours. You just ⁶ _____ the charger _____ . Then you put the game ⁷ _____ here and follow the instructions on the screen. Don't forget to switch it ⁸ _____ if you're not using it.

6 Think of a machine you often use. Describe how to use it but do not say what it is. Use the *Phrases2know*. Can other students guess what it is?

> **Phrases 2 know** (3.34)
>
> ### Giving instructions
> First of all, you switch it on.
> Then you select from the menu.
> You have to charge the battery/it.
> Just follow the instructions.
> Don't forget to switch it off.

MINI WORKBOOK exercises 5–6 page 117

Grammar Focus

Relative clauses

7 Read the brochure and discuss these questions.

- What two advantages of GoGreen! products are mentioned in the introduction?
- One of the gadgets does not belong in the GoGreen! brochure. Which one is it?
- Would you like to own any of these gadgets? Why?

8 Read *Grammar2know*. Find more examples of relative clauses with *which*, *that*, *who* and *where* in the article.

Grammar 2 know

Relative clauses

Use a relative pronoun to add extra information:
The latest gadget is a fridge. The fridge can throw you a drink.
The latest gadget is a fridge **which** *can throw you a drink.*

which, that, who, where

- Use *which* or *that* for things:
  It's a fridge **which/that** *serves lazy drinkers.*
- Use *who* or *that* for people:
  John Cornwall is the student **who** *invented the fridge.*
- Use *where* for places:
  He had a few accidents in the college room **where** *he keeps the fridge.*

9 (3.35) Complete the quiz with *where*, *which*, *that* or *who*. Then choose the correct definition, a or b, for each word. Listen and check.

vocabulary quiz

1 Photocopiers are
- a machines *that* make copies of documents.
- b people _____ do the photocopying in an office.

2 Drycleaners are
- a people _____ clean schools and offices.
- b shops _____ they clean your clothes for you.

3 Cookers are
- a people _____ cook professionally.
- b kitchen appliances _____ cook food.

4 Stationers are
- a shops _____ you buy paper, pens, etc.
- b people _____ work at a railway station.

10 What gadget would you like to invent? Think of three ideas and compare answers with the class.

I'd like to invent a robot that tidies my bedroom for me.

MINI WORKBOOK exercise 1 page 116

GoGreen! (3.36)

GoGreen! is a company which sells green alternatives of everyday gadgets. We interviewed Mike Rogers who started **GoGreen!** five years ago. 'Gadgets are part of our lives now,' he explains in the office in his garden where he runs the company. 'But we want to help the environment and save money, too.'

A THE BICYCLE THAT CHARGES YOUR PHONE!

Save money, get healthy AND charge your mobile! The Pedalcharger is a small gadget which you attach to your bike. Then you plug in your phone and start cycling. After thirty minutes, your phone is fully charged … and it costs nothing!

B THE ALARM CLOCK THAT USES WATER!

The new H²0 Multi-clock is unique. It has an amazing water battery which produces electricity. You don't plug it in, you just fill it with water! It has a thermometer and a radio, too!

C THE FRIDGE THAT SERVES LAZY DRINKERS!

The latest must-have gadget is a fridge which throws you a drink! Press the remote control and the drink flies across the room to you. John Cornwall, the student who invented the fridge, explains. 'One day, I thought, "I'm tired of going to the fridge for a drink … why don't the drinks come to me?"' He had a few accidents in the college room where he keeps his fridge but he says, 'The fridge is 99% safe … there's only a small danger that a drink will hit you!'

cool tech

69

Listening & Speaking

The question on this morning's phone-in radio breakfast show is: 'Which gadgets can't you live without, and which do you hate?'

1 **a** PREDICTING Read the caption for the photo. Guess which gadgets the radio listeners mention.

b (3.37) Listen and write down the gadgets you hear. Is your list the same?

2 (3.37) Read the statements a–f. Then listen again and match them with the speakers.

☐ Dan	**a**	I've thrown them both away now and my life is much better.
☐ Cathy	**b**	They smell nice and if you're hungry, you can even eat them.
☐ Tim	**c**	You realise how important it is when you can't find it.
☐ Alice	**d**	I hate all gadgets when they break down.
☐ Lucy	**e**	It wakes me up and makes me go to school.
☐ Nick	**f**	I don't get bored at all but people probably think I'm mad.

3 Answer the questions.
- Which gadget is each speaker talking about? Do they love it or hate it?
- Do you agree with them or not?

4 Write down your three most important possessions. In pairs, explain why they are important to you.

I can't live without my CD player. It's really important to me because it was a present. I use it when …

Grammar Focus

First conditional and future time clauses

5 Look at the photo on page 71 and answer the questions.
- What are the rules about using mobile phones in your school?
- Do you agree with them? Why? Why not?

6 Read the internet article and the debate. Answer the questions.
- Who wants to ban mobile phones from the school and why?
- Who agrees or disagrees with Mr Langley, and why?
- Who do you agree or disagree with?

7 <u>Underline</u> three sentences starting with *if* in the article and answer the questions. Then read *Grammar2know* to check.
- Are these sentences about the present or the future?
- Which tense comes after *if* ?

Grammar 2 know

First conditional

Use the first conditional to talk about a possible future situation:

*We **won't be able to** contact our families **if** we **don't have** our mobiles at school.*

Form: *If* + present simple, future simple

*If they **ban** mobile phones, people **will be** very angry.*

Future time clauses

Use the present tense after time words like *when, after* and *before*:

***After** school **finishes**, people will be able to use their phones.*
*Parents will discuss the situation **when** they **meet** next week.*

8 Read some more opinions about Mr Langley's ban on mobile phones. Put the verbs in the correct tense. Which sentences do you agree with?

1 If the school (ban) mobiles, pupils (concentrate) better in lessons.

2 There (not be) so much crime in the school if pupils (not take) mobiles to school.

3 If pupils (not have) mobiles with them, their parents (worry) about them more.

4 If the school (ban) mobiles, a lot of pupils (break) the rules.

5 Life (be) easier for teachers if there (not be) any mobiles in school.

Should we ban mobile phones from our schools? (3.39)

Robert Langley, Head Teacher of King George V School in Egham wants schools to become 'mobile phone free zones' after an incident at his secondary school. 'A student used his mobile phone to film part of a lesson in which several students fell asleep.'

'We also have students who text their friends and family during lessons or even play games. I have no problem with mobile phones but people need to use them in a sensible way. From now on, the school will have a new policy. If we see a student with a mobile during school hours, we will take the phone away.' Parents will discuss the situation when they meet the Head Teacher next week.

→ **What do you think? Join the debate!**

If they ban mobiles, people will get very angry. They'll bring them to school anyway but they'll just hide them.
✉ Laura 4.26 P.M. 04 Feb

We won't be able to contact our family in an emergency if we don't have our mobiles at school. It might be something really important.
✉ By Andy K 9.32 A.M. on 05 Feb

At the King George V School, the problem was not the phone but the rude students or the boring teacher! Why are they punishing everyone?
✉ By Bella 3.22 P.M. on Feb 05

I don't see why people have a problem. After school finishes, they'll be able to use their phones the same as usual.
✉ Greg B 6.24 P.M. on 06 Feb

I am a college student and I have seen students use their mobile phones to cheat during exams. If we ban them, a lot of cheating will stop.
✉ By Derek 11.02 P.M. 06 Feb

As a teacher, I often have to tell my students to stop playing games, texting, etc. during valuable lesson time. I find it really annoying.
✉ Liz Bailey 7.49 P.M. 09 Feb

9 (3.38) **Put the verbs in the correct forms in a–e. Then match 1–5 with a–e to make dialogues. Listen and check.**

1 ☐ Are you coming out tonight?

2 ☐ Sam, are you going to do the washing-up?

3 ☐ What time will you be home?

4 ☐ Are you going to tidy your room, Katie?

5 ☐ So we're meeting at six o'clock outside the café?

a Yeah, hopefully, but I _will text_ (text) you when my train _____ (arrive).

b I hope so. When I _____ (finish) my essay, I _____ (call) you, okay?

c Yeah, Mum, I _____ (do) it before I _____ (go) to bed. I promise!

d I don't know, I _____ (phone) you when I _____ (come) out of the cinema. Okay?

e I _____ (do) it after this programme _____ (finish).

10 **Complete the sentences with your own ideas.**

1 When I (get) home, I'_ll call you._

2 If I (have) enough time this evening, I …

3 If it (be) sunny tomorrow, I …

4 After this lesson (be) over, I …

5 After I (leave) school, I …

6 I (be able) to drive a car when …

MINI WORKBOOK exercises 2–4 page 116

cool tech

71

Listening & Speaking

Numbers and dates

1 (3.40) Match the numbers to the way you say them. Listen and check. Then listen again and repeat.

1 a sixth $\frac{1}{6}$

2 sixteen sixty-six _____

3 six thousand, six hundred and sixty-six _____

4 sixty thousand _____

5 six hundred and six _____

6 six billion _____

7 six hundred thousand _____

8 sixty-six percent _____

9 six point six _____

10 six million _____

2 (3.41) Listen and <u>underline</u> the number or date that you hear. Listen again and repeat.

1	33%	3.3	303
2	300,000	3,000,000	3,000,000,000
3	80,000	880,000	88,000
4	15	1.5	$\frac{1}{5}$
5	78%	87%	88%
6	1964	1946	1649
7	440	404	444
8	85	8.5	8.55
9	1958	1988	1588
10	992	229	292

3 Work in pairs. Write down a number for your partner to say. Take turns to test each other.

MINI WORKBOOK exercise 7 page 117

Reading & Vocabulary

4 Look at the photos on page 73 and answer the questions.

· What are the people doing in each photo?

· Do you do lots of things at the same time? What things?

5 SCANNING Read the text and match the numbers to the explanations, 1–5.

> sixty   two thousand three hundred   five
> one to two billion   four and a half

1 The number of channels on American TV: _____

2 The percentage of American children with their own TV: _____

3 The number of computers IBM expected to sell in 1943: _____

4 The number of people in the world who go online every day: _____

5 The number of hours every day that most Americans watch TV: _____

6 Find and <u>underline</u> two predictions in the text about the first TVs and computers. Did they come true?

7 Read the article again. Tick (✓) true and cross (✗) false. Correct the false statements.

1 ☐ In the past, most people listened to important radio news alone.

2 ☐ Many people like watching TV alone so that they can choose the programme they want.

3 ☐ Young people in Britain watch more TV than their parents.

4 ☐ Young people often do other things while they are watching TV.

5 ☐ TV executives think that everyone in the future will watch TV in the same way.

8 Find the missing word or phrase in the text.

1 *searching* : to be looking for (paragraph 3)

2 _____ : to get bigger (paragraph 5)

3 _____ : to talk about unimportant things (paragraph 5)

4 _____ : something you are not really listening to (paragraph 5)

5 _____ : people born around the same time (paragraph 6)

6 _____ : machines or tools that do a special job (paragraph 6)

9 Discuss these questions.

· Do you usually watch TV alone or with other people? Which do you prefer?

· Do you like the idea of watching TV on your mobile or a laptop? Why? Why not?

MINI WORKBOOK exercise 8 page 117

How screens took over our lives (3.42)

1 '**T**he problem with television is that people must sit with their eyes fixed on the screen and the average American just won't have time,' said the *New York Times* in 1939. In those days, TV sets were toys for rich Americans: the only screen that most people saw was in the cinema. When the President made an important speech, families and neighbours sat round a single radio set.

2 Today, there are more TV sets than people in the US. Sixty percent of children have one in their bedroom and the average American finds time to watch for four and a half hours a day! But with over 2300 channels to choose from, many people prefer to watch alone, rather than in a family group.

3 And, of course, TVs are not the only screens in our lives. When the first computer appeared in 1943, the chairman of IBM was also pessimistic. 'Worldwide, I expect to sell maybe five computers,' he said. Today, between one and two billion people use the internet every day! The average young Briton spends three hours a day online: socialising through sites like MySpace, watching videos on YouTube or just searching for information. And then there are video games …

4 When you add all this up, the average American child now consumes 8.5 hours of media every day! So how do people find the time?

5 Actually, it's not that bad. The total time that young people spend in front of screens hasn't increased that much. But today's teenagers are very good at 'multitasking' or doing several things at the same time. They chat to friends while searching for information and they listen to the TV as background noise. British teenagers actually watch less TV than their parents: many prefer the internet. 'I spend much more time online than watching TV,' says Saqib Khan, aged sixteen. 'It's more useful – you can get a lot more information.'

6 However, there is a big difference between generations: many over-fifties have no interest in the internet. For the future, TV executives are planning two different services. One service will be for the 'iPod generation', who will select what they want to watch on different devices (TVs, mobiles, laptops). The other service will be for the older generation, who prefer traditional TV. Only one thing seems certain: our eyes will be fixed to screens!

A

COMPLAINING

1 Look at the photos and answer the questions.

- What are Zack and Grace doing in the photos?
- Why do you think Zack is unhappy in Photo B? Think of three possible reasons.

  Maybe ... he's had bad news.

2 (3.43) Listen to Zack and Grace's conversation.

- What three problems does Zack mention?
- Tick the best summary of the situation with the camcorder:

  ☐ Zack wants to change it because it doesn't work properly.

  ☐ It doesn't work properly and Zack has discovered that it is available more cheaply.

  ☐ Zack has found a better model on the internet.

3 (3.44) Check the words in blue below and then listen to Zack's conversation at the shop. Tick (✓) true and cross (✗) false.

1 ☐ Zack hasn't got his receipt.
2 ☐ The assistant refuses to exchange the camera.
3 ☐ The manager refuses to give him a refund.
4 ☐ The manager gives Zack the address of the manufacturer.

4 (3.45) Listen and complete the *Phrases2know* with the words below. Then listen again and practise the intonation.

[refund   nothing   exchange   happy
  exactly   receipt   manager   properly   give]

Phrases 2 know

Complaints

What the customer says
It doesn't work _____ .
Could I speak to the _____ , please?
I'm really not _____ about this.
I'd like a _____ , please.

What the shop assistant says
Have you got the _____ ?
What _____ is the problem?
We can _____ it if you like.
I'm afraid we can't _____ refunds.
I'm sorry, there's _____ I can do.

5 (3.46) Put the dialogue in order, then listen and check. In pairs, act out the dialogue.

I'm sorry, I didn't keep it. ☐

Yes, I bought this CD here yesterday and it's scratched. I'd like a refund, please. ☐

Can I help you? 1

Yes, just a moment. 7

I'm really not happy about this. Could I speak to the manager, please? ☐

Have you got the receipt? ☐

I'm afraid we can't give refunds if you don't have the receipt. We can exchange it if you like. ☐

6 In pairs, take turns to act out the dialogues below. Follow the chart and use the *Phrases2know* in exercise 4.

CAN YOU DO IT IN ENGLISH?

Customer	Shop assistant
You are complaining because:	You can't give a refund because:
1 the headphones for your new MP3 player don't work	the customer bought it three months ago
2 you bought a printer and one of the wires is missing	the customer hasn't got a receipt
3 you discovered a stain on your new jumper	the customer bought it in a sale

Customer Service,
Megatron Electronics,
Kirkdale Industrial Estate,
Kirkdale KD2 7TP

25 Manorgate Road
London NW10 2PQ

30 August 2010

Dear Sir or Madam,

a <u>I am writing to complain about</u> an Ultrasonic 780X camcorder that I bought from Digital Superstore on 21 August.

b There are two problems with the camcorder. Firstly, the battery does not work properly: I have to recharge it every time I use it. According to the instruction book, it only needs recharging after sixty minutes of recording time. Secondly, there is a problem with the volume: sometimes it is very loud and sometimes there is no volume. I returned the camcorder to Digital Superstore, but they refused to give me a refund and advised me to contact you.

c I am enclosing the camcorder, together with the receipt. <u>Could you please give me a refund as soon as possible?</u>

<u>I look forward to hearing from you,</u>

<u>Yours faithfully,</u>

Zachery Garber

Zachery Garber

A LETTER OF COMPLAINT

7 Read Zack's letter to the manufacturer. Match what he says, 1–3 with paragraphs in the letter, a–c.

1 ☐ He says what he expects to happen.
2 ☐ He explains the problem.
3 ☐ He explains why he is writing.

8 a Which addresses does Zack write at the beginning of the letter and where? Where does he write the date?

b Add the phrases <u>underlined</u> in the letter to the correct section of the *Phrases2know*.

Phrases **2** know

A letter of complaint
Opening
Dear Mr Benton,
a _____ ,
Reasons for writing
I am writing because I would like to make a complaint.
b _____
Saying what you expect
Could you send me a replacement as soon as possible?
I think you should send me a refund.
c _____
Showing that you expect a reply
d _____
Closing
Yours sincerely,
e _____ ,

9 Write a letter of complaint about one of the items in exercise 6. In the letter:

- explain the reason for your complaint
- give details of the problem
- tell the company that you are returning it together with the receipt
- say what you expect the company to do.

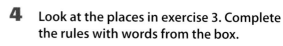

Grammar	*used to* Present perfect with *for* and *since*
Vocabulary	The natural world
Phrases	Telling an interesting story

Vocabulary Speaking

The natural world

1 Which *Words2know* can you see in the photo?

> **Words 2 know**
>
> a desert   a mountain range   an ocean/a sea
> a forest   a coast   a volcano   a lake   a river   an island
> a continent   waves   a field   a jungle   the Earth

2 (4.2) Put the *Words2know* into the categories a–c.
Listen and check. Add more words to each group.
  a Words connected with land   *a desert*
  b Words connected with water
  c Words connected with land and water

3 (4.3) Listen and repeat. Then <u>underline</u> the odd word
out and explain your answers.
  1 Argentina/Africa/Europe/Antarctica
  2 the Nile/the Amazon/the Sahara/the Mississippi
  3 the Caribbean/the Baltic/the Atlantic/the Mediterranean
  4 Switzerland/Japan/Great Britain/New Zealand
  5 the Andes/the Pyrenees/the Alps/the Canaries

Argentina is the odd word out because it's a country.
Africa, Europe and Antarctica are continents.

4 Look at the places in exercise 3. Complete
the rules with words from the box.
  • Use *the* with names of _rivers,_____
  • Don't use *the* with names of _____

> countries   rivers ✓   mountain ranges
> seas   oceans   deserts   continents
> groups of islands

5 Which of the *Words2know* are/aren't in
your country? Where are they?

" *There is a mountain range in the*
north. There aren't any volcanoes.

MINI WORKBOOK exercises 1 and 6 pages 118–119

Grammar Focus

used to

6 Read the fantastic facts about the Earth.
Which facts do you find most surprising?

7 Which facts describe the picture? Find
three mistakes in the picture.

8 Read *Grammar2know* and find another
example for rules a and b in the text.

> **Grammar 2 know**
>
> ### *used to*
>
> Use *used to*:
>
> **a** to talk about states in the past that are not
> true now:
> *Winters used to be much colder.*
>
> **b** to talk about things that happened
> regularly in the past but don't happen now:
> *The River Thames used to freeze regularly.*
>
> We can always use the past simple instead of
> *used to*:
> *It used to rain there regularly./It rained there regularly.*
>
> Use the past simple if things happened once:
> *Africa and North America separated.* (they
> separated only once)
>
> ### Form
>
> **+** *It used to rain there regularly.*
>
> **–** *It didn't use to rain there regularly.*
>
> **?** *Did it use to rain there? Yes, it did. / No, it didn't.*
> *When did it use to rain?*

Amazing Earth! (4.4)

FANTASTIC FACTS ABOUT THE WAY OUR PLANET USED TO BE

The continents didn't use to be separate! 250 million years ago there was just one 'super-continent', known as Pangaea. First North America and Africa separated. Then, about 140 million years ago, Africa, South America and Australia broke away. The continents are still moving and scientists believe that one day there may be a new super-continent.

The Sahara Desert was green until about 5000 years ago! It used to rain there regularly and it wasn't sandy. There were freshwater lakes with fish, rivers, forests and large areas of grassland. People farmed the area and elephants, giraffes, rhinoceros and crocodiles used to live there!

Winters used to be much colder than they are now. Between 1550 and 1850, Europe had extremely cold winters and cool summers. Scientists often call this the 'Little Ice Age'. The River Thames in London used to freeze regularly and there were fairs on the frozen river known as 'Frost Fairs'. The last one took place in 1814.

9 Rewrite the sentences with *used to* where possible.

1 There was one super-continent.
   There used to be one super-continent.
2 Australia broke away.
3 The Sahara was green.
4 The Sahara wasn't sandy.
5 Europe had extremely cold winters.
6 The last Frost Fair took place in 1814.

10 Write sentences about the picture with *used to* and these words and phrases.

> women/long skirts   not have cars
> skate/on the river
> not have mobile phones

Women used to wear long skirts.

11 Read what Jodie believed when she was young. Underline the correct option. Sometimes both options are possible.

I ¹ had/used to have some crazy ideas when I was a kid! When we ² studied/used to study volcanoes at school, our teacher ³ told/used to tell us that volcanoes came from cracks in the Earth's surface. I ⁴ was/used to be really frightened that the cracks in the pavement were a volcano … I ⁵ checked/used to check them every day to see if they were getting bigger.

12 Tell the class three things from your childhood. Use *used to* and the ideas below.

- things you believed/didn't believe in (Santa Claus, fairies, etc.)
- things you were frightened of (animals, the dark, etc.)
- things you loved/didn't like (food, toys, etc.)

❝ *I used to be really frightened of fire when I was little.*

13 a Read Hannah's memories of a place she used to visit as a child. What kind of place was it? Find the phrases Hannah uses to describe:

- what the place looked like
- why/when she went there
- what she did there
- how she felt when she was there.

We always used to go to the same place in Cornwall when I was a child and every year we used to go to the same beach. It was a tiny beach and not many people knew about it. Every day we used to take a picnic. It was a really beautiful place, with cliffs behind the beach, white sand and big waves. My sister and I used to spend hours climbing on the rocks and playing in the waves. It's one of my favourite places in the world. I loved it!

b WRITING Write a description of a place you used to visit when you were a child, like Hannah's.

MINI WORKBOOK exercise 2 page 118

out there

Grammar Focus

Present perfect with *for* and *since*

1 Look at the photos and answer the questions.
- What do you know about global warming?
- Match the *Words2know* with the photos.

 (4.5)

floods droughts hurricanes
species becoming extinct melting ice
rising sea levels high temperatures

2 **a** Read about global warming. Match the facts in the text 1–5 with the headings a–e.

a Many species are in danger.

b Global temperatures are rising. ✓

c Extreme weather is becoming more common.

d There are droughts in many parts of the world.

e Polar ice is melting and sea levels are rising.

b (4.6) Listen and check. Which facts do you find most worrying?

3 Complete these sentences from the text. What's the difference between *since* and *for*? Read *Grammar2know* to check.
- At the North Pole, 22% of the ice has melted *since* _____ .
- In parts of Australia, it hasn't rained *for* _____ .

Present perfect

Use the present perfect to talk about unfinished past actions:
*The global sea level **has risen** 20 cm.* (and it is still rising)

Time expressions: *this year, this week, all my life, all week, in the last few days*

We often ask questions with ***How long ...?*** + present perfect:
***How long has** the drought **lasted**?*

for and *since*

Use ***for*** with periods of time: ***for** ten days, **for** a long time.*
*It **hasn't rained for** seven years.*

Use ***since*** with points in time: ***since** last Christmas, **since** 10 a.m.*
*At the North Pole, 22% of the ice **has melted since** 1979.*

Five reasons to worry about global warming

1 *Global temperatures are rising.*
Global temperatures have risen by 1°C since 1900. Experts fear they will rise by 3–4°C in the next century.

2 _____
At the North Pole, 22% of the ice has melted since 1979. The global sea level has risen around 20 cm in the last century. Experts say it will rise between 11 cm and 77 cm in the twenty–first century.

3 _____
Between 1850 and 1990, there were about five serious hurricanes every year. Since 1990, there have been eight every year. There have also been many serious floods, especially around India.

4 _____
In parts of Australia, it hasn't rained for seven years. There have also been serious droughts in China and the USA.

5 _____
Since 1987, the number of polar bears has decreased by 22% and penguins by 35%. Scientists believe that 35% of all species will become extinct because of global warming.

4 Read the article about drought in Australia and <u>underline</u> the correct words.

The worst drought for 1000 years!

Australia ¹ *has had/had* its worst drought for 1000 years. Farmers near the Murray-Darling River are suffering badly. Ian Morris, a fruit farmer, is typical. 'I ² *'ve moved/moved* to this area in 1980 and I ³ *'ve owned/owned* this farm for twenty-five years. Since 2000, things ⁴ *have been/were* terrible – we ⁵ *'ve had/had* a drought for years and years now. This area here used to be a lake, Gidgee Lake, but now we call it the Gidgee Desert because it ⁶ *'s been/was* dry since 2005. In 2001, sixty people ⁷ *have worked/worked* on this farm but now there are only fifteen of us. A lot of farmers in this area ⁸ *have sold /sold* their farms in the last few years. I don't know what I'm going to do.'

5 (4.7) Complete the time phrases with *for* or *since*. Then listen and check your answers.

1 *for* four years 2 __ 15 May 3 __ 1999
4 __ six weeks 5 __ two hours 6 __ five minutes
7 __ 12.00 8 __ last Tuesday

6 Use the prompts to write at least four questions. Then ask and answer in pairs, using *for* and *since* to answer.

1 How long/be (at this school/in this class)?
2 How long/live in (this town/your house)?
3 How long/know (your best friend/your teacher/someone else)?
4 How long/have (your watch/mobile/iPod, etc.)?

❝ *How long have you been at this school?*
For two years./Since 2009.

MINI WORKBOOK exercises 3–5 and 7 pages 118–119

Listening & Speaking

Climate refugees

7 Look at the photo at the bottom of this page. What do you think a climate refugee is?

8 a (4.8) Listen to Part 1 of a radio programme, about the Carteret Islands. Write 1 next to the things below that the report mentions.

> mosquitoes and malaria   29 August 2005
> rising sea levels *1*   a thousand people
> sick children   high temperatures
> relatives who died   salty water
> expensive insurance   help from government

b (4.9) Listen to Part 2 of the programme about New Orleans. Write 2 next to the things that the report mentions.

9 (4.10) Listen to both parts of the programme again. Tick (✓) true and cross (✗) false.

1 ☐ The Carteret islanders have damaged their environment, so they have to leave.
2 ☐ The islanders cannot feed themselves properly.
3 ☐ Soon it will be impossible to live on the islands.
4 ☐ Most people who left New Orleans in 2005 have now returned.
5 ☐ Bill wanted to return to New Orleans but he could not afford to.
6 ☐ Scientists don't think Hurricane Katrina happened because of global warming.

10 Discuss these questions:

- Whose problems are worse in your opinion, Ursula Tobasi's or Bill Jackson's?
- Scientists believe global warming is happening because we use too much energy. Think of four things we can all do to save energy.

❝ *We can switch off gadgets when we aren't using them.*

New Orleans, 2005

Reading & Vocabulary

1 Work in pairs. Tick (✓) the words from the story that you know. Check the unknown words with your teacher or in a dictionary.

Words 2 know (4.11)

ash   a volcanic eruption   an explosion   a scream
a loud noise   an uninhabited island   a sailing ship
to crash   to destroy   to shake with fear   gunfire

2 PREDICTING Read the title of the story and look at the pictures. Can you guess what the story is about and when it happened?

Maybe it's about …
I think it happened … years ago.

3 Read the three diary extracts, written more than 120 years ago. What strange things did each writer notice?

a I was walking with my friends by the seashore, looking towards the south-west. Suddenly the sky turned blood red. I started shaking with fear and felt an awful scream passing through nature …

b Early this morning, as we were sailing past an uninhabited island, we saw something incredible: an enormous cloud of smoke rising into the air, like the beginning of a volcanic eruption. Fortunately, we continued our journey safely but the situation may be dangerous for other ships in the area.

c I was working at my desk as usual when I heard a loud noise outside my window – it sounded like gunfire. I went to see what was happening but I saw nothing unusual in the street outside. Many other people also heard the noise but no one knows of any gunfire on the island. There's no explanation …

4 (4.12) Read the text. Match diary extracts a–c in exercise 3 with gaps 1–3 in the text. Then listen to the whole story and check.

5 Read the text again. Put the events in the correct order.

☐ The world's weather returned to normal.

☐ The world's weather became colder.

1 A ship's captain saw smoke coming from Krakatoa.

☐ Big waves killed thousands of people.

☐ A new volcano appeared from under the sea.

☐ A volcano erupted and destroyed the island.

☐ The sky changed colour.

6 Read *Active Study*. Then complete the table with words from the text.

Notice noun/verb forms

ACTIVE STUDY

Some nouns are the same as the verb:
to scream   a scream

Some nouns have a special ending (suffix):
to erupt   an eruption

Verb	Noun
to smoke	_____
to explain	_____
to explode	_____
to _____	a disappearance
to _____	a crash
to _____	destruction
to inspire	_____

The biggest BANG in history

In May and June 1883, smoke was pouring out of the tiny uninhabited island of Krakatoa in Indonesia. The captain of *H.M.S. Elizabeth*, a passing ship, wrote in his diary that he could see smoke.

1 20 May 1883 (Indonesia) _____
Then, on 26 August 1883, Krakatoa began to erupt violently. The next morning the eruption ended suddenly: the island exploded into pieces and simply disappeared into the sea. A column of ash and smoke rose 50 km into the air, eight times higher than a modern aeroplane flies.

People heard the explosion in Australia and India. It was the loudest noise in history, an explosion ten times bigger than the atomic bomb at Hiroshima. A police officer 4600 km away, wrote about it in his diary.

2 27 August 1883 (Rodriguez Island, South Pacific) _____
Then came four enormous waves, or 'tsunami', 40 metres high. They crashed onto the shores of Java and Sumatra, destroying everything in their way and killing thousands. People felt the waves as far away as France!

One unfortunate man in the South Pacific was sitting on the veranda at the top of his house when the tsunami came. Suddenly, to his right, he saw a crocodile. To save himself, he jumped onto the crocodile's back and rode on top of the wave. He surfed like this for about three kilometres until the wave broke, leaving him and the crocodile on the jungle floor.

There were signs of the explosion all over the world for many months afterwards. Around Krakatoa, it was completely dark for two and half days after the explosion. All over the world, the sky turned a strange colour. The painter, Edvard Munch, wrote about it in his diary, as he walked near his home.

3 29 November 1883 (Norway) _____
People now believe that this was the inspiration for Munch's famous painting, *The Scream*. Because of the dust and ash in the atmosphere, global temperatures fell by 1.2°C and did not return to normal for five years.

Then, in 1925, a new volcano began to appear. Local people called it Anek Krakatoa, 'Son of Krakatoa'. It is still active today and experts believe that one day there will be another enormous explosion like the one in 1883.

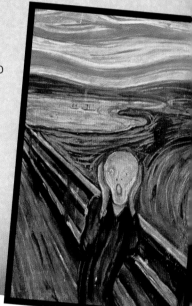

---

7 **a** Work in pairs, A and B. Read the cards below and plan what to say. Use the *Phrases2know*.

CAN YOU DO IT IN ENGLISH?

A: You are the man who survived the tsunami by riding on the crocodile's back.
A journalist is interviewing you about your experience. Think how to describe what happened and how to answer Student B's questions (you can invent information).

B: You are a journalist from 1887. You are going to interview the man who rode on the crocodile's back. Think of questions to ask. Use the ideas below:
• What/you do/when the tsunami/arrive?
• How/you feel/when you/see it?
• Crocodile/very big?
• You/frightened of him?
• How/you feel now?

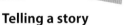

Phrases 2 know (4.13)

Telling a story
Describing how you felt
It was terrible/amazing/incredible!
I was terrified/frightened/scared!
I still can't believe it!

Responding with interest
That's amazing/incredible!
Wow!
Really?
Oh no!

b Act out the interview in front of the class.

MINI WORKBOOK exercises 8–9 page 119

out there

activestudy5 (EXAMS)

Vocabulary

ACTIVE STUDY | Learn the meaning of useful words

1 Choose the correct word for each definition.

1 These happen when there is a lot of rain and the land is covered in water.
a droughts   b floods   c waves

2 You receive one of these when you pay for something in a shop.
a a charger   b a gadget   c a receipt

3 People sometimes do this if they are very afraid.
a crash   b erupt   c shake

4 When a shop gives you your money back, it gives you …
a a desert   b a refund   c a sale

5 You have to do this with an electrical appliance to make it work.
a exchange it   b plug it in   c destroy it

6 The place where land and sea meet.
a forest   b lake   c coast

ACTIVE STUDY | Learn collocations

2 Match words from column A and column B to make collocations.

A	B
global	control
alarm	eruption
public	temperatures
remote	clock
volcanic	transport
high	warming

ACTIVE STUDY | Learn words in groups

3 Complete the sentences with the words below.

[charge   press   search   select   set   switch]

1 Will you _switch_ off the television, please? I'm trying to study.

2 May I use your charger to _____ the battery on my mobile?

3 I took the battery out of my mobile and now I have to _____ the time again.

4 Could you please _____ the button for the fifth floor?

5 You can use this computer to _____ for information on the internet.

6 Just _____ 'print' from the menu.

ACTIVE STUDY | Notice word stress

4 PRONUNCIATION (4.14) Listen and put the words into groups according to their stress pattern. Listen again and repeat.

■ ·	· ■	· ■ ·	■ · ·
jungle	machine	volcano	continent

1 jungle	5 message	9 select
2 machine	6 eruption	10 socialise
3 volcano	7 exchange	11 explosion
4 continent	8 desert	12 recognise

Grammar

5 Choose the best answer for each gap.

Jeffrey Sachs is an economist [1] *which/who/where* has written several books about world poverty. He was born in Detroit in the USA in 1954 and he has worked in American universities [2] *since/from/for* many years. In the 1980s and 90s, he advised governments in Bolivia and Poland about their economic problems. [3] *Since/From/For* 2002, he [4] *was/is/has been* the director of the Earth Institute at Columbia University. In 2005, he [5] *has written/wrote/used to write* The End of Poverty, a book [6] *who/which/where* suggests solutions to many of the problems in poor countries, especially in Africa, [7] *where/which/who* malaria and AIDS make the situation worse. [8] *From/For/Since* then, he has travelled to many countries around the world to talk about his ideas. He believes that if rich governments [9] *will help/help/are helping* poorer countries in the Third World, extreme poverty [10] *will disappear/disappear/is disappearing* by the year 2025.

6 Make correct sentences from the jumbled words. The first word is given.

1 about/meet/talk/it/we'll/we/when
We'll _____ .

2 love/little/teddy bears/was/I/when/used/I/to
When _____ .

3 have/lesson/this/after/I'll/sandwich/a/finishes
After _____ .

4 here/our/1995/lived/neighbours/since/have
Our _____ .

5 before/I'll/plane/you/the/off/text/takes
I'll _____ .

Reading Skills

7 Read the text about the Itelmen people of Kamchatka. Parts of sentences are missing. Match phrases a–g to gaps 1–6. There is one extra phrase.

a the stories explain the fire coming from the mountains at night

b and about thirty of them are still active today.

c who form 1% of the total population of the region

d the gomuls fly down from the mountain tops and into the sea

e an area which contains 50% of the world's volcanoes

f where temperatures can go down to 35 degrees below zero in winter

g which gave people fish to eat

ACTIVE STUDY Guess meaning from the context

8 a **Look at the words in blue. Decide if each word is a) a noun, b) an adjective or c) a verb.**

b <u>Underline</u> the best meaning for each word. Use the context to help you.

1 remote   far away/very small/very warm

2 huge   very big/very slow/very small

3 spear   a small knife/a weapon for hunting/a gun

4 roast   to catch/to cook/to hunt

5 summit   the top of a mountain/the side of a mountain/a cloud

Listening Skills

ACTIVE STUDY Learn words in groups

9 (4.15) **Listen to a conversation about a trip to Kamchatka. For statements 1–6, tick (✓) true, cross (✗) false and write (?) if the text doesn't say.**

1 ☐ Kamchatka is an eight-hour flight from Moscow.

2 ☐ Kamchatka is bigger than England.

3 ☐ The population of Kamchatka is about one million.

4 ☐ The main city of Kamchatka lies in the north.

5 ☐ You can see polar bears in Kamchatka.

6 ☐ It always rains in the summer.

Gomuls, Whales and Fire on the Mountain Top (4.16)

Kamchatka is a peninsula in the far eastern part of Russia. It is part of the so-called 'Ring of Fire', [1] _____. Kamchatka alone has more than 160 volcanoes, [2] _____. It is a remote place, more than 6,000 kilometres from Moscow. The people who live there have many traditional stories which explain the volcanic activity in the region.

One of the oldest peoples of the far North are the Itelmen, [3] _____ and who live mainly by rivers in the west of Kamchatka. For thousands of years, they have lived from fishing and from picking berries and mushrooms in the forest. Traditionally, they used to believe that there were spirits in everything: animals, rocks, rivers. The most important of all was the spirit of the sea, [4] _____.

In old Itelmen stories, all dangerous places – such as volcanoes – are inhabited by huge monsters called gomuls. At night, [5] _____. They hunt whales there, using their fingers as spears. With a whale on each finger, they then return to the mountain tops where they light fires to roast and eat the food they have caught. This is how [6] _____. The Itelmen used to believe that great piles of whale bones lie on the mountain tops … but it was bad luck to go up to the summit to see them!

Speaking Skills

10 In pairs, act out the following roleplay.

Student A (Customer)
You bought a gadget (decide what) a few days ago but it has already stopped working. Take it back to the shop and explain the problem. You'd like a refund but you didn't keep the receipt.

Student B (Shop Assistant)
You would like to help but you can't give a refund because the customer hasn't got the receipt.

SKILLS STRATEGIES back cover

11 must see

A

B   C

D

Listening & Vocabulary

Making a film

1 Discuss these questions in groups.

- Have you seen any of the films in the photos?
- What was the last film you saw at the cinema or on DVD? Did you enjoy it?
- What's your favourite film? Do you have any favourite actors?

The last film I saw was …
Did you like it?
I thought it was okay/really good.

2 **a** Match the photos, A–E, to the *Words2know*.

Words 2 know (4.17)

a romantic comedy   a historical drama   a thriller
fantasy/science fiction   a horror movie

b Work in pairs. Tell each other which types of film you like and don't like.

I like fantasy but I don't like romantic comedies.

3 (4.18) Listen to a description of how a film is made and put the *Words2know* in the order that you first hear them.

Words 2 know

☐ producer   ☐ special effects   ☐ director
☐ actors   ☑ film studios   ☐ script
☐ budget   ☐ editing   ☐ publicity   ☐ scenes

4 **a** (4.18) Listen again and answer the questions.

1 What's the typical budget of a big Hollywood film?
2 How much do the top stars earn?
3 How many minutes of the final film do they make each day?
4 Why don't they film all the scenes on location?
5 How long does it generally take to edit a film?
6 How much of the total budget do they spend on publicity?

b Which of these things surprise you?

I'm surprised that …

MINI WORKBOOK exercises 7–8 page 121

84

Grammar Focus

Present simple passive

5 In pairs, put the stages of making a film into the correct order. Compare your answers with another pair.

- ☐ Then the movie is filmed.
- ☐ They then plan the budget and choose a director.
- ☑ A story is chosen by the producers.
- ☐ The scenes are planned in detail.
- ☐ Music isn't added until the end.
- ☐ Finally, the film is printed.
- ☐ The director decides on the main actors.

6 Read *Grammar2know*. How many passive forms can you find in exercise 5?

Grammar 2 know

Present simple passive

Use the passive when the action is the most important thing in the sentence:
*The film **is printed**.* (it is not important who prints it)

Notice that often we do not say who does the action because it is not important or it is obvious.
*The movie **is filmed**.* (obviously the camera men do this)

To say who does the action, we use **by**:
*A story is chosen **by the producer**.*

Form: *is/are* + past participle

+ *The music **is added**.*

− *Most scenes **aren't filmed** on location.*

? *Is the story **chosen** by the producer?*
*When is the music **added**?*

7 **a** (4.19) Complete the text, using the passive. Then listen and check.

SUBBED OR DUBBED?

Do foreign language films have subtitles in your country? Or [1] *are they dubbed* (they/dub)? Foreign-language films [2] _____ (watch) all over the world nowadays … but people need to understand them!

In many countries, subtitles [3] _____ (use) to translate the dialogue. Usually the dialogue [4] _____ (not/translate) word for word but the general meaning [5] _____ (give). Often the dialogue [6] _____ (make) shorter so the audience can read the titles easily.

In other countries, dubbing is more popular. The dialogue [7] _____ (re-record) by voice actors and the original actors' voices [8] _____ (not/hear) by the audience. These days, famous actors [9] _____ (often choose) to do the dubbing.

A third method, the 'lector' method, [10] _____ (use) in some countries. Here, the audience [11] _____ (given) a translation by a single narrator but the original voices [12] _____ (hear) in the background.

b Which method in the text do you prefer when you watch a foreign language film?

8 Rewrite the sentences in the passive. Use *by* if necessary.

1 Big studios make most films these days.
Most films *are made by big studios these days.*

2 They spend millions of dollars on special effects.
Millions of dollars _____ .

3 The designers plan every scene in detail.
Every scene _____ .

4 They film some scenes on location.
Some scenes _____ .

5 The editors cut some scenes.
Some scenes _____ .

6 They send copies of the film all over the world.
Copies of the film _____ .

9 Look at exercises 5 and 8 and memorise ten stages in the making of a film in order. Close your book and tell the class.

❝ *First, a story is chosen, then …*

MINI WORKBOOK exercise 1 page 120

must see

Listening & Vocabulary

TV programmes

1 **a** Write down the name of a TV programme that you really like and one that you hate.

b Read out the programmes but do not say which is which. The other students guess whether you like or hate the programme.

2 Check you understand the *Words2know*. Think of an example of each type of programme from TV in your country.

Words 2 know (4.20)

advert   reality show   cookery programme
comedy series   soap opera   weather forecast
sports programme   cartoon   documentary
quiz show   news

3 (4.21) Listen to four extracts from TV programmes. What types of programme are they?

A _____   B _____

C _____   D _____

4 (4.21) Listen again and choose the correct answers.

A

1   Which ingredients are necessary for Frittata?
   a cheese   **b** oil   **c** onions
   d potatoes   **e** eggs   **f** tuna
   g peppers   **h** tomatoes

B

2   Where was Mrs Gray last night?
   a at the hospital   **b** with a friend
   c with her husband, John

3   How does Marianne feel about this?
   a angry   **b** interested   **c** sad

C

4   This is an advert for:
   a a dentist   **b** a health club
   c toothpaste

D

5   Jenny is talking to:
   a her boyfriend   **b** her father
   c someone called Jeremy

6   She's just come back from:
   a a date   **b** a party   **c** school

5 **a** Divide the programmes in the *Words2know* into three categories.

- There are too many programmes like this on TV: *cartoons*

- There aren't enough programmes like this on TV:

- There are the right number:

b Compare answers with other students. Which types of programme do you like best?

" *I think there are too many soap operas. To me, there aren't enough sports programmes.*
I like cartoons best.

MINI WORKBOOK exercise 9 page 121

Grammar Focus

Past simple and present perfect passive

6 Look at the photos and answer the questions.
- What kinds of TV programme do the photos show?
- Do you ever watch programmes like this?

7 SCANNING Work in pairs. Read the text and find the information below. Which pair finished first?

1   the date of the first *Doctor Who*
   23 November 1963

2   the name of the person who created *Pop Idol*

3   the year of Princess Diana's funeral

4   the number of British people who watched the 1966 World Cup Final

5   the day of the week that *Doctor Who* is shown

6   the year of the first episode of *The Simpsons*

8 **a** Which sentences below are active (A) and which are passive (P)? Which tenses are they in?

1   ☐ *Pop Idol* began in 2001.

2   ☐ *Doctor Who* was shown for the first time in 1963.

3   ☐ The cartoon has been sold all over the world.

4   ☐ A new version of the programme has appeared.

b Read *Grammar2know* and check. Find more examples of the past simple and present perfect passive in the text.

Records and Fantastic Facts ... from the world of TV (4.23)

MOST SUCCESSFUL CARTOON

The Simpsons first appeared on US TV in 1987 and since then it has been shown all over the world. In fact, Bart Simpson is probably the most famous face on the planet! But creator Matt Groening invented the cartoon family in just fifteen minutes because the characters were based on his own family!

MOST POPULAR TV SHOW

Pop Idol was originally a British television series and was first shown in October 2001. Viewers voted for their favourite new pop singer and the winners often sold millions of records! The idea was created by Simon Fuller – now one of Britain's richest men. Different versions of *Pop Idol* have been made all over the world, including *American Idol* and *Indian Idol*.

LONGEST RUNNING TV SHOW

Every British adult remembers watching the science fiction drama *Doctor Who* as a child. It was first shown on Saturday, 23 November 1963 and was a favourite for many years. Now, a new version has appeared and *Doctor Who* is again Britain's most popular Saturday night show. It is also popular in Australia and the USA, and has been sold to TV companies all over the world. So it's probably showing on a TV near you!

MOST WATCHED TV BROADCAST

The England–Germany final of the 1966 World Cup was the most watched broadcast in British history. It was watched by 32.3 million Britons. 32.1 million watched the funeral of Diana, Princess of Wales, in 1997.

9 Put the verbs in the correct form of the passive. Then choose the correct information to complete the sentence. If you don't know, guess!

Past simple passive

1 'The Lord of the Rings' books (write) by J R R Tolkien/C S Lewis/J K Rowling.

   'The Lord of the Rings' books were written by J R R Tolkien.

2 The 'Star Wars' films (direct) by George Lucas/ Alfred Hitchcock/Steven Spielberg.

3 The first 'Harry Potter' book (publish) in 1977/1987/1997.

4 The most successful film in history, *Titanic*, (release) in 1992/1997/2002.

Present perfect passive

5 Five/Six /All of the 'Harry Potter' books (make) into films.

6 The Bible (translate) into 500/2000/5000 languages and dialects.

7 Over 10 million/80 million/100 million copies of the 'Lord of the Rings' books (sell) around the world.

10 (4.22) Compare answers with a partner. Then listen and check.

> *I think the 'Star Wars' films were directed by Steven Spielberg but I'm not sure.*

MINI WORKBOOK exercises 2–6 pages 120–121

Grammar 2 know

Past simple passive
Form: *was/were* + past participle

+ *It was shown ...*   *They were shown ...*
− *It wasn't shown ...*   *They weren't shown ...*
? *Was it shown ...?*   *Were they shown ...?*
   When was it shown?

Present perfect passive
Form: *have/has been* + past participle

+ *It has been sold ...*   *They have been sold ...*
− *It hasn't been sold ...*   *They haven't been sold ...*
? *Has it been sold?*   *Have they been sold?*
   Who has it been sold to?

must see

Reading & Writing

1 Read the *Words2know*. Which of these do you read? Do you have any favourite writers?

Words 2 know (4.24)

novels   short stories   blogs
magazines   newspapers   poetry   comics

2 Look at the book cover and read the caption.

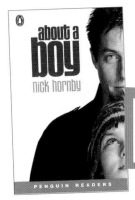

- Do you know other novels which are also films?
- Do you prefer to read the book or watch the film?

About a Boy is a novel by Nick Hornby. It has been made into a film, starring Hugh Grant.

3 Read the introduction to *About a Boy* and answer the questions.

- What do you learn about Will?
- Has Will got any children?
- Why has Will joined the single parents' group?
- What do you learn about Marcus?

Thirty-six-year-old Will Freeman has a life without responsibilities. He isn't interested in children, marriage or work but he is interested in attractive single mothers. He invents a two-year-old son called Ned so that he can join a single parents' group. There, he meets Suzie, an attractive young mother, and her daughter Megan. One day, Will goes to the park with a group of mothers and their children. There, he meets a twelve-year-old boy called Marcus, who is having problems at home and at school.

4 Read the extract from the novel on page 89. Match the characters to the descriptions.

[Will   Suzie   Marcus   the park-keeper]

1 _____ doesn't want to answer too many questions.
2 _____ is sympathetic to Will.
3 _____ kills a duck by mistake.
4 _____ is angry about the dead duck.
5 _____ lies about why Marcus was throwing bread at the duck.
6 _____ seems worried about what he has done.

5 Discuss these questions in groups.

- How do Marcus and Will feel about each other at the beginning? Does this change?
- Why does Will lie to the park-keeper?
- Do you think Will is a nice person? Why? Why not?

6 Tick the things you think will happen later in the novel. Do you have any other ideas? Check on page 124.

1 ☐ Will and Suzie fall in love.
2 ☐ Suzie finds out about Will's lies and won't forgive him.
3 ☐ Marcus and Will become friends.
4 ☐ Will has a bad influence on Marcus.
5 ☐ Marcus finds out about Will's lies and won't forgive him.
6 ☐ Will becomes a better person.

7 Complete the book review of *About a Boy* with the *Phrases2know*.

Phrases 2 know (4.25)

Describing a book or film

it's set in   It was written by   My favourite part is
It's about   (It) is called ✓   It was released
It stars   The characters are   I like it because

A book I've read recently

The book ¹ *is called* 'About A Boy'.
² _____ a man called Will and his relationship with a boy called Marcus.
³ _____ an English writer called Nick Hornby and ⁴ _____ London in the present day.

⁵ _____ it's a modern story and it's also very real and funny. ⁶ _____ realistic and interesting, especially Will, the main character, and Marcus, the boy. ⁷ _____ the scene where Will and Marcus first meet in the park.

'About a Boy' has also been made into a film. ⁸ _____ five or six years ago. ⁹ _____ Hugh Grant. It was quite funny but parts of it were sad. I really recommend the book and the film!

ABOUT A BOY

4.26

Will played with the children for most of the afternoon. He kept away from the adults sitting on blankets because he didn't want to have to answer any difficult questions about Ned. He kept away from Marcus, too. Marcus was walking
5 round the lake, throwing bits of his sandwich at the ducks.

Later, Suzie came to talk to him. 'You miss him, don't you?'

'Who?' He meant it; he had no idea who she was talking about. But then he remembered about Ned. 'I'll see him later.'
10 'What's he like?' asked Suzie.

'Oh … Nice. He's a really nice boy.'

Before Suzie could ask more questions, Marcus ran over to them. He seemed very nervous and upset.

'I think I've killed a duck,' he said.
15 Will, Suzie and Marcus stood on the path by the edge of the lake, staring at the duck's dead body in the water.

'What happened, Marcus?' Will asked.

'I don't know. I was just throwing a piece of my sandwich at it. I didn't mean to kill it.'
20 'What's that in the water next to it? Is that the bread you threw at it?'

'Yes,' said Marcus. He didn't like Will much so he didn't want to answer his questions.

'That's not a sandwich, that's a loaf,' said Will. 'I'm not surprised the duck was killed.'
25 'Perhaps I didn't kill it,' said Marcus. 'Perhaps it died because it was ill.'

Nobody said anything.

They were all staring so hard at the scene of the crime that they didn't notice the park-keeper standing next to them. Marcus felt very frightened. He would be in big trouble now.
30 'One of your ducks has died,' said Will. He made it sound like the saddest thing he'd ever seen. Marcus looked up at him. Maybe Will wasn't such a bad guy.

'I was told it was your boy's fault,' said the park-keeper. 'It's a crime to kill a duck, you know.'

'Are you suggesting that Marcus killed this duck? Marcus loves ducks, don't
35 you?'

'Yes,' said Marcus. 'They're my favourite animal. I mean, my favourite bird.' This was rubbish because he hated all animals, but he thought it helped.

'I was told he was throwing enormous loaves at it.'

'No,' said Will. 'He was throwing bread at the duck's body. He wanted to sink it
40 because the sight of the dead bird was upsetting my friend's little girl, Megan.'

There was a silence. At last the park-keeper spoke.

'Well, I'll have to go into the water and get it,' he said.

Marcus felt much better. He didn't have to go to prison.

8 Write a review of a book or film. Use the *Phrases2know* and include the following:

Paragraph 1
- The title
- What it's about
- Who it was written/ directed by
- Where it's set

Paragraph 2
- Your opinion of the book/ film/characters/story
- Your favourite characters/ part

Paragraph 3
- Other information (Has it been made into a film? When was it released? Who stars in it?)
- Do you recommend it?

must see

REAL TIME

ADVERTS AND NOTICES

1 SCANNING Read three notices on the students' notice board at Zack's college and <u>underline</u> the correct words.

1 Mark wants to *learn/teach other people* how to play the guitar. He *has/hasn't* given lessons before.

2 Carrie wants to *buy/sell* some tickets for a rock concert. They are *cheap/full price*.

3 Lauren has *lost/found* an iPod. The case is *easy/difficult* to recognise.

GUITAR LESSONS AVAILABLE

Private or small groups – eves and wknds only
£25–£30 p.h.

Experienced teacher

Phone Mark on 0208 445 8797
(mob 08823765491)

FOR SALE
2 Tickets for DEMONICA concert at U.L.U.
Saturday 28th August / 8.30
BARGAIN!   Only £10.00 each!!!
Call Carrie on 01243 567897

LOST!!!
IPOD NANO in red and black spotted case
Lost in cafeteria area Wednesday 25th August about 3.00
If you've found it,
please contact me ASAP!
Contact Lauren on 08762 787686

2 Read the notices again and complete the *Phrases2know*.

Phrases 2know

Notices

Heading	Contact details
Found!	Phone (Mark) on …
Wanted!	_____
Lost!	_____
_____	
_____	

Zack sees a notice for tickets for the Demonica concert. It's Grace's favourite band so he decides to invite her to the concert.

3 Notices are not usually written in full sentences and often use abbreviations. Look at the notices in exercise 1 again and

a tick which of these are often missing:

☐ pronouns (*I/he*, etc.)   ☐ prepositions
☐ the verb *be*   ☐ articles (*a/the*)

b match the abbreviations, 1–5, to the words, a–e, in the box:

1 p.h. ☐   3 a.s.a.p. ☐   5 wknds ☐
2 eves ☐   4 mob ☐

[a evenings   b as soon as possible
  c per hour   d weekends   e mobile]

4 Write notices for the situations below. Use the *Phrases2know* in exercise 2.

1 You have lost your mobile phone. It has a 'Simpsons' case. Decide where and when you lost it.

2 You want to sell your old PlayStation. It is in excellent condition. Decide the price.

3 You want to earn extra money by giving lessons (a sport, language, etc.) Decide how much to charge and when you are available.

MAKING PHONE CALLS

5 **(4.27)** Listen to Zack's phone calls. Choose the correct answer.

1 Zack *asks Grace to call him back/says he will try her mobile again later.*

2 Fran says Grace *hasn't got her phone with her/is in class.*

3 Grace *wants/doesn't want* to go to the concert.

4 Zack is worried that the tickets *are too expensive/have already been sold.*

5 The tickets are *still available/sold.*

6 Zack is going to pick the tickets up *from Carrie's house/at college.*

6 **(4.28)** Which dialogue, a–d, do the *Phrases2know* come from? Listen again and practise the intonation.

Phrases 2 know

Telephoning

It's Zack. *a, b and c*
Is Grace there?
Could I speak to Carrie, please?
Hi, Carrie speaking.
Who's calling?
Just a minute, I'll get her.
She isn't here at the moment. Can I take a message?
Why don't you try her mobile?
Could you call me as soon as you can?
Speak to you soon.

7 **(4.29)** Complete the dialogue with the *Phrases2know*. Listen and check. In pairs, practise the dialogue, using your own names.

A: Hello?

B: Hello, ¹ _____ Anna, please?

A: Who's calling?

B: ² _____ Greg.

A: Just a minute, I'll ³ _____ . I'm sorry, but she isn't here at the moment. ⁴ _____ a message?

B: Oh don't worry, it's okay.

A: ⁵ _____ her mobile? It's her lunchtime now.

B: Oh yes, good idea, thanks.

8 In pairs, take turns to act out the dialogue below. Follow the chart and use the *Phrases2know*.

A: Answer the phone.

B: Ask to speak to A's sister/brother/another friend.

A: Say he/she's gone shopping. Suggest you take a message.

B: Ask A to leave a message for him/her to call you about the party tomorrow night.

A: Suggest that B tries his/her mobile.

B: Agree and say 'thank you'.

> While Zack and Grace are at the concert, lots of people try to phone him!

9 Read the phone messages that Rosie has taken for Zack and answer the questions.

1 Why did Auntie Pat phone?

2 What is the surprising news about Lily?

3 Who is Monika and what does she want?

Zack

Auntie Pat called. Expecting you for dinner tonight at 8 – It's already 9 – did you forget?! BAD BOY!!! Call her tonight before 10.00 or first thing tomorrow. ☹

R XXX

Zack

Lily called – she's in London!!!
Will call back tomorrow.

R XXX

Zack ♡

Monika ??? called (Polish girl from new students' party at college)
Do you want to go for walk with her tomorrow morning? (Or perhaps you'll be too busy??!!!)

R XXX

---

10 **(4.30)** Listen to Zack's voicemail messages and find the mistakes that Rosie made in the messages.

11 Lily arrives to see Zack the next day! In groups, prepare and act out a dialogue between Zack, Grace and Lily. Think about:

• how Lily/Zack/Grace feel
• who Zack likes best, Grace or Lily
• how the story ends.

Which ending do you like best?

Grammar	**Second conditional**
	Reported requests and comma
Vocabulary	**Crime**
	Adjectives ending in -ed and -i
Phrases	**Reporting events**
	Giving your opinion

Vocabulary & Speaking

Serious crimes?

1 **Look at the CCTV pictures.**

- Where is each picture taken?
- What crimes might happen next?

2 **Check you understand the crimes in *Words2know*. Then match them to the descriptions.**

> **Words 2 know** (4.31)
>
> shoplifting   downloading music illegally
> using fake ID   speeding   dropping litter
> playing truant   vandalism   burglary
> attacking someone   robbery ✓

1 Someone goes into a shop and steals all the money from the till. *robbery*

2 Someone damages a new statue in the centre of your town.

3 Someone goes shopping when he/she should be at school.

4 Someone uses a passport with a false photo, name or age.

5 Someone comes up to you and hits you.

6 Someone drives through your town centre at 70 km.p.h.

7 Someone eats some chocolate and then throws the paper on the ground.

8 Someone gets a new single from the internet without paying for it.

9 Someone takes a book from a shop without paying.

10 Someone goes into a house and steals the TV.

3 **Put the crimes in exercise 2 in order from most to least serious. Compare lists with other students.**

 I think ... is a serious crime.
 I don't agree.

MINI WORKBOOK exercise 6 page 123

Grammar Focus

Second conditional

4 **Read the newspaper extract about British teenagers. Then answer the questions.**

- Which four crimes are mentioned?
- Which crimes are the same in your country?

In a recent survey, 80% of British sixteen-year-olds say they would never steal anything but 20% admit that they 'tried shoplifting when they were younger'. 63% say they have downloaded music illegally from the internet.

90% of teenagers in the survey believe that they are 'honest' or 'very honest' but 70% admit that they have lied about their age to get into an '18' film!

5 (4.32) Read and listen to the opinions of five teenagers. Which crimes in exercise 4 are they talking about? Who do you agree with?

1 'I know it's illegal, but I do it … music's really expensive. If it was cheaper, I'd pay for it legally.' (Ollie, 17)

2 'Some young kids would see really violent films if we didn't have these laws. Some parents just don't care about their children.' (Jack, 17)

3 'People don't think it's stealing because it's online but it is. If people didn't pay for music, artists wouldn't make any more records … Then what would happen?' (Bella, 15)

4 'I'd definitely lie about my age if I really wanted to see a movie! Everyone does it!' (Pete, 16)

5 'I'd never steal anything. I'd feel too guilty! And if my parents found out, they'd be furious!' (Lily, 15)

6 Read *Grammar2know* and then <u>underline</u> two more examples of the second conditional in exercise 5.

Grammar 2 know

Second conditional

Use the second conditional to describe imaginary situations and their results:

If music *was* cheaper (it isn't), *I'd pay* for it. (but I don't)
If people *didn't pay* for music, artists *wouldn't make* records.
Some young kids *would see* violent films *if* we *didn't have* these laws.

Form: *If* + past simple, *would/wouldn't* + verb

Sometimes we use *would* on its own, without the *if* clause:

+ *I'd* (= *would*) *lie* about my age.

− *I wouldn't* (= *would not*) *use* fake ID.

? *Would* you ever *do* any of these things?
Yes, I would. / No, I wouldn't.

7 (4.33) Complete the opinions with the correct tense. Then listen and check.

1 'I _____ (not want) to watch a film if it _____ (be) really violent.'

2 'If the police _____ (be) stricter, young kids _____ (not try) shoplifting.'

3 'A lot of new bands _____ (not become) famous if people _____ (not listen) to their music free on the internet.'

4 'If there _____ (be) other things for teenagers to do, they _____ (not get) so bored.'

5 'I _____ (not feel) guilty about downloading music illegally if the artist _____ (be) super-rich.'

8 Write the questions with the correct verb forms. Then circle the best answers for yourself.

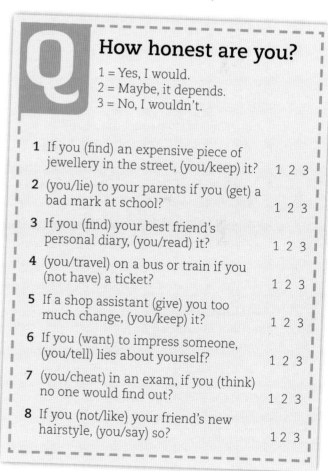

How honest are you?

1 = Yes, I would.
2 = Maybe, it depends.
3 = No, I wouldn't.

1 If you (find) an expensive piece of jewellery in the street, (you/keep) it?   1 2 3

2 (you/lie) to your parents if you (get) a bad mark at school?   1 2 3

3 If you (find) your best friend's personal diary, (you/read) it?   1 2 3

4 (you/travel) on a bus or train if you (not have) a ticket?   1 2 3

5 If a shop assistant (give) you too much change, (you/keep) it?   1 2 3

6 If you (want) to impress someone, (you/tell) lies about yourself?   1 2 3

7 (you/cheat) in an exam, if you (think) no one would find out?   1 2 3

8 If you (not/like) your friend's new hairstyle, (you/say) so?   1 2 3

9 In pairs, ask and answer the quiz questions. Count your partner's score and then read the quiz key on page 135.

10 Choose four situations from the quiz and say what you would do.

If a shop assistant gave me too much change, I'd give it back.

MINI WORKBOOK exercises 1–4 page 122

Vocabulary & Listening

Adjectives ending in -ed and -ing

1 a Check you understand the *Words2know*. Then put them in the right group in the table.

> bored ✓   interested   worried   annoyed   frustrated
> pleased   surprised   frightened   terrified   embarrassed
> disappointed   excited

Positive feelings	Negative feelings
	bored

b (4.34) Listen and repeat. How many syllables are there in each word?

2 Ask and answer in pairs. Use the *Words2know*.

How would you feel if someone stole your school bag?
I'd be really annoyed and a bit worried.

How would you feel if:

1 … someone stole your schoolbag?

2 … you locked yourself out of your house?

3 … someone followed you home on a dark night?

4 … a friend copied your essay and handed it in, without telling you?

5 … your friends didn't remember your birthday?

6 … your teacher found you cheating in a test?

7 … you found £100 in the street?

8 … you failed your driving test for the third time?

3 (4.35) Listen to four teenagers answering some of the questions in exercise 2.

• Which question is each person answering?

• Which *Words2know* does each speaker use?

4 Look at the picture and answer the questions.

• Who/What is terrified?

• Who/What is terrifying?

5 Read *Active Study*. What are the *-ing* forms of the adjectives in exercise 1?

bored → boring

Notice -ed and -ing endings in adjectives

Adjectives ending in *-ed* describe the person's feelings:
The girl is terrified.

Adjectives ending in *-ing* describe the thing that makes the person feel that way:
The film is terrifying.

6 Choose the correct adjective.

1 I was really *pleased/pleasing* with my French test. I got 90 percent!

2 There was a really *worried/worrying* programme about crime on TV last night.

3 We didn't enjoy the concert much. The bands were *disappointed/ disappointing*.

4 Josh and Amy are going out together – I'm really *surprised/surprising*.

5 Do you ever get *bored/boring* watching TV?

6 I didn't have enough money to pay the bill … it was so *embarrassed/ embarrassing*!

MINI WORKBOOK exercises 7–8 page 123

Grammar Focus

Reported requests and commands

7 Look at the pictures on page 95. Match a–c with the speech balloons 1–3.

a 'Put down that baseball bat right now!'

b 'Please, can you help me?'

c 'Be quiet, lady!'

8 Read the three news articles about crimes that went wrong. Answer these questions for each story.

• What did the criminal want to do?

• What went wrong?

• What happened to the criminal in the end?

I read it in ...
the tabloids (4.36)

Sorry, I don't understand.

A San Francisco man decided to burgle the home of a seventy-three-year-old woman but she woke up and heard him. He told the old lady to be quiet and not to move. But unfortunately she spoke very bad English and didn't understand what he wanted. So instead of doing what he said, she started showing him photos of her grandchildren. After a while, the burglar was so bored that he fell asleep! The old lady quickly went to another room and phoned the police.

Oh no! It's Grandma!

A nineteen-year-old who tried to rob a grocery store in New York was surprised to find that he knew one of the customers. Pedro Alvarez and his two friends ordered the shopkeeper to give them the money in the till but the shopkeeper refused. Then Pedro heard a voice he knew well coming from the back of the shop: his grandmother's. She marched angrily to the till, ordered the boy to put down his baseball bat and told the boys to go home immediately. All three did as they were told!

Help! I can't do this!

A fifty-eight-year-old man from the Japanese city of Kumagaya decided to rob his local bank. But in the middle of the robbery he became frightened and asked the staff to help him! They advised him to get out of the bank as quickly as possible and he politely agreed. Unfortunately he was so terrified that he fell over, stabbed himself in the leg and the police soon arrested him!

9 In exercise 7, you see people's exact words. Find and <u>underline</u> the sentences in the text that match them. Read *Grammar2know* to check.

Reported requests and commands

When we want to describe what someone said, we can:

- give the person's exact words (direct speech)
  'Be quiet, lady!'

- or use a verb to report what the person said (reported speech)
  *He **told** the old lady to be quiet.*

Direct speech	Reported speech
'Be quiet!'	*He **told** her **to be** quiet.*
'Please, can you help me?'	*He **asked** them **to help** him.*
'Put down that baseball bat right now!'	*She **ordered** him **to put** it down.*
'You should go quickly.'	*She **advised** him **to go** quickly.*

Notice the word order in the negative:

'Don't move!'	*He told her **not to move**.*

10 Rewrite the direct speech from the stories in reported speech. Use the prompts in brackets.

1 'Don't wake the burglar up!'
(the policeman → the old lady)
The policeman told the old lady not to wake the burglar up.

2 'Lie on the floor.'
(the police → the burglar)

3 'Put better locks on your door.'
(the police → the old lady)

4 'Don't call the police.'
(Pedro → the shopkeeper)

5 'Don't do this again!'
(the grandmother → the boys)

6 'Please don't tell my mother.'
(Pedro → his grandmother)

7 'Can you call a doctor, please?'
(the bank robber → the bank clerk)

8 'Put your hands up!'
(the police → the bank robber)

11 Ask/Tell your partner to do five things. Report them to the class.

" *Please can you lend me a pen?*
She asked me to lend her a pen.

MINI WORKBOOK exercise 5 page 122

Listening & Reading

1 Answer the questions.

- Are young people worried about crime in your area?
- Do you think the boys in the photo are criminals or are they worried about crime?

2 In pairs, check the *Words2know*.

Words 2 know (4.37)

to threaten   to commit a crime   to blame
victim   violence   to protect   to get hurt
fear   valuable possessions

3 **a** Read the newspaper article below. Tick (✓) true and cross (✗) false. Correct the false statements.

1 ☐ Teenagers are more often the victims of crime than adults.

2 ☐ Teenagers nowadays have more expensive possessions than before.

3 ☐ More young women are victims of crime than young men.

4 ☐ Half the teenagers in Central London have committed a crime recently.

5 ☐ Most London teenagers aren't worried about crime.

b Which problems mentioned in the article are the same in your country?

4 (4.38) Listen to Part 1 of a radio phone-in about teenagers and crime. For each caller, choose two correct answers.

1 Josh:
   a had to give his money to a group of boys.
   b had to give them his mobile phone.
   c was robbed but not attacked physically.

2 Judy:
   a doesn't understand why teenagers carry so many valuable things.
   b is the parent of teenagers herself.
   c blames teenagers' parents for the problem.

3 Becky:
   a feels safer with a mobile phone.
   b has stopped listening to music on her iPod.
   c thinks teenagers should have the same rights as everyone else.

5 Read the advice, 'Stay Safe', about how to avoid crime. Which pieces of advice do you find most and least useful?

(4.41)

Teenage victims of crime

Statistics show that there has been a rise in crime against teenagers in the last few years. But why is this? A new report suggests one reason: teenagers nowadays have more to steal.

According to the report, the average UK teenager now walks around in clothes and equipment worth £700. As well as clothes, trainers and jewellery, this includes valuable equipment such as MP3 players, mobile phones and watches. The authors of the report believe that this is the main reason why crime against teenagers is increasing. They say that teenagers should leave their phones and iPods at home if they want to be safe on the streets.

Teenagers – particularly young men – are more likely to be the victims of crime than adults: about half of all fifteen–sixteen-year-olds in Central London have been victims in the last eighteen months. It's not surprising that 51 percent of London teenagers say that crime is their biggest worry.

STAY SAFE

Follow these rules and cut the risk of crime

1 Before you use your mobile in the street, look around – if you don't feel safe, don't use it.

2 Cover your jewellery when you are in the street.

3 Don't keep all your valuable possessions together.

4 If anyone threatens you with violence, give them what they want – it's better than getting hurt.

5 Keep your bag where you can see it and keep it closed.

6 If possible, sit near the driver on trains and buses.

7 If your phone is stolen, report it immediately.

8 Stay in places where there are other people, especially after dark.

6 (4.39) Listen to Part 2 of the phone-in. Tick the advice in 'Stay Safe' that Alison mentions.

7 Imagine that you are a caller on the phone-in. Do one of the tasks below:

CAN YOU DO IT IN ENGLISH?

- Describe a crime that happened to you or someone you know.
- Say how you or this person felt afterwards. (You can invent a story.)
- Give your opinion about one of the things that Judy, Becky or Alison said.

MINI WORKBOOK exercise 9 page 123

Reading Writing

8 Read the newspaper article and answer the questions.

- What is the biggest worry for pensioners in Peterborough?
- What does Mr Robinson want the government to do?

Pensioners fear 'hoodies'*

ACCORDING TO a survey by Peterborough Council, 72% of pensioners say that their biggest worry is walking past groups of teenagers in the street. They find young people dressed in hoods particularly frightening. 'The government should ban these hoodies,' says George Robinson, aged 74. 'I don't understand why young people want to walk around in these hoods. Older people find it very threatening.'

---

* hoodie: a top with a hood; also describes a young person who wears a hoodie and who looks like a criminal.

9 Read the letter a reader wrote in response to the article. Does she agree with the article? Why? Why not?

Letters to the editor

¹ _Dear Sir_ ,

² _____ 'Pensioners fear hoodies', ³ _____ 17 January.

As a teenager myself, I am sorry that pensioners are frightened of us.

⁴ _____ teenagers in hoods sometimes look frightening. ⁵ _____ , many teenagers put their hoods up because they are worried about crime themselves, not to frighten older people.

⁶ _____ Mr George Robinson when he says that the government should ban hoods for young people. I think everyone has the right to wear what they want, including teenagers. What do we do if it is raining or cold? Why should older people have the right to wear a hood but not teenagers?

⁷ _____ , older people should see teenagers as individuals and not judge them by their clothes.

⁸ _____ ,

Alex Whittaker

10 Complete the letter in exercise 9 with the *Phrases2know*.

Phrases 2 know (4.40)

A letter from a reader

I agree that   I disagree with   However
which appeared on   Dear Sir ✓
Yours faithfully   In my opinion
I am writing in connection with your article

11 Write a letter responding to the article in exercise 3. Use the *Phrases2know* and the ideas below.

- **Paragraph 1:** Say which article you are writing about and if you generally agree/disagree with it.
- **Paragraph 2:** Say what you agree with and why.
- **Paragraph 3:** Say what you disagree with and why.
- **Paragraph 4:** Suggest a solution to the problem.

activestudy6

Vocabulary

ACTIVE STUDY | Learn words in groups

1 Write in the missing letters. Then add one more word to each category.

crimes: b _ r g l _ r _ ; r _ b b _ r _ ; v _ n d _ l _ s m; s p _ _ d _ n g

things connected with films: a _ t _ r; p r _ d _ c _ r; s c _ _ e; s _ r _ p _

types of TV programme: c _ r t _ _ n; s _ _ p op _ _ a; d _ c _ m _ n t _ r _

things you can read: n _ v _ l; c _ m _ c; sh _ rt st _ r _; m _ g _ z _ n _

ACTIVE STUDY | Understanding word endings

2 Complete these pairs of sentences with the -*ed* or -*ing* form of the words. There is one extra adjective.

[annoy   disappoint   embarrass
interest   surprise]

1 a I'm seriously _interested_ in cinema. I'd like to become a director.
   b It's an _____ story but I don't believe it!

2 a My brother always takes my things without asking. It's so _____ !
   b The shop didn't give me a refund on that broken MP3. I was very _____ .

3 a I'm so _____ . I've been waiting for this trip for six months and now I can't go!
   b This test result is rather _____ . I was hoping to get a better score.

4 a Everyone was looking at me. It was very _____ .
   b I was terribly _____ . How could I have said something so stupid?

ACTIVE STUDY | Notice the pronunciation of consonants

3 PRONUNCIATION (4.42) Is the <u>underlined</u> letter 's' pronounced /s/ or /z/ in the words 1–12? Listen and put the words in the right column.

1 fru<u>s</u>trated ✓   5 surpri<u>s</u>ed   9 advi<u>s</u>e
2 new<u>s</u>   6 <u>s</u>cript   10 fanta<u>s</u>y
3 embarra<u>ss</u>ed   7 choo<u>s</u>e   11 vandali<u>s</u>m
4 di<u>s</u>appointed   8 serie<u>s</u>   12 plea<u>s</u>ed

/s/	/z/
frustrated	

Grammar

4 Choose the correct forms to complete the article.

The world's most expensive advert?

Millions of pounds [1] _____ on TV and cinema adverts every year. One of the world's most expensive adverts – for Chanel No 5 Perfume – cost an incredible £18 million and it's only three minutes long! It [2] _____ by the movie director, Baz Luhrmann, and the top fashion designer, Karl Lagerfeld, [3] _____ the costumes. Australian actress Nicole Kidman [4] _____ £2 million for her appearance in the ad, which has been shown in cinemas and on TV all over the world. It [5] _____ for the first time on British TV on 20 November 2004. It [6] _____ the story of a mysterious megastar and her romance with a handsome stranger. One critic [7] _____ it as 'more like a one-minute movie than an ad!'

1 **a** are spent   **b** spend   **c** spent
2 **a** directed   **b** directs   **c** was directed
3 **a** designed   **b** was designed **c** were designed
4 **a** paid   **b** was paid   **c** pays
5 **a** saw   **b** seen   **c** was seen
6 **a** tells   **b** is told   **c** was told
7 **a** describes   **b** described   **c** was described

5 Complete the second sentence so that it means the same as the first sentence.

1 I don't go to the cinema because I don't have the time.
   If I _had the time, I'd_ go to the cinema.

2 The doctor said, 'You should get more sleep, Alice.'
   The doctor advised _____ sleep.

3 They have built a new cinema in our town.
   A new cinema _____ in our town.

4 'Put your hands up!' said the policeman to the robber.
   The policeman ordered _____ up.

5 My mother said to me, 'Don't forget to buy the tickets!'
   My mother told _____ the tickets.

The Making of a Classic The Godfather

(4.44)

1 ___

The Godfather by Francis Ford Coppola is one of the most famous films of all time. It won Oscars for Best Picture, Best Screenplay and Best Actor and always appears in lists of 'best movies'. When we think about great mafia movies, we immediately think of *The Godfather*, and of the roles of Marlon Brando as Don Vito Corleone and Al Pacino as his son, Michael.

2 ___

Paramount Pictures wanted to make the bestselling novel *The Godfather*, by Mario Puzo, into a film. They asked Coppola to direct *The Godfather* because he was the only Italian director in Hollywood. However, even though Coppola was not rich or successful at the time, he didn't want to direct it because he didn't want to present the leaders of organised crime as heroes. In the end, he agreed to make the film but only if he could tell it as a family story.

3 ___

Coppola chose Al Pacino for the key role of Michael Corleone. Paramount thought he was too short, too Italian and unknown – they wanted a handsome, tall, 'American-looking' star like Robert Redford or Ryan O'Neal. Coppola believed that Al Pacino was exactly right for this role. He believed in Pacino's talent and threatened to stop working on the film if he was not chosen for the role of Michael.

4 ___

Coppola also wanted Marlon Brando for the title role of the 'Godfather'. Again, the producers disagreed. Coppola made a terrible scene and the producers gave in. Brando was paid very little for starring in the film but after its great success, his percentage of the profits brought in $16 million.

5 ___

Soon, a second 'Godfather' film was planned. It included an earlier part of the family story. Robert de Niro – another young, little-known actor – played young Vito Corleone. Audiences and critics were amazed by how de Niro learned to copy Brando's gestures and way of speaking. *The Godfather II* won more Oscars and made more money than *The Godfather* and many critics thought it was better than the original film.

Reading Skills

ACTIVE STUDY **Read for gist**

6 Read the article about the film, *The Godfather*. Match headings a–f with the paragraphs 1–5. There is one extra heading.

a A moral problem
b A movie classic
c Problems with the script
d Even greater
e Too Italian
f A star at a bargain price

Listening Skills

ACTIVE STUDY **Listen for specific information**

7 (4.43) Listen to a radio programme which gives information about concerts in the Portsmouth area. Give short answers (maximum five words) to the questions below.

1 How many Trash concerts will there be?
2 How often does the regular acoustic night at the Portsmouth Folk Club take place?
3 Where is the band Boys from the Glen from?
4 On which day will the classical concert at St. John's Arts Centre take place?
5 How much does it cost to go to the classical concert?

Speaking Skills

8 Look at these photos of people watching different TV programmes. Compare and contrast them. Include the following points:

- What kind of programme do you think they are watching?
- How do you think they are feeling?
- What are the good and bad sides of television?
- What should children be allowed to watch?
- What do you like watching?

SKILLS STRATEGIES **back cover**

1 mini workbook

* ☀ easy to do
* ☀☀ a bit harder
* ☀☀☀ extra challenge

Grammar

1 ☀ **Present simple: affirmative, negative and question forms**

a **Make the sentences negative.**

1 You spend a lot of money on clothes.

You don't spend a lot of money on clothes.

2 Maria comes to school by bus.

3 It rains a lot in summer.

4 The shops close at lunchtime.

5 Michael speaks German.

6 I need to buy a ticket.

b **Make the sentences into questions.**

Do you spend a lot of money on clothes?

2 ☀☀ Read *Grammar Plus*. Then put the words in the correct order to make sentences.

Grammar + Plus

Present simple: word order with time expressions

* With most verbs, put the time expression before the main verb:
  He **never travels** by bus.

* Put the time expression after the verb **to be** and auxiliary verbs:
  She **is often** late for class.
  We **don't always have** lunch at home.

* Put longer time expressions at the end of the sentence:
  My brother and I go to the cinema **every week**.

1 to school/walk/every morning/I

I walk to school every morning.

2 never/to the theatre/goes/he

3 Josh/at home/in the evening/is/usually

4 sometimes/I/my little sister/look after

5 once a week/their grandmother/visit/they

6 Emily/every evening/the piano/practises

7 usually/I/on Saturday night/don't/go out

8 the bus/Sam/often/is/for/late

9 eat/I/at one o'clock/lunch/always

3 ☀☀ **Present continuous: form**

Complete the conversation with the correct form of the verbs in brackets.

Hannah: Hello, Alice! It's me.

Alice: Hi, Hannah. Where are you?

H: I'm out with my mum and dad. We ¹ *'re doing* (do) some shopping.

A: Cool. Is there anything nice?

H: Not really. I ² _____ (look) for a pair of shoes but there's nothing I like.

A: I see. So what ³ _____ (you/do) now?

H: I ⁴ _____ (wait) for my mum. She ⁵ _____ (try) on a hat at the moment. My dad ⁶ _____ (look) bored. Oh no …

A: What? What's the matter? What ⁷ _____ (happen)?

H: It's my mum … that hat is just … uuhh … she ⁸ _____ (look) at herself in the mirror. Now she ⁹ _____ (ask) my dad what he thinks. He ¹⁰ _____ (not say) anything, as usual. And how about you? ¹¹ _____ (you/do) your homework?

A: Yeah, well … yeah … I ¹² _____ (think) about it but I ¹³ _____ (not really/do) anything at the moment.

H: Oh! My mum ¹⁴ _____ (come) over. Talk to you later.

4 (✱✱✱) Present simple or present continuous?

Put the verbs in the correct form.

1 'What are <u>you watching</u> (you/watch)?'
   'It's a programme about dolphins.'

2 I usually walk to school but this week
   _____ (I/take) the bus.

3 'How many languages _____ (he/speak)?'
   'Two … English and Polish.'

4 What's that noise? What _____ (they/do)
   up there?

5 '_____ (your parents/watch) football on TV?'
   'No, never. They hate all sport!'

6 His exams are next week so _____
   (he/study) hard at the moment.

7 'Why _____ (smile)?'
   'Oh, no reason … I just feel happy today!'

5 (✱✱) Question words

Complete the questions about the invitation with the correct question words. Then find the answers.

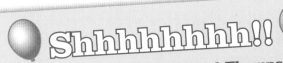

Shhhhhhhh!!

Surprise party for Michael Thompson

About thirty of his friends and family
will be there!!

On: Friday, 16 June

At: La Cabana Club, 108 High Street

(Take the 165 bus and get off at the Odeon
Cinema)

Please be there by 6 p.m.

Party starts about 6.15

Please reply to Lily on 07055750976

Remember!! It's a secret!!

1 <u>Where</u>'s the party?   _At La Cabana Club_
2 _____ is the party for?
3 _____ is the address of La Cabana?
4 _____ does the party start?
5 _____ people will be there?
6 _____ can you get there?
7 _____ bus do I take?
8 _____ does the card say 'Shhh!'?

6 (✱✱) Word order in questions

Correct the word order in the questions only if necessary. Tick the correct answers.

1 What's your address? ✓
2 How many brothers and sisters ~~you have got?~~
   have you got?
3 What time it is, please?
4 How do you spell your surname?
5 How much this does cost?
6 What kind of books do you like?
7 Which your favourite subject is at school?
8 Which part of Britain you are from?

Vocabulary

7 (✱✱) Social life

Find ten words in the long word below. Then put the words in the correct column.

go	go to the	do	meet	make
	beach			

8 (✱✱) Family and relationships

Find eleven family and relationships words. Look → and ↓.

s	t	e	p	s	i	s	t	e	r
o	d	m	m	l	l	e	c	t	e
n	i	e	c	e	a	n	n	w	l
i	v	b	w	s	s	p	w	s	a
n	o	o	i	p	c	a	u	n	t
l	r	n	f	m	m	r	h	d	i
a	c	n	e	p	h	e	w	w	v
w	e	h	s	g	u	n	c	l	e
p	d	b	w	c	b	t	c	g	s
q	b	r	c	o	u	s	i	n	o

2 miniworkbook

* easy to do
** a bit harder
*** extra challenge

Grammar

1 (**) Past simple: affirmative and negative forms

Complete the gaps with the correct forms of the verbs in brackets.

NAOMIE HARRIS

Naomie Harris is one of Britain's hottest young actresses. She ¹ _was born_ (be born) in London in 1976 and still lives there with her mother. Naomie ² _____ (begin) acting while she ³ _____ (be) at school and she ⁴ _____ (make) her first appearance on British TV at the age of ten. After school, she ⁵ _____ (study) Political Science at Cambridge University but she ⁶ _____ (not/enjoy) life at university and she ⁷ _____ (go) back to London every weekend to visit her family.

After graduating, she ⁸ _____ (train) as an actress in Bristol. She ⁹ _____ (travel) to Hollywood to make films and in 2006, she ¹⁰ _____ (play) Tia Dalma, an exotic fortune-teller in *Pirates of the Caribbean 2*.

2 (**) Past simple: questions

a Put the words in the correct order to make questions about Naomie Harris.

1 born?/was/Where/Naomie
   Where was Naomie born?

2 on TV?/first/Naomie/did/When/appear
   _____

3 at Cambridge University?/study/she/What/did
   _____

4 happy/at university?/Was/Naomie
   _____

5 did/as an actress?/Where/train/she
   _____

6 did/Which part/play/she/in *Pirates of the Caribbean 2*?
   _____

b Read the text in exercise 1 again and answer the questions 1–6.

1 *Naomie was born in London.*

3 (**) Past simple: with *ago*

Rewrite the phrases in bold using *ago*.

1 It's now 2008. I started learning English **in 2004**.
   four years ago

2 It's now Saturday. I sent you an email **on Monday**.

3 It's November. My birthday was **in February**.

4 It's now 12 o'clock. The party began **at 8 o'clock**.

5 It's now 10.00. The film started **at 9.45**.

4 (**) Read *Grammar Plus*. Then complete the sentences with *in*, *on* or *at*. Who are the sentences about? (Check your answers on page 135.)

Grammar + Plus

Time phrases with *in*, *on*, *at*

- Use *in* with decades, years and months:
  in the 1990s *in 1929* *in April*

- Use *on* with days:
  on Monday *on 21 May* *on your birthday*

- Use *at* with a specific time or a period of time:
  at 11 o'clock *at midnight* *at Christmas*

1 He was born _in_ 1935.
2 He gave his first concert ___ 15 November 1952.
3 He made his first record ___ July 1953.
4 He first became famous ___ the 1950s.
5 He got married ___ 1 May 1967.
6 He gave his last concert ___ 26 June 1977.
7 He died ___ 3.30 p.m. ___ 16 August 1977.

5 (**) Past continuous

What was Paul doing at these times yesterday? Write a sentence for each picture with the verbs below.

[watch   travel to school   have   play   study]

1 *Paul was having his breakfast at 8 a.m.*

6 (**) Past simple and past continuous

Put the verbs in the correct tense, past continuous or past simple.

A Blind Date*

It [1] ___was___ (be) a cold evening and it [2] ________ (rain) hard. Harry [3] ________ (wait) on the street corner for his blind date. Suddenly, he [4] ________ (see) a young woman on the other side of the street. She [5] ________ (carry) an umbrella and she [6] ________(look) at him carefully. Harry [7] ________ (smile) at her and [8] ________ (cross) the road.

'Hello. Are you Jane White?' he [9] ________ (ask) her.

'Are you Harry Black?' she [10] ________ (reply).

'Yes, I am,' Harry [11] ________ (say).

'Then I'm not Jane White,' she [12] ________ (answer) and [13] ________ (walk) away.

* A date between two people who don't know each other.

Vocabulary

7 (**) Icons

Unscramble the letters to make sentences about the icons on pages 12–13.

Life was very difficult for Audrey Hepburn's family during the [1] ___Second World War___ (Sonced Wrodl Wra).

Kurt Cobain had a happy [2] ________ (lohdichod) and he became very [3] ________ (cuscefluss) in the 1990s. But he was often [4] ________ (redspesed) and he finally [5] ________ (hots) himself in 1994.

The boxer Muhammad Ali became [6] ________ (wrodl namichop) in 1964 but he lost his title when he refused to [7] ________ (ghift) for his country.

8 (**) Life events

Complete the text with the words below.

[engaged fell got leave left met (x2) moved passed started ✓ went (x2)]

As children, Monica and Sophie [1] ___started___ school together and were best friends. Then one day, Sophie's parents [2] ________ house. Sophie [3] ________ to a different school and the two girls lost contact.

At sixteen, Monica decided to [4] ________ school and she [5] ________ a job as a waitress in a pizza restaurant.

Meanwhile, Sophie [6] ________ her exams and [7] ________ to university. There she [8] ________ a young student called Tony. They [9] ________ in love and after a few months, they got [10] ________ .

But six months later, Tony [11] ________ someone else – in a pizza restaurant.

Sophie [12] ________ university and never saw Tony – or his new girlfriend – again. Until one day she went for a pizza …

9 (*) Greatest Britons

Write the words to complete the definitions, 1–6.

1 to make a new product or idea: d e v e l o p
2 something you see at the theatre: p _ a _
3 to be in charge of something: l _ a _
4 to find or learn something for the first time: d _ s _ o _ e _
5 the opposite of war: p _ a _ e
6 to draw or plan something: d _ s _ g _

10 (**) Personal characteristics

Complete the definitions with the adjectives.

[brave cruel determined glamorous brilliant talented ✓]

1 A ___talented___ person is naturally very good at something.
2 Someone who wants to make people suffer is ________ .
3 Being ________ means that you really want to do something and nothing will stop you.
4 ________ people are rich, attractive and have exciting lives.
5 A ________ person is not afraid to do dangerous things.
6 A ________ person is very intelligent or good at something.

3 miniworkbook

* easy to do
** a bit harder
*** extra challenge

Grammar

1 (*) **Comparative forms**

Complete the sentences with *as* or *than*.

1 The weather isn't _as_ cold _as_ it was yesterday.
2 This question is easier ___ the last one.
3 This question is not ___ difficult ___ the next one!
4 London isn't ___ expensive ___ Tokyo but it's more expensive ___ Madrid.
5 My sister is taller ___ me but she's not ___ tall ___ my brother.

2 (**) **Comparative and superlative adjectives**

Complete the sentences about finalists in a TV talent show. Use the information in the table and the correct form of the adjectives in brackets.

***** = Fantastic!   *** = Average   * = Bad

	Jason Burke	Danny Boyd	Andy Martin
Age	18	25	40 +
Looks	*****	***	*
Singing ability	*	***	*****
Popularity	***	*****	*

1 Jason is _younger_ (young) than Danny.
2 Andy is _____ (old) of the three singers.
3 Danny is _____ (good-looking) than Andy.
4 Danny isn't _____ (good-looking) as Jason.
5 Andy is _____ (good) singer.
6 Jason is _____ (bad) singer.
7 Andy isn't _____ (popular) Jason and Danny.
8 Danny is _____ (popular) than Jason.

3 (***) **Comparative and superlative adjectives**

Complete the fact file with the correct form of the adjectives in brackets.

What's in a name?

Which names are popular in your country? In the UK, names like David and Peter aren't [1] _as fashionable as_ (fashionable) they were thirty years ago.

The [2] _____ (popular) first name for boys in 2006 was Jack. And nowadays, it's [3] _____ (common) to find names like Olivia and Jessica than [4] _____ (traditional) names like Elizabeth or Anne.

A village in Scotland (Ae) has [5] _____ (short) name in Britain – but even that name isn't [6] _____ (short) a place in Norway (Å). A hill in New Zealand has [7] _____ (long) place name in the world: it has 57 letters!

And one website voted Ynysybwl – a town in Wales – [8] _____ (difficult) place name to pronounce!

4 (**) Read *Grammar Plus*. Then <u>underline</u> the correct form of the verbs.

Grammar + Plus

Countable, uncountable and plural nouns

- Countable nouns have a singular and a plural form:
  building(s)   friend(s)   idea(s)

- Uncountable nouns do not have a plural form:
  money   music   snow

- Some nouns are always in the plural form and take a plural verb:
  clothes   jeans   people
  *These jeans **are** too big for me.*

Notice that we can use ***a lot of*** with a singular or plural verb:
*There **is** a lot of time (= uncountable) before the bus comes.*
*There **are** a lot of expensive shops (= plural) in this area.*
*There **were** a lot of people at the concert.*

1 All Zoe's clothes *comes/come* from 'Top Girl': it's her favourite shop.

2 A lot of your ideas *is/are* very useful.

3 People often *says/say* that life was better in the old days.

4 Money *doesn't/don't* buy happiness.

5 A lot of snow *falls/fall* during the winter.

6 Those jeans *is/are* too small for you: try a bigger size.

5 (✲✲) *too much, too many, not enough*

George lost his shopping list on the way to the shops.

Shopping list

1 kg pasta

2 tomatoes

6 lemons

1 kg rice

Lemonade (1 small bottle)

1 egg

Look at the things he bought and write six sentences with *too much*, *too many* and *not enough*.

He bought too much pasta.

He didn't buy ...

6 (✲✲) *too and enough*

Complete the sentences with *too* or *enough*.

1 At sixteen, she isn't old ∧ to start driving lessons. *enough*

2 It was dark to see what was happening.

3 We haven't got money to go on holiday this year.

4 I'm tired to go out this evening.

5 There isn't time to stop for lunch.

6 He isn't tall to be a professional basketball player.

Vocabulary

7 (✲) My favourite place

Choose the correct answer.

1 Which of these do you sit on?
   a a chair ✓ b a cupboard c pictures

2 Which of these can you usually find on the wall?
   a cushions b posters c plants

3 Which of these do you put on the floor?
   a a table b a poster c a rug

4 Which of these can two or more people sit on?
   a a chair b a sofa c a stool

8 (✲✲) Describing personal style

Match an adjective from column A with a noun from column B.

A	B
a well-dressed	clothes
bright	colours
a noisy	desk
a tidy	ears
casual	hair
pierced	person
wavy	street

9 (✲✲) Money and spending

Complete the definitions with the 'money' verbs below.

[buy ✓ lend owe borrow afford sell
save spend earn pay … back]

1 If you *buy* something, you give money for it. The opposite is _____.

2 You _____ money when you use it to pay for something.

3 If you can't _____ something, it is too expensive for you.

4 You _____ money from work that you do.

5 You _____ money by keeping it instead of spending it.

6 If you _____ money to someone, you give it to them for a short time: later they must _____ it _____ .

7 You _____ money when someone gives it to you for a short time.

8 When you borrow money from someone, you _____ it to them until you give it back.

4 miniworkbook

✱	easy to do
✱✱	a bit harder
✱✱✱	extra challenge

Grammar

1 ✱✱ *would like to, want to, going to, planning to*

Put the words in the correct order to make sentences.

1 to buy/your parents/are/going/a new car?

Are your parents going to buy a new car?

2 to visit/we/next year/are/Disneyworld/planning

3 to study/next year/not/German/I'm/going

4 to have/do/you/this evening?/a pizza/want

5 like/would/your friend/to the concert?/to come

6 after school?/to go/do/want/you/where

2 ✱✱ **Describing intentions and wishes**

<u>Underline</u> the correct form to complete the sentences.

1 Are you *go/go to/<u>going to</u>* have a holiday this year?

2 My sister wants *be/being/to be* a model when she's older.

3 *I'd like to/I like/I'm going* visit China one day.

4 How many people are you *plan/planning/plans* to invite to your party?

5 Where *are/do/would* you like to go after lunch today?

6 Would you like *be/to be/to being* famous?

3 ✱✱ **Gerunds and infinitives**

Complete the sentences with the infinitive or *-ing* form of the verbs.

1 Toni really likes <u>*working*</u> (work) with children. She wants <u>*to be*</u> (be) a primary school teacher when she's older.

2 I enjoy _____ (read) about South America. I'd love _____ (go) there one day.

3 Stephanie hates _____ (get up) early! She'd like _____ (stay) in bed till 11 o'clock every day!

4 I hope _____ (live) abroad after I finish school. I really love _____ (learn) about other cultures.

5 Adam spends all his time _____ (play) computer games. He'd like _____ (get) a job as a computer game designer one day.

4 ✱✱✱ **Gerunds and infinitives**

Complete the interview with the correct form of the verbs in brackets.

I = Interviewer

AS = Albie Schroder

I: I'm here with Hollywood superstar Albie Schroder – and we're talking about his new book, *My Fantastic Life Part I*. Albie, why did you decide [1] <u>*to write*</u> (write) this book?

AS: Well, all my fans enjoy [2] _____ (read) about me … and I love [3] _____ (talk) about myself! So I'm just trying [4] _____ (make) my fans happy.

I: I'd like [5] _____ (change) the subject for a moment. Are you planning [6] _____ (marry) your lovely fiancé, Tammy Jones?

AS: Well, Tammy and I hope [7] _____ (get) married one day soon. We would love [8] _____ (have) lots of children. But you need [9] _____ (buy) my book if you want [10] _____ (know) more about Tammy and me.

I: I see. And do you intend [11] _____ (write) any more books, Albie?

AS: Sure! I'm going to start [12] _____ (work) on *My Fantastic Life Part II* … right after this interview!

5 (✱✱) Read *Grammar Plus*. Then write the correct form of the verbs in brackets: infinitive or gerund.

Grammar ✚ Plus

More about gerunds and infinitives

- After prepositions (*at*, *about*, *by*, etc.) use the gerund (*-ing*) form of the verb:
  *Are you worried **about** finding a job?*
  *He learned English **by** listening to pop songs.*

- After adjectives, use the infinitive form of the verb:
  *It's very **difficult to get** a good job without any experience.*
  *It's **easy to travel** abroad nowadays.*

1 Our teacher is very good at *remembering* (remember) people's names!

2 I'm very happy _____ (be) here again.

3 I'm tired of _____ (stay) at home every evening: let's go out.

4 It was very difficult _____ (understand) what she was saying.

5 It was very nice _____ (see) all my friends again.

6 She left without _____ (say) goodbye.

Vocabulary

6 (✱✱) Education

Complete the text with these words.

> compulsory   course   mixed   pass   A-levels
> secondary ✓   single-sex   take   drop   marks

Hi! my name's Neeraj and I'm sixteen years old. I go to Woodland High School – it's a large
¹ *secondary* school near London with about 1500 students. It's a ² _____ school, so there are boys and girls studying together. It's better than going to a ³ _____ school – how do the boys ever meet any girls??!!!

   At the moment, I'm in Year 10, so next year I'm going to ⁴ _____ my GCSE exams. Maths, English, Science and a foreign language are
⁵ _____ at my school – so I can't ⁶ _____ French until next year! It's my worst subject! But I'm getting good ⁷ _____ in all my other subjects and I hope to ⁸ _____ all my exams.

   Then I'd like to stay at Woodland and take my
⁹ _____ when I'm eighteen. Then I want to do a ¹⁰ _____ in journalism at university.

7 (✱) Getting a job

Use the clues to write in the missing letters.

1 If there are v _a_ c _a_ n _c_ i _e_ s at the supermarket, it means there are jobs there.

2 You read these in the newspaper when you are looking for a job: a _ v _ r _ s

3 Something you have to complete when you apply for a job: a _ p _ i _ a _ i _ n   f _ r _

4 In a job like this you only work a small number of hours: p _ r _-t _ m _

5 A meeting with people about a possible job: i _ t _ r _ i _ w

6 To say you are going to give a job to someone: o _ f _ r

7 To complete a form: f _ l _   i _

8 To get money from a job: e _ r _

8 (✱✱✱) Describing jobs

Put the words in bold into the correct form in the sentences.

1 His job in a bank isn't very interesting, but it's *secure* .   **security**

2 It's difficult to relax when you have such a _____ job.   **stress**

3 Working with children is very _____ for me.   **reward**

4 Cristina is very _____ ; she loves drawing pictures and writing stories.   **create**

5 I'm sure film stars have a very _____ life.   **glamour**

9 (✱✱) Match the words 1–5 and the definitions a–e.

1 salary   **a** happening for only a short time
2 temporary   **b** a job you have for a long time
3 career   **c** the money you receive for working
4 experience   **d** the people who give you a job
5 employers   **e** the skills you learn in a job

5 miniworkbook

* easy to do
** a bit harder
*** extra challenge

Grammar

1 (*) *must/mustn't*

Complete the rules with *must* or *mustn't*.

> **Volleyball is one of the world's most popular sports … but how well do you know the rules?**
>
> 1 Each team _must_ have six players.
>
> 2 You _____ touch the ball more than three times before returning it.
>
> 3 The server _____ use his/her hand to serve the ball.
>
> 4 The players _____ touch the net.
>
> 5 You _____ go into the other team's area.

2 (**) *should/shouldn't*

Look at the street scene. What *should* the people do? What *shouldn't* they do? Write two sentences about each person with the phrases below.

> listen to music   use a mobile phone
> wear a helmet   look carefully
> wear a seat belt ✓   read a newspaper

The driver … while she's driving.

The cyclist … while he's cycling.

The pedestrian … while he's crossing the road.

The driver should wear a seat belt while she's driving.

3 (**) *should/shouldn't/must/mustn't*

Read the interview with Ben Hardcastle, an expert on internet dating, and <u>underline</u> the correct form of *should* or *must*.

Meeting people online

Interviewer: Dan, more and more people are making friends online … have you got any advice?

Ben: Of course. The internet is a great way to make friends … but remember, you ¹ *should/<u>shouldn't</u>* believe everything people tell you about themselves online. You ² *should/shouldn't* always be careful when you give information about yourself …

Interviewer: For example?

Ben: Well, you really ³ *must/mustn't* give personal information such as your address or phone number.

Interviewer: I see. And what ⁴ *should I/I should* do if someone asks to meet me?

Ben: Well, you really ⁵ *must/mustn't* be very careful before you meet someone face to face. If you arrange a meeting, you ⁶ *should/shouldn't* always meet in a public place.

Interviewer: ⁷ *I should/Should I* tell someone about the meeting?

Ben: Definitely. You ⁸ *should/shouldn't* definitely ask your parents' permission first or tell someone you know where you're going to meet.

4 (***) *should/shouldn't/must/mustn't*

Rewrite the sentences, replacing the phrases in bold with *should(n't)* or *must(n't)*.

1 **It's a good idea for you** to eat fresh fruit and vegetables.
   You should eat fresh fruit and vegetables.

2 **It's very very important for you** to get up early tomorrow.
   You _____ .

3 **Is it a good idea for me** to phone you later?
   _____ ?

4 **Don't** be late for the new students' meeting!!
   You _____ !!

5 **It's not a good idea to** drink coffee before going to bed.
   You _____ .

5 (✱✱✱) Articles

Complete the text with _a(n)_ or _the_.

Allyson Scott: The world's fastest teenager

Nineteen-year-old Allyson Scott is from Santa Cristina,
[1] _a_ small town in California … but she is certainly not
[2] ___ ordinary teenager. She began running when
she was [3] ___ child. Her mother – who is [4] ___ sports
teacher – always helped her. In 2006, Allyson became
[5] ___ fastest teenager in the world when she ran 200 m
in 23 seconds in [6] ___ race in California. After [7] ___ race,
Allyson said, 'This medal is really for my mom … she's
the best!'

[8] ___ biggest moment of Allyson's career was at [9] ___
Olympic Games in China, where she won [10] ___ bronze
medal. Her ambition now is to win [11] ___ gold medal in
London in 2012.

6 (✱✱) _the_ and ø article

Write _the_ where necessary.

the

1 Can you turn ∧ music off? I'm trying to work!

2 Can you pass me salt, please?

3 Do you like Italian food?

4 Everyone says food at Gino's is very good.

5 Football players can earn a lot of money these
days.

6 We lost because players were so tired.

7 Milk is very good for young children.

8 Where's milk?

7 (✱✱✱) Read _Grammar Plus_. Then complete the sentences with _a_, _the_ or _ø_.

Grammar + Plus

More phrases with _a_, _the_ and _ø_

- Use _a_ with these time expressions:
  three times **a** day   once **a** month

- Don't use _a_ with these phrases with _go_:
  go home   go to school   go to work

- Other phrases with _the_:
  in **the** world
  **the** whole (= all the) _thing/day/class_

1 I visit my cousin once _a_ week.

2 We spent ___ whole evening playing cards.

3 You should take this medicine three times ___
day, after meals.

4 It's nearly 3.30 … time to go ___ home!

5 How do you get to ___ school in the morning?

6 Dentists say you should brush your teeth
twice ___ day.

Vocabulary

8 (✱✱) Healthy lifestyle

Complete the sentences with the words below.

> contain   energy ✓   healthy   heart
> skin   lose   put on

1 I don't have any _energy_ at the moment – I
just want to stay in bed all day!

2 If you want to _____ weight, you should do
more exercise!

3 Put some cream on your _____ before you
go out in the sun.

4 My grandfather went into hospital for a
_____ operation.

5 Eating fresh fruit is an important part of a
_____ diet.

6 Potato crisps _____ a lot of salt.
You shouldn't eat too many of them.

7 I love chocolate but if I eat a lot of it, I
_____ weight.

9 (✱) Food and drink

**Rearrange the letters to find food and drink
words.**

four things that you drink:

1 l i m e r a n   r a t e w   _mineral water_

2 k i l m h a s e k

3 m a l e d o n e

4 r a g e n o   c u j i e

four types of fruit or vegetable:

5 b a b e c a g

6 n i o n o s

7 w a r t s b i s e e r r

8 p a g r e s

four types of meat or meat products:

9 k a s t e

10 b o n a c

11 k i c c h e n

12 u s e a g s s a

6 miniworkbook

* easy to do
** a bit harder
*** extra challenge

Grammar

1 (**) Obligation: present

Look at the signs at a school. Complete each sentence with the words below.

[are allowed   aren't allowed   have to
can   can't   don't have to]

**STAFF PARKING ONLY (FREE)
VISITORS' PARKING →**

---

1 Only teachers _are allowed_ to use this car park.

2 Teachers _____ park their cars here if they want to.

3 Teachers _____ pay to use this car park.

4 Students _____ to park here.

5 Visitors to the school _____ park somewhere else.

6 Students _____ use this car park.

STUDENTS' LIBRARY

SHOW LIBRARY CARD FOR ALL BOOKS BORROWED

MAXIMUM 4 BOOKS PER PERSON, UP TO 7 DAYS

---

7 You _have to_ show your library card if you want to borrow a book.

8 You _____ borrow a book without a library card.

9 You _____ to borrow up to four books.

10 You _____ to borrow eight books.

11 You _____ return the books the next day.

12 You _____ keep the books for up to a week.

2 (**) Obligation: past and present

a Write the negative form of these sentences.

1 We have to get up early tomorrow.
   We don't have to get up early tomorrow.

2 You can leave your bicycle here.

3 We are allowed to eat in class.

4 I have to be home early.

b Write the past form of these sentences.

5 We have to leave very early in the morning.
   We had to leave very early in the morning.

6 We can't use a dictionary in the exam.

7 I'm not allowed to watch TV in my room.

8 I have to walk to school.

3 (***) Obligation: past and present

Complete the sentences with the correct form of the verbs in brackets.

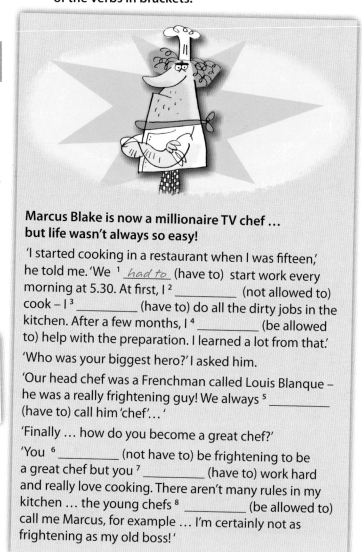

**Marcus Blake is now a millionaire TV chef …
but life wasn't always so easy!**

'I started cooking in a restaurant when I was fifteen,' he told me. 'We ¹ _had to_ (have to) start work every morning at 5.30. At first, I ² _____ (not allowed to) cook – I ³ _____ (have to) do all the dirty jobs in the kitchen. After a few months, I ⁴ _____ (be allowed to) help with the preparation. I learned a lot from that.'

'Who was your biggest hero?' I asked him.

'Our head chef was a Frenchman called Louis Blanque – he was a really frightening guy! We always ⁵ _____ (have to) call him 'chef'… '

'Finally … how do you become a great chef?'

'You ⁶ _____ (not have to) be frightening to be a great chef but you ⁷ _____ (have to) work hard and really love cooking. There aren't many rules in my kitchen … the young chefs ⁸ _____ (be allowed to) call me Marcus, for example … I'm certainly not as frightening as my old boss!'

4 (**) Read Grammar Plus. Then complete the questions and answers with the correct infinitive form.

Grammar + Plus

Infinitive with and without to

- Remember to use the infinitive without **to** after **can/can't**, **must/mustn't** and **should/shouldn't**:
  *You can **wear** your normal clothes.*
  *You mustn't **be** late.*
  *You shouldn't **say** that.*

- Use the infinitive with **to** with **allowed** (**to**) and **have** (**to**):
  *I wasn't allowed **to tell** you.*
  *We really have **to go** soon.*

1 'Were you allowed _to use_ (use) a dictionary?'
'Yes, but I thought I should _try_ (try) to guess the meaning first.'

2 'Do we have _____ (bring) our dictionary to class every day?'
'Yes … you must always _____ (have) it with you.'

3 'Should we _____ (finish) this exercise for homework?'
'No! You have _____ (finish) it now!'

4 'Can we _____ (go) home now?'
'You can't _____ (leave) until I tell you!'

Vocabulary

5 (✱✱) **Brat Camp**

<u>Underline</u> the correct verbs to complete each sentence.

1 Martin *did/<u>had</u>/made/took* an argument with his parents and decided to leave home.

2 After leaving school, Laurence soon *got/made/took/went* into trouble with the police.

3 Perhaps Lisa is *doing/having/making/taking* badly at school because of her problems at home.

4 England started the game well but things started to *do/get/go/make* wrong after fifteen minutes.

5 Sometimes people say unkind things but you shouldn't *do/get/have/take* any notice.

6 Philip doesn't *do/get/go/take* on well with his sister. They argue almost every day.

6 (✱✱) **Rules and behaviour**

Match each word below with a definition.

> easy-going   strict   fair   to punish
> to guide   to control ✓   to bring up
> freedom

1 _to control_ : to have power over what someone does

2 _____ : to look after and educate children

3 _____ : to make someone suffer because they did something wrong

4 _____ : having a lot of rules for people to follow

5 _____ : relaxed and calm – not often upset or angry

6 _____ : being able to do what you want

7 _____ : treating everyone in an equal way

8 _____ : to teach or show someone how to do something

7 (✱✱) *make* and *do*

Harry and Louis are flatmates. Harry is the lazy one and Louis has to do all the work!

Complete the sentences with a name and *does* or *makes*.

1 _Louis does_ all the housework.

2 _____ nothing to help!

3 _____ the breakfast every morning.

4 ____ never ____ any cooking.

5 _____ all the cooking and washing-up.

6 _____ about twenty phone calls every evening.

8 (✱✱) **Society and the law**

Match a word or phrase in Column A with a word or phrase in Column B.

A   B
1 to be   a the army
2 to commit   b sweets
3 to   c illegal
4 to go to   d your driving test
5 to join   e prison
6 to steal   f a crime
7 to take   g vote

7 miniworkbook

* ★ easy to do
* ★★ a bit harder
* ★★★ extra challenge

Grammar

1 ⊛ **Present continuous for future**

Complete the conversation between the President (P) and his assistant (A) by putting the verbs in brackets into the correct form of the present continuous.

P: So, how long before we get there?

A: About two hours, Mr President. The British Prime Minister ¹ _'s coming_ (come) to the airport to meet us.

P: Good! I'm very happy to meet Mr … uh …

A: Mr Black. The British Prime Minister's name is Mr George Black, Mr President.

P: Sure. George Black. And what ² _____ (happen) after that?

A: Well, first we ³ _____ (drive) to 10 Downing Street for a meeting.

P: OK. And what ⁴ _____ (I/do) after the meeting?

A: Then you ⁵ _____ (have) tea with Mr Black and his wife.

P: I see. And then?

A: You ⁶ _____ (go) to Buckingham Palace with Mr Black. You and Mr Black ⁷ _____ (have) dinner with the Queen.

P: That's great. And where ⁸ _____ (we/stay)?

A: At the Grand Hotel, Mr President. It's the best hotel in London …

2 ⊛⊛ Read *Grammar Plus*. Then complete the email with *in, on, at* or *ø* (= no preposition).

Grammar ✚ Plus

Prepositions with future time expressions

* Notice how prepositions are used in future time expressions:
  *My friends are having a party **on** Saturday.*
  *We're moving house **in** two weeks' (time). (= two weeks from now)*
  *I'm seeing my cousins **at** the weekend.*

* Phrases with *next* and *this* do not have a preposition:
  We're going on holiday ø next week/this weekend/ tomorrow.

Hi Hannah,

Amazing news! We're finally moving house … and it's happening ¹ _in_ only three weeks' time!

We've got a new house in Penley and we're moving there ² _____ next month: ³ _____ March 12th to be exact.

So we're having a leaving party for family and friends ⁴ _____ Saturday night. Sorry I didn't tell you earlier … but if you're not doing anything ⁵ _____ this weekend, please come!

Text me tomorrow if you can … or I'll phone ⁶ _____ a few days to check if you can come.

We're SOOOOO excited about the move!! Hope to see you ⁷ _____ the weekend!

Love
Annie xxxxxxxxxxx

3 ⊛⊛ *may/may not/might/might not*

Rewrite the sentences using *may/may not* or *might/might not*.

1 Perhaps he won't get to the airport on time. (may)
   He may not get to the airport on time.

2 It's possible that he'll miss his flight. (might)

3 Maybe he'll have to spend the night at the airport. (may)

4 It's possible that he'll have to fly tomorrow. (might)

5 Maybe he won't get a seat on tomorrow's flight. (might)

6 Perhaps he'll miss his holiday! (may)

4 (✱✱) will probably/definitely

Put the words in the correct order to make sentences.

1 Liverpool/probably/this year/won't/the cup/win
   Liverpool probably won't win the cup this year.

2 any snow/be/definitely/There/this Christmas/won't

3 Carla/home/be/later/probably/will

4 definitely/finish/I/my homework/today/will

5 You/have to/will/again/probably/take the test

6 be able/to come/I/to your party/won't/probably

Vocabulary

5 (✱✱) Holidays

Read the definitions and complete the words.

1 sleeping in a tent on holiday:
   c a m p i n g

2 the place you are travelling to:
   d _ _ _ n _ _ _ _ n

3 a short holiday trip:
   e _ _ _ r _ _ _ n

4 a place where you see art:
   g _ _ l _ _ y

5 when you travel from one place to another:
   j _ _ r _ _ y

6 the opposite of 'early morning':
   l _ t _   n _ g _ t

7 evening entertainment:
   n _ g _ t l _ _ e

8 something you see in the countryside:
   s _ _ n _ _ y

9 to stay in contact = to keep in _____:
   t _ u _ h

10 to go and see a place:
   v _ s _ t

6 (✱✱) Flying

Match each word in Column A with a word in Column B.

A	B
1 check-in	a luggage
2 passport	b shop
3 departures	c card
4 boarding	d desk
5 hand	e control
6 duty-free	f board

7 (✱✱) Describing holidays

Complete Jo and Fiona's conversation with the words below.

> accommodation sunburnt delicious traffic jam delayed disgusting relax food poisoning fun ✓

F: Hi Jo! How was your Easter holiday? Did you have lots of ¹ _fun_ ?

J: No, we didn't!! It was awful!

F: Why? What happened?

J: Well, first of all our flight was ² _____ and we got there about five hours late! And then the ³ _____ was really terrible – it was an old hotel a long way from the beach.

F: Oh, dear!

J: On the first day we took a bus to the beach … but we spent too much time in the sun and we all got ⁴ _____ .

F: Oh, no! And how was the food?

J: Well, the food in the hotel was ⁵ _____ – we just couldn't eat it – so one day we went to a restaurant and had the local speciality … but we all got ⁶ _____ and had to stay in bed for two days!

F: Well, at least you got back okay …

J: Hmmm!! On the last day we spent hours in a ⁷ _____ on our way to the airport and we nearly missed our flight! But how about you? How was your holiday?

F: Well, we didn't do much really. We had a lot of time to ⁸ _____ and do nothing. On Sunday, Mum cooked us a ⁹ _____ meal. It was great!!

J: Hmm …

8 (✱✱) The sea is full of fish!

Complete the sentences with the words below.

> blamed compensation deal genuine startled ✓ wildlife

1 She looked _startled_ when someone shouted her name.

2 As a hotel receptionist, David sometimes has to _____ with difficult customers.

3 Many people _____ the manager for losing the match.

4 After his terrible holiday, he received £1000 _____ from the travel company.

5 Only an expert can know if these diamonds are _____ or not.

6 Many people visit South Africa to see the wonderful _____ .

113

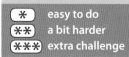

8 miniworkbook

* easy to do
** a bit harder
*** extra challenge

Grammar

1 (*) Past participles

Write the missing letters to complete the forms.

Infinitive	past form	past participle
1 g i v e	g a v e	g i v e n
2 s e e	s _ w	s _ _ n
3 t a k e	t _ _ k	t _ k _ n
4 f a l l	f _ l l	f _ l l _ n
5 s p e a k	s p _ k _	s p _ k _ n
6 e a t	a t _	e _ t _ n
7 c a t c h	c _ _ g h _	c _ _ g h _
8 w r i t e	w r _ t _	w r _ t t _ n

2 (**) Present perfect: positive, negative and question forms

Complete the gaps with the correct form of the verbs in brackets.

1 _Have_ you _heard_ (hear) of an actor called Ben Crossley?

2 My dad _____ _____ (give) me a pair of earrings.

3 _____ you ever _____ (meet) a famous person?

4 I _____ _____ (not/see) this film before.

5 _____ you _____ (speak) to Kate about the party?

6 My brother _____ _____ (buy) a new MP3 player.

7 I always buy a lottery ticket but I _____ never _____ (win) anything.

8 I hope I _____ _____ (not/make) too many mistakes in this exercise!

3 (**) Present perfect or past simple?

Underline the correct form of the verbs.

1 I *have been/went* to a really cool concert last night.

2 'Did you ever lose/Have you ever lost something important?'
'Yes … I *have lost/lost* my mobile phone last month.

3 I *'ve never read/never read* any books by Philip Pullman.

4 My parents *have taken/took* me to a fantastic restaurant on my birthday.

5 *Did you ever eat/Have you ever eaten* Mexican food?

6 Pete Sampras *has been/was* the world's top tennis player in the 1990s.

4 (***) Read Grammar Plus. Then complete the sentences with *been* or *gone*.

Grammar + Plus

been vs gone

*He's **gone** to the supermarket.* (= he's on his way to the supermarket or he's there now)

*He's **been** to the supermarket.* (= he went to the supermarket but he's not there now)

1 'How many times have you _been_ to Germany?' 'Two or three.'

2 'Where's Michael?' 'I'm not sure … perhaps he's _____ to the shops.'

3 My grandmother's nearly seventy and she's never _____ abroad.

4 Where's the cat _____? He was here a minute ago.

5 I've _____ to Switzerland twice on holiday.

6 My friends have all _____ on holiday so I've got no one to talk to!

5 (**) Present perfect with *just*

What have these people just done? Write a sentence for each picture with the verbs below.

get married   score a goal   have a baby
leave the station   get up   open the box

   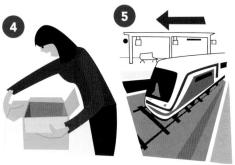 

1 *He's just scored a goal.*

114

6 (✶✶) Present perfect with *already* and *yet*

Danni has made a list of things to do for her fancy dress birthday party. Write six sentences about what she has *already* done and hasn't done *yet*.

Things to do
- *put up the decorations* ✓
- *buy a costume* ✓
- *go to the supermarket*
- *borrow a CD player*
- *put on her costume*
- *make the sandwiches* ✓

😊

1 *She's already put up the decorations.*

Vocabulary

7 (✶✶) Sports equipment

Read the definitions of eight pieces of sports equipment and write the correct word next to the definition.

1 You hit this when you play tennis and kick it when you play football.
   ball
2 You hit the ball with this in games like tennis or badminton.
3 You wear these to protect your eyes when you go skiing.
4 In tennis, you need to hit the ball over this.
5 You wear these on your feet when you play football.
6 These help you move quickly on ice.
7 You wear these on your hands when boxing or when you go skiing.
8 You wear these on your legs when playing sport … or on a hot day.

8 (✶✶✶) Verbs/phrases

Complete the paragraph with the correct form of the verbs.

[beat   play (x2) ✓   score   train   meet   win]

Marta Vieira da Silva

Brazil's footballers are famous all over the world – but have you heard of Marta Vieira da Silva – better known as Marta? Many people say she is the best woman football player in the world. She started ¹ *playing* football at the age of eight. As a child, her hero was the famous Brazilian Pelé … but up to now she has never ² _____ Brazil's most famous footballer.

In the 2007 Women's World Cup in China, Marta ³ _____ seven goals … but sadly for Marta, her team didn't ⁴ _____ the competition. Germany ⁵ _____ Brazil 2–0 in the final.

She is now ⁶ _____ for Umeå, a team in Sweden. Marta knows that you can't succeed without hard work. 'I want to be the best and that is why I always ⁷ _____ hard,' she says.

9 (✶✶) Champions against the odds

Complete the sentences with the words below.

[champion   medal   speed   athlete ✓
  tournament   opponent   strength   disabled]

1 Donovan Bailey was a famous *athlete* in the 1990s.
2 The world _____ is the best person in the world at a particular sport.
3 The World Cup is the world's most important football _____ .
4 Only _____ people can compete in the Para-Olympics.
5 Everyone at the Olympic Games hopes to win a gold _____ .
6 Your _____ is the person you are playing against.
7 Tennis players can hit the ball at a _____ of more than 200 km per hour!
8 Physical _____ is very important for a boxer.

* easy to do
** a bit harder
*** extra challenge

Grammar

1 (**) Relative clauses

<u>Underline</u> the correct relative pronouns to complete the sentences.

Tokyo: The World's No1 technology city!!

1 Shibuya is an area *that/where/who* you can find all the best shops and the latest technology.

2 'Tokyoers' are people *where/which/who* come from Tokyo.

3 The Shinkansen is the name of the train *where/which/who* connects Tokyo and the city of Kyoto.

4 Narita is one of the airports *that/where/who* serve Tokyo.

5 The Sumida is a river *where/which/who* runs through Tokyo.

6 The Imperial Palace is the place *that/where/which* the Japanese emperor lives.

7 The Sanja Festival is a street festival *that/where/who* happens every May in Japan.

2 (**) First conditional

Put the verbs in brackets into the correct tense.

1 If the weather *is* (be) good this weekend, we _____ (go) to the beach.

2 If you _____ (not buy) a ticket, you _____ (not get) into the concert.

3 The teacher _____ (be) really angry if you _____ (be) late for class again.

4 He _____ (miss) the bus if he _____ (not get up) soon.

5 If we _____ (run), we _____ (be) there in five minutes.

6 I _____ (do) the washing-up if you _____ (cook) the dinner.

3 (**) Read *Grammar Plus*. Then complete the sentences with *if* or *when*.

Grammar + Plus

if vs when

- Use *if* + present simple to talk about a future possibility:
  If it rains tomorrow, we'll stay at home.

- Use *when* + present simple to talk about something you are sure will happen in the future:
  I'll start cooking when the children get home.

1 You can use your mobile phone *when* the plane lands.

2 We'll go inside _____ it starts raining.

3 The town will be much busier _____ the holiday season starts.

4 I'll be very surprised _____ he gets home before 8 o'clock.

5 I'll have a great party _____ I'm eighteen!

6 _____ you don't hurry up, you'll miss the bus.

4 (**) Future time clauses

Match 1–7 with a–g and *after*, *before* and *when* to form complete sentences.

1 Please check you have your luggage with you
2 Can you do the washing-up
3 Don't forget to give me your email address
4 I'd like to get a weekend job
5 You should start revising for your exams
6 I'd like to get home
7 I'll call you

after
before
when

a I'm old enough.
b it's too late.
c it gets dark.
d lunch is ready.
e you finish your meal?
f you go home.
g you leave the train.

1 Please check you have your luggage with you before you leave the train.

Vocabulary

5 ✱✱ Operating machines

Match words from Column A and Column B to make the name of gadgets.

A		B	
1	a flat screen	a	player
2	a mobile	b	console
3	an answering	c	TV
4	an MP3	d	clock
5	a games	e	phone
6	an alarm	f	machine

1 c = a flat screen TV

6 ✱✱ Two-word verbs

Complete the sentences with the verbs below.

> plug   press   charge   put
> record   switch   turn ✓

1 Can you _turn_ the volume up, please? I can't hear anything!!

2 This machine doesn't use batteries: you need to _____ it in.

3 You open the camera here if you want to _____ some new batteries in.

4 What happens if I _____ this button?

5 I can't use my phone at the moment: I need to _____ the battery.

6 Can you _____ the light off, please? I'm trying to sleep!

7 'If you want to _____ a message, please speak after the tone … BEEEEP!'

7 ✱✱ Numbers and dates

Rewrite the numbers in bold as words.

Radio Facts!

Do you listen to the radio? Here are some radio facts that may surprise you!!

Radio – not television – is the most popular medium today. [1] **44%** of people in the UK listen to the radio every day – but only [2] **41%** watch television! The music station Radio 2 is the nation's favourite station, with an audience of [3] **13.2 million** people.

The BBC World Service is available on radio and online all over the world and broadcasts in [4] **33** languages. It began in [5] **1932** and it now has more than [6] **160,000,000** regular listeners around the world, with [7] **61.1 million** listeners in Asia alone.

The United States has more than [8] **13,000** radio stations – more than any other country in the world. The state of Texas alone has [9] **940** stations! There are more than [10] **600,000,000** radios in the country – that's [11] **5.6** radios per household!

1 Forty-four percent

8 ✱✱ How screens took over our lives

Complete the sentences with one of these words.

> search   background noise ✓   devices   chats   generation

1 I couldn't hear what she was saying because there was a lot of _background noise_ .

2 I often _____ for information on the internet.

3 She always _____ with her friends for hours when they meet.

4 I don't agree that the older _____ are afraid of computers. My grandma sends me an email every week!

5 Computers and mobile phones are _____ that we all use now.

10 miniworkbook

* easy to do
** a bit harder
*** extra challenge

Grammar

1 (*) **Articles with geographical names**
Complete the sentences. Use *the* or no article (Ø).

South America

Did you know that ¹ _Ø_ South America is the world's fourth largest continent? It's smaller than ² ____ Asia but much bigger than ³ ____ Europe. Here are some other things you may not know about the world's fourth largest continent.

• ⁴ ____ Andes is the world's longest mountain range. It stretches from ⁵ ____ Pacific Ocean in the north right down to ⁶ ____ Chile in the south. The highest point is Mount Aconcagua in ⁷ ____ Argentina.

• Also in ⁸ ____ Andes, you can find the world's highest lake – Lake Titicaca. It's on the border between ⁹ ____ Bolivia and ¹⁰ ____ Peru.

• Many people believe that ¹¹ ____ Amazon River is the longest river in the world but, in fact, ¹² ____ Nile River in ¹³ ____ Africa is longer.

• The biggest country, ¹⁴ ____ Brazil, has an area of 8.4 million square kilometres. It's nearly as big as ¹⁵ ____ United States and eight times bigger than ¹⁶ ____ UK, ¹⁷ ____ France and ¹⁸ ____ Poland combined!

2 (**) *used to*
Rewrite the sentences with *used to* where possible.

1 My sister had long hair.
   My sister used to have long hair.
2 I met an old friend in the street yesterday.   ✗
3 I loved ice-cream as a small child.
4 My father took me to the park every Saturday.
5 My parents went to Spain last year.
6 People didn't go abroad very often.
7 Summers were much warmer when I was a child.
8 She visited her friend last week.

3 (**) *for* and *since*
Which phrases go with *for* and which go with *since*? Put each phrase into the correct column.

> 1947 ✓   a week   we started school
> fifteen minutes   8 o'clock this morning
> he was eight years old   fifty years
> six months

for	since
	1947

4 (***) **Present perfect with *for* and *since***
Choose one of the phrases from exercise 3 to complete each sentence.

1 India has been an independent country
   since 1947 .
2 It's the last day of our holiday today – we've been here _____ .
3 I'm so hungry! I haven't eaten anything _____ .
4 Hurry up! The taxi has been outside _____ and we're all waiting for you!
5 Alonso hasn't played _____ because of a foot injury.
6 My grandparents have their golden wedding anniversary next week. They have been married _____ .
7 Lucia and I have been best friends _____ .
8 Andy has been an Arsenal fan _____ .

5 (✱✱) Read *Grammar Plus*. Then complete the sentences with *very* or *absolutely*.

Grammar + Plus

Adjectives with *very* and *absolutely*

- Use *very* to make most adjectives stronger:
  *He made a **very** big mistake.*
  *There was a **very** loud noise coming from outside.*
- Use *absolutely* instead of *very* with 'strong' adjectives like *incredible*, *enormous* and *awful*:
  *The food was **absolutely** awful.*
  (NOT *The food was **very absolutely** awful.*)

1 There was a (n) _very_ large crowd outside the door of his house.

2 Come and look at this spider! It's _____ enormous!!

3 Travelling to India was an _____ incredible experience for me.

4 It's _____ unusual to see snow at this time of year.

5 It was a _____ small hotel with no bar or restaurant.

6 We can't go outside at the moment – the weather is _____ awful.

Vocabulary

6 (✱✱) **The natural world**

Complete the words to match the definitions.

1 an area where there is no rain: d _e_ _s_ _e_ _r_ t

2 an area of land with water all around it:
  i _ _ _ _ d

3 a large area of water with land all around it:
  l _ _ e

4 a large area of trees: f _ _ _ _ t

5 a large sea such as the Atlantic or the Pacific:
  o _ _ _ n

6 water which rises up and moves towards the land: w _ _ _ s

7 a mountain which may explode with fire and melted rock: v _ _ _ _ _ o

8 the area of land next to the sea: c _ _ _ t

7 (✱✱) **Global warming**

Complete the fact file with the words below.

> floods   droughts   species   extinct
> melt   rise   levels   temperatures ✓

Global warming: the facts

If [1] _temperatures_ around the world continue to [2] _____ , here are some of the things that may happen:

- The polar ice of the Arctic and Antarctic will [3] _____: this means that sea [4] _____ around the world will become higher. It is also possible that many [5] _____ of animal – such as polar bears – could become [6] _____ in the next few years.

- In areas near rivers, there will be a bigger danger of [7] _____ because of heavy rain.

- Low rainfall and a lack of water could mean serious [8] _____ in many areas of southern Europe.

8 (✱✱) **The Biggest Bang in History**

Choose the correct answers (more than one answer may be correct).

1 Which of these can you find after something has burnt?
  a ash ✓   b crash   c eruption

2 Which of these can you hear?
  a an explosion   b gunfire   c fear

3 What do people sometimes do when they are frightened?
  a crash   b scream   c shake

4 Which of these means to break or ruin something?
  a destroy   b sail   c shake

5 Which word describes a noise?
  a fear   b loud   c uninhabited

9 (✱✱) **Noun/verb forms**

Complete the sentences with the correct form of the words in brackets.

1 We need to do something about the _destruction_ (destroy) of the natural environment.

2 There is no _____ (explain) for what he did.

3 The bomb could _____ (explosion) at any moment.

4 The _____ (inspire) for the painting was the artist's father.

5 Police are still looking for the young girl, two months after her _____ (disappear).

* easy to do
** a bit harder
*** extra challenge

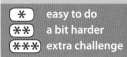

Grammar

1 (**) **Present simple passive**

Complete the sentences with the present simple passive of the verbs in brackets.

Did you know that in the UK …

1 More than three hundred languages are _spoken_ (speak) by London schoolchildren.

2 More than 350,000 emails _____ (send) every second!

3 More than 30% of the food which people buy _____ (throw) away.

4 More than 10 million packets of potato crisps _____ (eat) every day.

5 More than 1.2 million bags _____ (lose) at Heathrow Airport every year.

6 A car _____ (sell) over the internet every two minutes.

2 (**) **Past simple passive**

Complete the paragraph about John Lennon's piano with the past simple passive of the verbs in brackets.

NEWS

A very special piano [1] _was used_ (used) by ex-Beatle John Lennon when he wrote his most famous song *Imagine*. The Steinway Model Z piano [2] _____ (make) in Germany. It [3] _____ (buy) by Lennon in 1970 and it [4] _____ (keep) at his home studio in Berkshire, near London. Lennon played the song to his wife Yoko Ono when the original video for *Imagine* [5] _____ (record) in 1971. Interest in his music increased after Lennon [6] _____ (murder) by Beatles fan Mark Chapman in New York in 1980. Twenty years after Lennon's death, the piano [7] _____ (sell) for £1.67m in an online auction in October 2000. It [8] _____ (buy) by rock star and Lennon fan George Michael.

3 (***) **Present simple and past simple passive**

Put the verbs in blue into the present simple passive and the verbs in red into the past simple passive.

Sir Ian McKellen

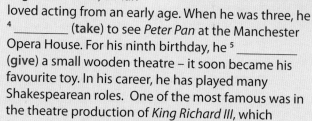

Nowadays, the British actor Sir Ian McKellen [1] _is recognised_ (**recognise**) everywhere. He [2] _____ (**know**) all over the world for his roles in the *X-men* and *The Lord of the Rings* films. But for many years, he [3] _____ (**know**) only as a theatre actor.

Born in the north-west of England in 1939, Sir Ian loved acting from an early age. When he was three, he [4] _____ (**take**) to see *Peter Pan* at the Manchester Opera House. For his ninth birthday, he [5] _____ (**give**) a small wooden theatre – it soon became his favourite toy. In his career, he has played many Shakespearean roles. One of the most famous was in the theatre production of *King Richard III*, which [6] _____ (**make**) into a film in 1991. In the same year, he became Sir Ian McKellen. Very few actors [7] _____ (**give**) this important title.

In 2001, Sir Ian [8] _____ (**choose**) to play the part of the wizard in Peter Jackson's *The Lord of the Rings* film trilogy. Also, he [9] _____ (**ask**) to appear in a special British edition of *The Simpsons* with Tony Blair and J K Rowling. But he has never lost his love of theatre and even now he [10] _____ (**see**) in small theatres in the UK and abroad.

4 (**) **Passives: negative and question forms**

a Make the sentences negative.

1 This jacket is made of real leather.
   This jacket isn't made of real leather.

2 This poem was written by Shakespeare.

3 We're invited to Tom's party.

4 My friends were injured in the crash.

b Make the sentences into questions.

1 Your dog is called Billy.
   Is your dog called Billy?

2 The church was built in the 16th century.

3 Her books are translated into Spanish.

4 You were taught English by an Australian.

5 (✱✱) Present perfect passive

Complete the news items by putting the verbs into the present perfect passive.

1 A new album by the Scottish group McFlea _has been released_ (release) on the internet.

2 The President of Italy _____ (invite) to Britain to visit the Queen.

3 More than 10,000 new jobs _____ (create) this year.

4 A new type of computer _____ (invent) by scientists.

5 A new supermarket _____ (open) by the mayor.

6 (✱✱✱) Read *Grammar Plus*. Then put the words into the correct order to make sentences.

Grammar + Plus

Time expressions in passive sentences

If you use a time expression (*always*, *never*, *sometimes*, etc.) in a passive sentence, it goes between the verb *to be* and the past participle:
*International matches are **sometimes** played on Saturdays.*
*His last novel was **never** finished.*

1 is/in tourist areas/understood/usually/English
English is usually understood in tourist areas.

2 are/people/bitten/sometimes/by snakes

3 in Italian cooking/tomatoes/used/are/often

4 are/made of/new buildings/steel and glass/often

5 am/by aircraft noise/sometimes/woken up/I

Vocabulary

7 (✱✱) Types of film

Match 1–5 with a–e to make definitions.

1 A historical drama *b*

2 A horror movie

3 A romantic comedy

4 Science fiction

5 A thriller

a ... is a film where strange and frightening things happen.

b ... is about important events in the past.

c ... is about things that happen in an imaginary future.

d ... is a funny story about love.

e ... is an exciting story about murder or crime.

8 (✱✱) Making a film

Rearrange the letters to make words connected with making a film.

1 t r e c o d i r *director*   2 p e r c u d r o

3 t e d b u g   4 p e s c a l i f e f t e c s

5 s o r c a t   6 t r i p c s

7 d e t i   8 s o i d u t

9 n e e s c   10 c u l p i t i b y

9 (✱✱) TV programmes

What type of TV programme is the TV guide describing?

> a comedy series   a cookery programme
> the news   a documentary   a reality show ✓
> the weather forecast   a soap opera
> a sports programme

1 'Who will the public vote out of the Celebrity Cave? Find out at 10 p.m. tonight.'   *a reality show*

2 All the latest headlines and information from around the world.

3 Find out if you need a sun hat or an umbrella when you go out tomorrow!

4 What's happening on Lawrence Street? Will Caroline tell her daughter the truth about Mike? And what is Matthew's terrible secret?

5 Celebrity chef Rick Payne shows you how to cook fish Spanish-style.

6 Plenty of laughs as Dan and Mary try to impress their new neighbours.

7 The best of today's action from the International Athletics Championships in Helsinki.

8 Global warming and you: a look at how climate change is affecting our daily lives.

12 mini workbook

* easy to do
** a bit harder
*** extra challenge

Grammar

1 (**) **Second conditional**

Underline the correct forms in each sentence.

1 If I <u>had to</u>/would have to live abroad, I went/I would go to live in Canada.

2 If I was/would be President of my country, I'd ban/I banned smoking everywhere.

3 I went/would go out with you tonight if I didn't have/wouldn't have so much homework.

4 If you can/could interview a famous person, who was it/would it be?

5 I would buy/bought tickets for the concert if I had/would have enough money.

2 (***) **Second conditional**

Put the verbs in brackets in the correct tense to make a second conditional sentence.

1 If I _could_ (can) travel anywhere in the world, I _would go_ (go) to Florida.

2 I think we _____ (get) really bored if we _____ (live) in the country.

3 If I _____ (have) more time, I _____ (be) happy to help you.

4 You _____ (look) better if you _____ (have) shorter hair.

5 You _____ (not/be) late for school if you _____ (get) up earlier.

6 Jane _____ (get) better marks at school if she _____ (do) her homework.

3 Complete the sentences about you.

1 If I had a free afternoon today, I _____ .

2 I _____ if I had a private airplane.

3 I _____ if I got more pocket money.

4 If I didn't have to go to school every day, I _____ .

5 If I could travel anywhere, I _____ .

4 (**) Read *Grammar Plus*. Match sentences 1–5 with advice a–e. Then write sentences with *If I were you, …*

Grammar + Plus

If I were you, I'd …

The conditional phrase **If I were you, I'd …** is often used to give advice:

A: *It takes me hours to walk to school in the morning!*

B: *If I were you, I'd buy a bicycle.*

C: *I'd take the bus if I were you … it's much quicker.*

1 'Help! I'm so nervous about the exam!' _c_

2 'I don't know which university to go to.'

3 'I've got a terrible headache.'

4 'Oh dear! We're lost!'

5 'I can't get up in the morning.'

a … ask that lady for directions

b … buy a new alarm clock

c … sit down and relax for a few minutes

d … take an aspirin

e … talk to your careers teacher

1 *If I were you, I'd sit down and relax for a few minutes.*

5 (**) **Reported requests and commands with *tell*, *ask*, *order* and *advise***

Complete the sentences in reported speech.

1 'Be careful!' (Joanna → her son)
Joanna told _her son to be careful._

2 'Could you turn off your mobile phones, please?' (the speaker → the audience)
The speaker asked _____ .

3 'Don't worry about me.' (I → my mother)
I told _____ .

4 'Please don't ask any more questions.' (the teacher → Jenny)
The teacher asked _____ .

5 If I were you, I'd take the bus to the airport.' (the travel agent → us)
The travel agent advised _____ .

6 'Put down the knife!' (the policeman → the robber)
The policeman ordered _____ .

Vocabulary

6 (✳✳) Serious crimes?

Use the clues to write in the missing letters.

1 To break something: d *a* m *a* g *e*
2 To try to hurt or kill someone: a _ t _ c _
3 Paper that people throw away: l _ t _ e _
4 The crime of stealing from a house: b _ r _ l _ r _
5 Not real: f _ k _
6 To move files from the internet onto a computer: d _ w _ l _ a _
7 Damaging or writing on public places such as bus stops: v _ n _ a _ i _ m
8 To miss school without permission: p _ a _ t _ u _ n _
9 The crime of stealing money from banks, shops, etc: r _ b _ e _ y
10 The crime of driving faster than the official speed limit: s _ e _ d _ n _
11 The crime of taking things from shops without paying for them: s _ o _ l _ f _ i _ g
12 In a way which is not allowed by the law: i _ l _ g _ l _ y

7 (✳) -ed adjectives

Write one of the adjectives next to the correct picture.

> annoyed   bored ✓   embarrassed
> frightened   interested   surprised

bored

8 (✳✳✳) -ed and -ing adjectives

Underline the correct adjectives in Cindy's blog.

Cindy's Blog – 26 February

Remember last week I told you about AJ and how [1] *frustrated*/*frustrating* I feel about him? Sure, he's a nice boy. But spending all your time outside school with the same person gets [2] *bored*/*boring*!! And all my friends are really [3] *annoyed*/*annoying* with me now because I never hang out with them any more. AJ never wants to do anything [4] *excited*/*exciting*.

And I feel s-o-o-o [5] *embarrassed*/*embarrassing* when he calls me 'his girl' when he's talking to people! I told him we had to talk. He looked so [6] *worried*/*worrying*! Well, we talked and everything is fine now … we're going to see each other a little less in future. My mum's [7] *pleased*/*pleasing* – she thinks I'll have more time to spend on my homework … hmmm …

Anyway, on Friday my friends and I are going to hire some DVDs and have a looooong chat. It's going to be an [8] *interested*/*interesting* evening …

Peace and love everyone.

Cindy

9 (✳✳) Victims of crime

Complete the sentences with these words.

> blame ✓   commit   hurt   threatens
> valuable   victims   violence

1 Many people _blame_ young people for the vandalism in the town centre.
2 _____ at football matches is a problem in some countries.
3 Young people who _____ serious crimes can go to prison.
4 If someone _____ you with violence, you should give them what they want.
5 Do you think it's a good idea for _____ of crime to receive money?
6 It's a good idea to leave _____ possessions such as watches and MP3 players at home.
7 Luckily, no one was _____ in the robbery.

Quiz answers and activities

Unit 1, page 6, exercise 2

Quiz key

If most of your answers were c:
Well you're certainly 'chilled' aren't you? Okay, you don't worry much but you don't do much either! Why not try a few new activities – and getting a bit less sleep!

If most of your answers were a:
You never stop but do you always enjoy what you're doing? It's great to have a busy life but sometimes it's nice to have time to think or just to do nothing.

If most of your answers were b:
You have a good balance in your life. You enjoy lots of different activities but you know when to relax.

Unit 1, page 11, Real Time, exercise 7

Course options	Dates
English Language	2 July – 5 August
European History	2 July – 9 September
Film Studies	8 August – 9 September
Media Studies	8 August – 9 September

University Enrolment

1 **Name of course** _____
2 **Dates of course** _____

3 Full name _____
4 Date of birth _____
5 Place of birth _____
6 Nationality _____
7 Passport number _____
8 Home address _____
9 Mobile number _____
10 Email address _____
11 Emergency
   contact details: _____

NAME: _____
ADDRESS: _____
TELEPHONE: _____

Unit 2, page 16, exercise 3
The winner of the BBC poll is Winston Churchill.

Unit 11, page 88, exercise 6

1 Will and Suzie don't fall in love. They stop seeing each other.
2 Suzie does find out about Will's lies. At first, she is angry but then she forgives him.
3 Marcus and Will do become friends.
4 Will has a good influence on Marcus. He helps Marcus to dress like a kid.
5 Marcus finds out about Will's lies but he doesn't get angry with Will.
6 Will becomes a better person: 'He couldn't remember feeling as good as this before. He had made an unhappy boy happy, and there hadn't been any advantage in it for him at all.' (*About a Boy*, page 42)

Student A

Unit 2, page 13, exercise 7

Put the verbs in the correct forms. Use the irregular verb list on the back cover to help you.

Marilyn Monroe

1 She _____ (be) a famous movie star in the 1950s. After she _____ (die) she _____ (become) a legend.
2 She _____ (be born) on 1 June 1926 in Los Angeles, California.
3 She _____ (not have) a happy childhood. She never _____ (know) her father.
4 She _____ (make) a lot of films in the 1950s. Her best film _____ (be) *Some Like it Hot* in 1959.
5 She _____ (get) married three times but _____ (not have) any children. All her husbands were very famous.
6 She _____ (kill) herself in 1962 when she _____ (be) just 36 years old.

Unit 4, page 33, exercise 9
Katrina

- twenty years old
- good French and Italian, is learning English
- good cook and lots of experience of cleaning (was a hotel cleaner)
- likes children (but no experience)
- can ski and ice-skate
- good sense of humour!

Word List

Unit 1

Pages 4–5

A-level (n)	/'eɪ ˌlevəl/
crazy about sth. (adj)	/'kreɪzi əbaʊt ˌsʌmθɪŋ/
divorced (adj)	/dɪ'vɔːst/
electrician (n)	/ɪˌlek'trɪʃən/
fitness freak (n)	/'fɪtnəs ˌfriːk/
lazy (adj)	/'leɪzi/
nurse (n)	/nɜːs/
nursery (n)	/'nɜːsəri/
personality (n)	/ˌpɜːsə'næləti/
private school	/'praɪvət skuːl/
similar (adj)	/'sɪmələ/
similarity (n)	/ˌsɪmə'lærəti/
twin (n)	/twɪn/
wonder (v)	/'wʌndə/

Pages 6–7

activity (n)	/æk'tɪvəti/
arrange (v)	/ə'reɪndʒ/
arrangement (n)	/ə'reɪndʒmənt/
chilled (adj)	/tʃɪld/
complain (v)	/kəm'pleɪn/
do nothing (v)	/ˌduː 'nʌθɪŋ/
do sport (v)	/ˌduː 'spɔːt/
go on the internet (v)	/ˌgəʊ ɒn ði 'ɪntənet/
go out (v)	/ˌgəʊ 'aʊt/
go running (v)	/ˌgəʊ 'rʌnɪŋ/
go shopping (v)	/ˌgəʊ 'ʃɒpɪŋ/
go to the beach (v)	/ˌgəʊ tə ðə 'biːtʃ/
go to the cinema (v)	/ˌgəʊ tə ðə 'sɪnəmə/
have a party (v)	/hæv ə 'pɑːti/
hyper (adj)	/'haɪpə/
make plans (v)	/ˌmeɪk 'plænz/
meet friends (v)	/ˌmiːt 'frendz/
meet new people (v)	/ˌmiːt njuː 'piːpəl/
play computer games (v)	/ˌpleɪ kəm'pjuːtə geɪmz/
stay in (v)	/ˌsteɪ 'ɪn/
terrible (adj)	/'terəbəl/

Pages 8–9

alive (adj)	/ə'laɪv/
appearance (n)	/ə'pɪərəns/
aunt (n)	/ɑːnt/
brother (n)	/'brʌðə/
brother-in-law (n)	/'brʌðər ɪn ˌlɔː/
complain (v)	/kəm'pleɪn/
cousin (n)	/'kʌzən/
daughter-in-law (n)	/'dɔːtər ɪn ˌlɔː/
exam pressure (n)	/ɪg'zæm ˌpreʃə/
ex-wife (n)	/ˌeks 'waɪf/
freedom (n)	/'friːdəm/
get on well with sb (v)	/ˌget ɒn 'wel wɪð ˌsʌmbədi/
great grandfather (n)	/ˌgreɪt 'grænˌfɑːðə/
great grandmother (n)	/ˌgreɪt 'grænˌmʌðə/
log on (v)	/ˌlɒg 'ɒn/
(the) media (n)	/ðə 'miːdiə/
mood (n)	/muːd/
nephew (n)	/'nefjuː/
niece (n)	/niːs/
older (adj)	/'əʊldə/
only child (n)	/ˌəʊnli 'tʃaɪld/
opinion (n)	/ə'pɪnjən/
relationship (n)	/rɪ'leɪʃənʃɪp/
relative (n)	/'relətɪv/
respect (v)	/rɪ'spekt/

sense of humour (n)	/ˌsens əv 'hjuːmə/
sister (n)	/'sɪstə/
stepfather (n)	/'step ˌfɑːðə/
stepmother (n)	/'step ˌmʌðə/
support (n)	/sə'pɔːt/
survey (n)	/'sɜːveɪ/
teenager (n)	/'tiːneɪdʒə/
treat sb like (a child)	/ˌtriːt sʌmbədi laɪk ə 'tʃaɪld/
uncle (n)	/'ʌŋkəl/
worry (n)	/'wʌri/
younger (adj)	/'jʌŋgə/

Pages 10–11

be in (= at home) (v)	/ˌbi 'ɪn/
contact details (n)	/'kɒntækt ˌdiːteɪlz/
emergency (n)	/ɪ'mɜːdʒənsi/
enrolment form (n)	/ɪn'rəʊlmənt fɔːm/
fill in (v)	/ˌfɪl 'ɪn/
flight (n)	/flaɪt/
form (n)	/fɔːm/
garage (n)	/'gærɑːʒ/
introduce sb (v)	/ˌɪntrə'djuːs ˌsʌmbədi/
journey (n)	/'dʒɜːni/
meet sb (v)	/'miːt ˌsʌmbədi/
overseas student (n)	/ˌəʊvəsiːz 'stjuːdənt/
postcode (n)	/'pəʊstkəʊd/
receptionist (n)	/rɪ'sepʃənɪst/
summer course (n)	/ˌsʌmə 'kɔːs/

Unit 2

Pages 12–13

actor (n)	/'æktə/
actress (n)	/'æktrəs/
admire sb (v)	/əd'maɪə ˌsʌmbədi/
childhood (n)	/'tʃaɪldhʊd/
depressed (adj)	/dɪ'prest/
depression (n)	/dɪ'preʃən/
fame (n)	/feɪm/
grow up (v)	/ˌgrəʊ 'ʌp/
icon (n)	/'aɪkɒn/
legend (n)	/'ledʒənd/
miserable (adj)	/'mɪzrəbəl/
model (n)	/'mɒdl/
musician (n)	/mjuː'zɪʃən/
popular (adj)	/'pɒpjələ/
raise money (v)	/ˌreɪz 'mʌni/
refuse to fight (v)	/rɪˌfjuːz tə 'faɪt/
Second World War (n)	/ˌsekənd wɜːld 'wɔː/
shoot (v)	/ʃuːt/
sportsman (n)	/'spɔːtsmən/
sportswoman (n)	/'spɔːtsˌwʊmən/
successful (adj)	/sək'sesfəl/
world champion (n)	/ˌwɜːld 'tʃæmpiən/

Pages 14–15

band (n)	/bænd/
church fair (n)	/ˌtʃɜːtʃ 'feə/
close friend (n)	/ˌkləʊs 'frend/
degree (n)	/dɪ'griː/
dump sb (v)	/'dʌmp ˌsʌmbədi/
fall in love (v)	/ˌfɔːl ɪn 'lʌv/
get a degree (v)	/ˌget ə dɪ'griː/
get a job (v)	/ˌget ə 'dʒɒb/
get engaged (v)	/ˌget ɪn'geɪdʒd/
get married (v)	/ˌget 'mærid/
go to university (v)	/ˌgəʊ tə ˌjuːnə'vɜːsəti/

happily ever after (adv)	/ˌhæpəli evər 'ɑːftə/
have an argument (v)	/ˌhæv ən 'ɑːgjəmənt/
hit (n)	/hɪt/
leave school (v)	/ˌliːv 'skuːl/
leave university (v)	/ˌliːv juːnə'vɜːsəti/
memory (n)	/'meməri/
move house (v)	/ˌmuːv 'haʊs/
notice (v)	/'nəʊtɪs/
pass your exams (v)	/ˌpɑːs jər ɪg'zæmz/
performance (n)	/pə'fɔːməns/
primary school (n)	/'praɪməri ˌskuːl/
rent a flat (v)	/ˌrent ə 'flæt/
secondary school (n)	/'sekəndəri ˌskuːl/
stare at sb (v)	/'steər ət ˌsʌmbədi/
start school (v)	/ˌstɑːt 'skuːl/

Pages 16–17

aristocratic (adj)	/ˌærɪstə'krætɪk/
battle (n)	/'bætl/
brave (adj)	/breɪv/
brilliant (adj)	/'brɪljənt/
brutal (adj)	/'bruːtl/
car crash (n)	/'kɑː kræʃ/
composer (n)	/kəm'pəʊzə/
cruel (adj)	/'kruːəl/
design (v)	/dɪ'zaɪn/
determined (adj)	/dɪ'tɜːmɪnd/
develop (v)	/dɪ'veləp/
discover (v)	/dɪs'kʌvə/
engineer (n)	/ˌendʒɪ'nɪə/
execute (= kill) (v)	/'eksɪkjuːt/
famous (adj)	/'feɪməs/
feeble (adj)	/'fiːbəl/
friendly (adj)	/'frendli/
glamorous (adj)	/'glæmərəs/
habit (n)	/'hæbɪt/
inspire (v)	/ɪn'spaɪə/
intelligent (adj)	/ɪn'telɪdʒənt/
lead (v)	/liːd/
military leader (n)	/ˌmɪlətri 'liːdə/
peace (n)	/piːs/
peace campaigner (n)	/'piːs kæmˌpeɪnə/
play (n)	/pleɪ/
poetry (n)	/'pəʊətri/
political leader (n)	/pəˌlɪtɪkəl 'liːdə/
political party (n)	/pəˌlɪtɪkəl 'pɑːti/
popular (adj)	/'pɒpjələ/
pupil (n)	/'pjuːpəl/
retire (v)	/rɪ'taɪə/
royalty (n)	/'rɔɪəlti/
scientist (n)	/'saɪəntɪst/
speech (n)	/spiːtʃ/
statue (n)	/'stætʃuː/
successful (adj)	/sək'sesfəl/
sympathetic (adj)	/ˌsɪmpə'θetɪk/
talented (adj)	/'tæləntɪd/
theory (n)	/'θɪəri/
violent (adj)	/'vaɪələnt/
weak (adj)	/wiːk/
wit (n)	/wɪt/
writer (n)	/'raɪtə/

Unit 3
Pages 20–21

armchair (n)	/'ɑːmtʃeə/
bright (adj)	/braɪt/
chair (n)	/tʃeə/
coffee bar (n)	/'kɒfi bɑː/
coffee table (n)	/'kɒfi ˌteɪbəl/
colourful (adj)	/'kʌləfəl/
comfortable (adj)	/'kʌmftəbəl/
creative (adj)	/kri'eɪtɪv/
cupboard (n)	/'kʌbəd/
cushions (n)	/'kʊʃənz/
dark (adj)	/dɑːk/
feminine (adj)	/'femənɪn/
messy (adj)	/'mesi/
mirror (n)	/'mɪrə/
modern (adj)	/'mɒdn/
noisy (adj)	/'nɔɪzi/
owner (n)	/'əʊnə/
personality (n)	/ˌpɜːsə'næləti/
picture (n)	/'pɪktʃə/
plant (n)	/plɑːnt/
poster (n)	/'pəʊstə/
quiet (adj)	/'kwaɪət/
rug (n)	/rʌg/
sofa (n)	/'səʊfə/
stool (n)	/stuːl/
stylish (adj)	/'staɪlɪʃ/
table (n)	/'teɪbəl/
tidy (adj)	/'taɪdi/
well-organised (adj)	/ˌwel 'ɔːgənaɪzd/

Pages 22–23

baggy (adj)	/'bægi/
casual (adj)	/'kæʒuəl/
dye (your hair) (v)	/daɪ/
dyed (adj)	/daɪd/
jewellery (n)	/'dʒuːəlri/
long (adj)	/lɒŋ/
make-up (n)	/'meɪk ʌp/
match (v)	/mætʃ/
piercing (n)	/'pɪəsɪŋ/
ribbon (n)	/'rɪbən/
sandal (n)	/'sændəl/
short (adj)	/ʃɔːt/
skirt (n)	/skɜːt/
smart (adj)	/smɑːt/
straight (adj)	/streɪt/
suit (n)	/suːt/
tattoo (n)	/tə'tuː/
tight (adj)	/taɪt/
trousers (n)	/'traʊzəz/
well-dressed (adj)	/ˌwel 'drest/

Pages 24–25

(not) afford sth (v)	/ˌnɒt ə'fɔːd ˌsʌmθɪŋ/
bargain (n)	/'bɑːgɪn/
behave (v)	/bɪ'heɪv/
borrow (v)	/'bɒrəʊ/
business plan (n)	/'bɪznɪs ˌplæn/
buy (v)	/baɪ/
check into a hotel (v)	/ˌtʃek ɪntʊ ə həʊ'tel/
crazy (adj)	/'kreɪzi/
designer clothes (n)	/dɪˌzaɪnə 'kləʊðz/
earn (v)	/ɜːn/
generous (adj)	/'dʒenərəs/

give (n)	/gɪv/
go sightseeing (v)	/ˌgəʊ ˈsaɪtˌsiːɪŋ/
hire (v)	/haɪə/
invest (v)	/ɪnˈvest/
lend (v)	/lend/
limousine (n)	/ˈlɪməziːn/
lovely (adj)	/ˈlʌvli/
luxury (adj)	/ˈlʌkʃəri/
mean (adj)	/miːn/
owe (v)	/əʊ/
pay sth back (v)	/ˌpeɪ sʌmθɪŋ ˈbæk/
pilot (n)	/ˈpaɪlət/
pocket money (n)	/ˈpɒkɪt ˌmʌni/
present (n)	/ˈprezənt/
record (v)	/rɪˈkɔːd/
save (v)	/seɪv/
saver (n)	/ˈseɪvə/
school project (n)	/ˌskuːl ˈprɒdʒekt/
sensible (adj)	/ˈsensəbəl/
shopping trip (n)	/ˈʃɒpɪŋ trɪp/
spend (v)	/spend/
spender (n)	/ˈspendə/
suit (v)	/suːt/
wardrobe (n)	/ˈwɔːdrəʊb/

Pages 26–27

bag (n)	/bæg/
corner shop (n)	/ˈkɔːnə ʃɒp/
excited (adj)	/ɪkˈsaɪtɪd/
file (n)	/faɪl/
fitting room (n)	/ˈfɪtɪŋ ruːm/
high street (n)	/ˈhaɪ striːt/
local (adj)	/ˈləʊkəl/
look forward to sth (v)	/lʊk ˈfɔːwəd tə ˌsʌmθɪŋ/
medium (size) (adj)	/ˈmiːdiəm/
PIN (number) (n)	/pɪn/
receipt (n)	/rɪˈsiːt/
shampoo (n)	/ʃæmˈpuː/
size (n)	/saɪz/
supermarket (n)	/ˈsuːpəˌmɑːkɪt/
sweater (n)	/ˈswetə/
toothpaste (n)	/ˈtuːθpeɪst/
try sth on (v)	/ˌtraɪ sʌmθɪŋ ˈɒn/

Unit 4
Pages 28–29

A-Level (n)	/ˈeɪ ˌlevəl/
Art (n)	/ɑːt/
Biology (n)	/baɪˈɒlədʒi/
Chemistry (n)	/ˈkeməstri/
compulsory (adj)	/kəmˈpʌlsəri/
course (n)	/kɔːs/
Design and Technology (n)	/dɪˌzaɪn ən tekˈnɒlədʒi/
drop (a subject) (v)	/drɒp/
Foreign Language (n)	/ˌfɒrən ˈlæŋgwɪdʒ/
GCSE (= General Certificate of Secondary Education) (n)	/ˌdʒiː siː es ˈiː/
gap year (n)	/ˈgæp jɪə/
Geography (n)	/dʒiˈɒgrəfi/
get (good marks) (v)	/get/
high school	/ˈhaɪ skuːl/
History (n)	/ˈhɪstəri/
journalist (n)	/ˈdʒɜːnəlɪst/
lawyer (n)	/ˈlɔːjə/
Literature (n)	/ˈlɪtərətʃə/
Maths (n)	/mæθs/

Medicine (n)	/ˈmedsən/
mixed school (n)	/ˈmɪkst skuːl/
pass (an exam) (v)	/pɑːs/
Physics (n)	/ˈfɪzɪks/
private school (n)	/ˈpraɪvət skuːl/
Psychology (n)	/saɪˈkɒlədʒi/
school subject (n)	/ˌskuːl ˈsʌbdʒɪkt/
secondary school (n)	/ˈsekəndəri ˌskuːl/
single-sex school (n)	/ˌsɪŋgəl ˈseks ˌskuːl/
take (an exam) (v)	/teɪk/
useful (adj)	/ˈjuːsfəl/

Pages 30–31

accountancy (n)	/əˈkaʊntənsi/
advert (n)	/ˈædvɜːt/
application form (n)	/ˌæplɪˈkeɪʃən fɔːm/
babysitting (n)	/ˈbeɪbiˌsɪtɪŋ/
badly-paid (adj)	/ˌbædli ˈpeɪd/
career (n)	/kəˈrɪə/
company (n)	/ˈkʌmpəni/
CV (= Curriculum Vitae) (n)	/ˌsiː ˈviː/
deliver (v)	/dɪˈlɪvə/
earn money (v)	/ˌɜːn ˈmʌni/
experience (n)	/ɪkˈspɪəriəns/
farm (n)	/fɑːm/
fill in (v)	/ˌfɪl ˈɪn/
interview (n)	/ˈɪntəvjuː/
leaflet (n)	/ˈliːflət/
nightmare (n)	/ˈnaɪtmeə/
offer (v)	/ˈɒfə/
paint (n)	/peɪnt/
part-time job (n)	/ˌpɑːt taɪm ˈdʒɒb/
salary (n)	/ˈsæləri/
start work	/ˌstɑːt ˈwɜːk/
striped (adj)	/straɪpt/
unemployment (n)	/ˌʌnɪmˈplɔɪmənt/
vacancy (n)	/ˈveɪkənsi/
well-paid (adj)	/ˌwel ˈpeɪd/

Pages 32–33

accountant (n)	/əˈkaʊntənt/
au pair (n)	/əʊ ˈpeə/
career (n)	/kəˈrɪə/
cleaner (n)	/ˈkliːnə/
concentrate (v)	/ˈkɒnsəntreɪt/
creative (adj)	/kriˈeɪtɪv/
employer (n)	/ɪmˈplɔɪə/
experience (n)	/ɪkˈspɪəriəns/
glamorous (adj)	/ˈglæmərəs/
good with numbers (adj)	/ˌgʊd wɪð ˈnʌmbəz/
good with people (adj)	/ˌgʊd wɪð ˈpiːpəl/
good with your hands (adj)	/ˌgʊd wɪð jə ˈhændz/
graphic designer (n)	/ˌgræfɪk dɪˈzaɪnə/
housework (n)	/ˈhaʊswɜːk/
ironing (n)	/ˈaɪənɪŋ/
IT consultant (n)	/ˌaɪ ˈtiː kənˌsʌltənt/
joke (n)	/dʒəʊk/
look after sb (v)	/lʊk ˈɑːftə ˌsʌmbədi/
monk (n)	/mʌŋk/
nanny (n)	/ˈnæni/
qualification (n)	/ˌkwɒləfəˈkeɪʃən/
rewarding (adj)	/rɪˈwɔːdɪŋ/
salary (n)	/ˈsæləri/
sales representative (n)	/ˈseɪlz reprɪˌzentətɪv/
secure (adj)	/sɪˈkjʊə/
shy (adj)	/ʃaɪ/

Word List

social worker (n) /ˈsəʊʃəl ˌwɜːkə/
stressful (adj) /ˈstresfəl/
temporary (adj) /ˈtempərəri/
TV presenter (n) /ˌtiː ˈviː prɪˌzentə/
volunteer teacher /ˌvɒləntɪə ˈtiːtʃə/
well-paid (adj) /ˌwel ˈpeɪd/
work (long hours) (v) /wɜːk/

Unit 5
Pages 36–37
alarm clock (n) /əˈlɑːm klɒk/
amount (n) /əˈmaʊnt/
computer game (n) /kəmˈpjuːtə geɪm/
contain (v) /kənˈteɪn/
dangerous (adj) /ˈdeɪndʒərəs/
digestion (n) /daɪˈdʒestʃən/
egg (n) /eg/
energy (n) /ˈenədʒi/
exercise (n) /ˈeksəsaɪz/
fizzy (adj) /ˈfɪzi/
fresh (adj) /freʃ/
ham (n) /hæm/
healthy diet (n) /ˌhelθi ˈdaɪət/
heart (n) /hɑːt/
lose weight (v) /ˌluːz ˈweɪt/
low fat (adj) /ˌləʊ ˈfæt/
overweight (adj) /ˌəʊvəˈweɪt/
pastry (n) /ˈpeɪstri/
put on weight (v) /ˌpʊt ɒn ˈweɪt/
running shoes (n) /ˈrʌnɪŋ ʃuːz/
salt (n) /sɔːlt/
skin (n) /skɪn/
slim (adj) /slɪm/
sweet (adj) /swiːt/
toast (n) /təʊst/
warm up (v) /ˌwɔːm ˈʌp/

Pages 38–39
athlete (n) /ˈæθliːt/
bacon (n) /ˈbeɪkən/
baked potato (n) /ˌbeɪkt pəˈteɪtəʊ/
ballet dancer (n) /ˈbæleɪ ˌdɑːnsə/
banana (n) /bəˈnɑːnə/
bar (of chocolate) (n) /bɑː/
bottle (n) /ˈbɒtl/
box (n) /bɒks/
brain (n) /breɪn/
bread (n) /bred/
cabbage (n) /ˈkæbɪdʒ/
can (n) /kæn/
carton (n) /ˈkɑːtn/
cereal (n) /ˈsɪəriəl/
cheese (n) /tʃiːz/
chicken (n) /ˈtʃɪkən/
concentration (n) /ˌkɒnsənˈtreɪʃən/
cornflakes (n) /ˈkɔːnfleɪks/
cream (n) /kriːm/
dairy product /ˈdeəri ˌprɒdʌkt/
digest (v) /daɪˈdʒest/
footballer (n) /ˈfʊtbɔːlə/
glass (n) /glɑːs/
grape (n) /greɪp/
hungry (adj) /ˈhʌŋgri/
lemon (n) /ˈlemən/
lemonade (n) /ˌleməˈneɪd/
lettuce (n) /ˈletəs/

loaf (n) /ləʊf/
margarine (n) /ˌmɑːdʒəˈriːn/
milkshake (n) /ˌmɪlkˈʃeɪk/
mineral water (n) /ˈmɪnərəl ˌwɔːtə/
olive oil (n) /ˌɒlɪv ˈɔɪl/
onion (n) /ˈʌnjən/
orange juice (n) /ˈɒrɪndʒ dʒuːs/
packet (n) /ˈpækɪt/
pasta (n) /ˈpæstə/
piece (n) /piːs/
plate (n) /pleɪt/
potato (n) /pəˈteɪtəʊ/
professional (adj) /prəˈfeʃənəl/
rice (n) /raɪs/
sausage (n) /ˈsɒsɪdʒ/
soft drink (n) /ˌsɒft ˈdrɪŋk/
steak (n) /steɪk/
strawberry (n) /ˈstrɔːbəri/
sumo wrestler (n) /ˌsuːməʊ ˈreslə/
teeth (n) /tiːθ/
tomato sauce (n) /təˌmɑːtəʊ ˈsɔːs/
waistline (n) /ˈweɪstlaɪn/
wrestler (n) /ˈreslə/
yoghurt (n) /ˈjɒgət/

Pages 40–41
bedtime (n) /ˈbedtaɪm/
biscuit (n) /ˈbɪskɪt/
breakfast (n) /ˈbrekfəst/
coffee break (n) /ˈkɒfi breɪk/
cream cake (n) /ˈkriːm keɪk/
department store (n) /dɪˈpɑːtmənt stɔː/
dinner (n) /ˈdɪnə/
elevenses (n) /ɪˈlevənzɪz/
fruit juice (n) /ˈfruːt dʒuːs/
hot meal (n) /ˌhɒt ˈmiːl/
lunch (n) /lʌntʃ/
lunchtime (n) /ˈlʌntʃtaɪm/
marmalade (n) /ˈmɑːməleɪd/
national dish (n) /ˌnæʃənəl ˈdɪʃ/
packed lunch (n) /ˌpækt ˈlʌntʃ/
ready meal (n) /ˌredi ˈmiːl/
separately (adv) /ˈsepərətli/
snack (n) /snæk/
special occasion (n) /ˌspeʃəl əˈkeɪʒən/
stay (in a hotel) (v) /steɪ/
supper (n) /ˈsʌpə/
takeaway (meal) (n) /ˈteɪkəweɪ/
tasty (adj) /ˈteɪsti/

Pages 42–43
accept (v) /əkˈsept/
arrange (v) /əˈreɪndʒ/
fancy dress (n) /ˌfænsi ˈdres/
farewell party (n) /feəˈwel ˌpɑːti/
invitation (n) /ˌɪnvəˈteɪʃən/
invite (v) /ɪnˈvaɪt/
live band (n) /ˌlaɪv ˈbænd/
party (n) /ˈpɑːti/
refuse (v) /rɪˈfjuːz/
suggest (v) /səˈdʒest/

Unit 6

Pages 44–45

battle (n)	/ˈbætl/
behave badly (v)	/bɪˌheɪv ˈbædli/
behave well (v)	/bɪˌheɪv ˈwel/
break a rule (v)	/ˌbreɪk ə ˈruːl/
camp counsellor (n)	/ˌkæmp ˈkaʊnsələ/
check on sb (v)	/ˈtʃek ɒn ˌsʌmbədi/
discipline (n)	/ˈdɪsəplɪn/
discipline (v)	/ˈdɪsəplɪn/
do badly at school (v)	/ˌduː ˈbædli ət ˈskuːl/
do well at school (v)	/ˌduː ˈwel ət ˈskuːl/
get into trouble (v)	/ˌget ɪntə ˈtrʌbəl/
(not) get on with sb (v)	/ˌnɒt get ˈɒn wɪð ˌsʌmbədi/
go wrong (v)	/ˌgəʊ ˈrɒŋ/
have an argument with sb (v)	/hæv ən ˈɑːgjəmənt wɪð ˌsʌmbədi/
miss lessons (v)	/ˌmɪs ˈlesənz/
prepare a meal (v)	/prɪˌpeər ə ˈmiːl/
rest (n)	/rest/
reward (n)	/rɪˈwɔːd/
spend time with sb (v)	/ˌspend ˈtaɪm wɪð ˌsʌmbədi/
steal (v)	/stiːl/
strict (adj)	/strɪkt/
(not) take any notice (v)	/ˌnɒt teɪk ˌeni ˈnəʊtɪs/
tent (n)	/tent/
uniform (n)	/ˈjuːnəfɔːm/

Pages 46–47

bring up sb (v)	/ˌbrɪŋ ˈʌp ˌsʌmbədi/
by myself (prep)	/baɪ maɪˈself/
control (v)	/kənˈtrəʊl/
do a job (v)	/ˌduː ə ˈdʒɒb/
do homework (v)	/ˌduː ˈhəʊmwɜːk/
do nothing (v)	/ˌduː ˈnʌθɪŋ/
do the cooking (v)	/ˌduː ðə ˈkʊkɪŋ/
do the hoovering (v)	/ˌduː ðə ˈhuːvərɪŋ/
do the housework (v)	/ˌduː ðə ˈhaʊswɜːk/
do the ironing (v)	/ˌduː ði ˈaɪənɪŋ/
do the shopping (v)	/ˌduː ðə ˈʃɒpɪŋ/
do the washing-up (v)	/ˌduː ðə ˌwɒʃɪŋ ˈʌp/
easy-going (adj)	/ˌiːzi ˈgəʊɪŋ/
fair (adj)	/feə/
fed up (adj)	/ˌfed ˈʌp/
freedom (n)	/ˈfriːdəm/
guide (v)	/gaɪd/
lipstick (n)	/ˈlɪpˌstɪk/
make a bed (v)	/ˌmeɪk ə ˈbed/
make a cake (v)	/ˌmeɪk ə ˈkeɪk/
make a mess (v)	/ˌmeɪk ə ˈmes/
make a phone call (v)	/ˌmeɪk ə ˈfəʊn kɔːl/
make a sandwich (v)	/ˌmeɪk ə ˈsænwɪdʒ/
make breakfast (v)	/ˌmeɪk ˈbrekfəst/
make lunch (v)	/ˌmeɪk ˈlʌntʃ/
play time (n)	/ˈpleɪ taɪm/
punish (v)	/ˈpʌnɪʃ/
rules (n)	/ruːlz/
stay out late (v)	/ˌsteɪ aʊt ˈleɪt/
strict (adj)	/strɪkt/
tidy your room (v)	/ˌtaɪdi jə ˈruːm/
wages (n)	/ˈweɪdʒɪz/
walk around (v)	/ˌwɔːk əˈraʊnd/

Pages 48–49

according to (prep)	/əˈkɔːdɪŋ tə/
affect (v)	/əˈfekt/

army (n)	/ˈɑːmi/
banned (adj)	/bænd/
commit a crime (v)	/kəˌmɪt ə ˈkraɪm/
commit a murder (v)	/kəˌmɪt ə ˈmɜːdə/
death penalty (n)	/ˈdeθ ˌpenlti/
drop out of school (v)	/ˌdrɒp aʊt əv ˈskuːl/
go to prison (v)	/ˌgəʊ tə ˈprɪzən/
illegal (adj)	/ɪˈliːgəl/
involve (v)	/ɪnˈvɒlv/
join (v)	/dʒɔɪn/
law (n)	/lɔː/
patient (adj)	/ˈpeɪʃənt/
permission (n)	/pəˈmɪʃən/
responsibility (n)	/rɪˌspɒnsəˈbɪləti/
responsible (adj)	/rɪˈspɒnsəbəl/
take a driving test (v)	/ˌteɪk ə ˈdraɪvɪŋ test/
theoretically (adv)	/ˌθɪəˈretɪkli/
vote (v)	/vəʊt/

Unit 7

Pages 52–53

accommodation (n)	/əˌkɒməˈdeɪʃən/
activity (n)	/ækˈtɪvəti/
boat trip (n)	/ˈbəʊt trɪp/
charming (adj)	/ˈtʃɑːmɪŋ/
comfortable (adj)	/ˈkʌmftəbəl/
destination (n)	/ˌdestəˈneɪʃən/
eat out (v)	/ˌiːt ˈaʊt/
excursion (n)	/ɪkˈskɜːʃən/
fishing (n)	/ˈfɪʃɪŋ/
flight (n)	/flaɪt/
gallery (n)	/ˈgæləri/
go camping (v)	/ˌgəʊ ˈkæmpɪŋ/
go shopping (v)	/ˌgəʊ ˈʃɒpɪŋ/
go swimming (v)	/ˌgəʊ ˈswɪmɪŋ/
go to a club (v)	/ˌgəʊ tə ə ˈklʌb/
go to the beach (v)	/ˌgəʊ tə ðə ˈbiːtʃ/
go walking (v)	/ˌgəʊ ˈwɔːkɪŋ/
hang out with sb (v)	/ˌhæŋ ˈaʊt wɪð ˌsʌmbədi/
holiday (n)	/ˈhɒlədi/
holiday brochure (n)	/ˈhɒlədi ˌbrəʊʃə/
internet access (n)	/ˈɪntənet ˌækses/
island (n)	/ˈaɪlənd/
journey (n)	/ˈdʒɜːni/
keep in touch (v)	/ˌkiːp ɪn ˈtʌtʃ/
late-night shopping (n)	/ˌleɪt naɪt ˈʃɒpɪŋ/
lively (adj)	/ˈlaɪvli/
museum (n)	/mjuːˈziːəm/
nightlife (n)	/ˈnaɪtlaɪf/
paragliding (n)	/ˈpærəˌglaɪdɪŋ/
relax (v)	/rɪˈlæks/
relaxing (adj)	/rɪˈlæksɪŋ/
resort (n)	/rɪˈzɔːt/
scenery (n)	/ˈsiːnəri/
sight (n)	/saɪt/
sightseeing (n)	/ˈsaɪtˌsiːɪŋ/
sunbathing (n)	/ˈsʌnˌbeɪðɪŋ/
theme park (n)	/ˈθiːm pɑːk/
tip (n)	/tɪp/
unforgettable (adj)	/ˌʌnfəˈgetəbəl/
visit (v)	/ˈvɪzɪt/
water sports (n)	/ˈwɔːtə spɔːts/
wildlife (n)	/ˈwaɪldlaɪf/
windsurfing (n)	/ˈwɪndˌsɜːfɪŋ/
world-class (adj)	/ˌwɜːld ˈklɑːs/

Word List

Pages 54–55

airline (n)	/ˈeəlaɪn/
arrivals gate (n)	/əˈraɪvəlz ˈgeɪt/
board (v)	/bɔːd/
boarding card (n)	/ˈbɔːdɪŋ kɑːd/
check in (n)	/ˈtʃek ɪn/
check-in desk (n)	/ˈtʃek ɪn ˌdesk/
collect (v)	/kəˈlekt/
delayed (adj)	/dɪˈleɪd/
departure gate (n)	/dɪˈpɑːtʃə ˈgeɪt/
departures board (n)	/dɪˈpɑːtʃəz ˌbɔːd/
duty-free shop (n)	/ˌdjuːti ˈfriː ˌʃɒp/
fasten (v)	/ˈfɑːsən/
flight (n)	/flaɪt/
get off sth (v)	/get ˈɒf ˌsʌmθɪŋ/
go through (v)	/ˌgəʊ ˈθruː/
hand luggage (n)	/ˈhænd ˌlʌgɪdʒ/
land (v)	/lænd/
low income (n)	/ˌləʊ ˈɪŋkʌm/
luggage (n)	/ˈlʌgɪdʒ/
noise (n)	/nɔɪz/
passport control (n)	/ˈpɑːspɔːt kənˌtrəʊl/
pollution (n)	/pəˈluːʃən/
return flight (n)	/rɪˌtɜːn ˈflaɪt/
seat belt (n)	/ˈsiːt belt/
security (n)	/sɪˈkjʊərəti/
take off (v)	/ˌteɪk ˈɒf/

Pages 56–57

accommodation (n)	/əˌkɒməˈdeɪʃən/
air-conditioning (n)	/ˌeə kənˈdɪʃənɪŋ/
bite (v)	/baɪt/
blame (v)	/bleɪm/
compensation (n)	/ˌkɒmpənˈseɪʃən/
complaint (n)	/kəmˈpleɪnt/
deal with (v)	/ˈdiːl wɪð/
delayed (adj)	/dɪˈleɪd/
delicious (adj)	/dɪˈlɪʃəs/
disgusting (adj)	/dɪsˈgʌstɪŋ/
double bed (n)	/ˌdʌbəl ˈbed/
extreme (adj)	/ɪkˈstriːm/
food poisoning (n)	/ˈfuːd ˌpɔɪzənɪŋ/
genuine (adj)	/ˈdʒenjuɪn/
get sunburnt (v)	/get ˈsʌnbɜːnt/
have fun (v)	/hæv ˈfʌn/
holidaymaker (n)	/ˈhɒlədiˌmeɪkə/
hotel staff (n)	/həʊˈtel stɑːf/
lose sth (v)	/ˈluːz ˌsʌmθɪŋ/
luggage (n)	/ˈlʌgɪdʒ/
mosquito (n)	/məˈskiːtəʊ/
pregnant (adj)	/ˈpregnənt/
queue (v)	/kjuː/
relax (v)	/rɪˈlæks/
sand (n)	/sænd/
spokesman (n)	/ˈspəʊksmən/
startled (adj)	/ˈstɑːtld/
take sth seriously (v)	/ˌteɪk sʌmθɪŋ ˈsɪəriəsli/
tour operator (n)	/ˈtʊər ˌɒpəreɪtə/
traffic jam (n)	/ˈtræfɪk ˌdʒæm/
treat (n)	/triːt/
twin-bedded room (n)	/ˌtwɪn bedɪd ˈruːm/
visit (v)	/ˈvɪzɪt/
weather (n)	/ˈweðə/

Pages 58–59

amazing (adj)	/əˈmeɪzɪŋ/
book (v)	/bʊk/
coach (= bus) (n)	/kəʊtʃ/
guidebook (n)	/ˈgaɪdbʊk/
huge (adj)	/hjuːdʒ/
knee (n)	/niː/
recommend (v)	/ˌrekəˈmend/
recommendation (n)	/ˌrekəmenˈdeɪʃən/
take a guided tour (v)	/ˌteɪk ə ˌgaɪdɪd ˈtʊə/

Unit 8

Pages 60–61

achievement (n)	/əˈtʃiːvmənt/
award (n)	/əˈwɔːd/
baseball (n)	/ˈbeɪsbɔːl/
basketball (n)	/ˈbɑːskɪtbɔːl/
Congratulations! (n)	/kənˌgrætʃəˈleɪʃənz/
cricket (n)	/ˈkrɪkɪt/
cycling (n)	/ˈsaɪklɪŋ/
football (n)	/ˈfʊtbɔːl/
golf (n)	/gɒlf/
hockey (n)	/ˈhɒki/
horse (n)	/hɔːs/
long distance (adj)	/ˌlɒŋ ˈdɪstəns/
prize (n)	/praɪz/
receive (v)	/rɪˈsiːv/
ride (v)	/raɪd/
rock climbing (n)	/ˈrɒk ˌklaɪmɪŋ/
score a goal (v)	/ˌskɔːr ə ˈgəʊl/
skiing (n)	/ˈskiːɪŋ/
sporting competition (n)	/ˈspɔːtɪŋ kɒmpəˌtɪʃən/
sporting event (n)	/ˈspɔːtɪŋ ɪˌvent/
sporting hero (n)	/ˌspɔːtɪŋ ˈhɪərəʊ/
surfing (n)	/ˈsɜːfɪŋ/
table tennis (n)	/ˈteɪbəl ˌtenɪs/
take place (v)	/teɪk ˈpleɪs/
team (n)	/tiːm/
tennis (n)	/ˈtenɪs/
volleyball (n)	/ˈvɒlibɔːl/
win (v)	/wɪn/
yoga (n)	/ˈjəʊgə/

Pages 62–63

badminton (n)	/ˈbædmɪntən/
ball (n)	/bɔːl/
bat (n)	/bæt/
beat (v)	/biːt/
boot (n)	/buːt/
equipment (n)	/ɪˈkwɪpmənt/
exciting (adj)	/ɪkˈsaɪtɪŋ/
fantastic (adj)	/fænˈtæstɪk/
fast (adj)	/fɑːst/
fit (adj)	/fɪt/
fitness programme (n)	/ˈfɪtnəs ˌprəʊgræm/
glove (n)	/glʌv/
goggles (n)	/ˈgɒgəlz/
hockey stick (n)	/ˈhɒki stɪk/
ice rink (n)	/ˈaɪs rɪŋk/
indoor game (n)	/ˌɪndɔː ˈgeɪm/
kids (n)	/kɪdz/
leisure activity (n)	/ˈleʒər ækˌtɪvəti/
make progress (v)	/meɪk ˈprəʊgres/
net (n)	/net/
opponent (n)	/əˈpəʊnənt/
outdoor game (n)	/ˌaʊtdɔː ˈgeɪm/

persuade (v)	/pə'sweɪd/
player (n)	/'pleɪə/
point (n)	/pɔɪnt/
race (n)	/reɪs/
retired (adj)	/rɪ'taɪəd/
shorts (n)	/ʃɔːts/
skates (n)	/skeɪts/
sponsor (v)	/'spɒnsə/
substitute (n)	/'sʌbstɪtjuːt/
take part in (v)	/teɪk 'pɑːt ɪn/
tennis racket (n)	/'tenɪs ˌrækɪt/
train (hard) (v)	/treɪn/
trainers (= shoes) (n)	/'treɪnəz/
unfit (adj)	/ʌn'fɪt/

Pages 64–65

able-bodied (adj)	/ˌeɪbəl 'bɒdid/
athlete (n)	/'æθliːt/
chess grandmaster (n)	/ˌtʃes grændˌmɑːstə/
compete (v)	/kəm'piːt/
competition (n)	/ˌkɒmpə'tɪʃən/
disabled (adj)	/dɪs'eɪbəld/
educate (v)	/'edjʊkeɪt/
gold medal (n)	/ˌɡəʊld 'medl/
grow up (v)	/ˌɡrəʊ 'ʌp/
have an accident (v)	/hæv ən 'æksədənt/
injury (n)	/'ɪndʒəri/
inspire (v)	/ɪn'spaɪə/
ordinary (adj)	/'ɔːdənəri/
refuse (v)	/rɪ'fjuːz/
represent (a country) (v)	/ˌreprɪ'zent/
scooter (n)	/'skuːtə/
speed (n)	/spiːd/
statue (n)	/'stætʃuː/
strength (n)	/streŋθ/
take up (a sport) (v)	/ˌteɪk 'ʌp/
terrible (adj)	/'terəbəl/
top (adj)	/tɒp/
tournament (n)	/'tʊənəmənt/
tragedy (n)	/'trædʒədi/
unique (adj)	/juː'niːk/
unusual (adj)	/ʌn'juːʒuəl/
weigh (v)	/weɪ/
world champion (n)	/ˌwɜːld 'tʃæmpiən/

Unit 9
Pages 68–69

alternative (n)	/ɔːl'tɜːnətɪv/
answering machine (n)	/'ɑːnsərɪŋ məˌʃiːn/
battery (n)	/'bætəri/
charge (v)	/tʃɑːdʒ/
charger (n)	/'tʃɑːdʒə/
cooker (n)	/'kʊkə/
digital camera (n)	/ˌdɪdʒɪtl 'kæmərə/
dishwasher (n)	/'dɪʃˌwɒʃə/
dry cleaners (n)	/ˌdraɪ 'kliːnəz/
environment (n)	/ɪn'vaɪrənmənt/
flat-screen TV (n)	/ˌflæt skriːn tiː 'viː/
gadget (n)	/'ɡædʒɪt/
games console (n)	/'ɡeɪmz ˌkɒnsəʊl/
hairdryer (n)	/'heəˌdraɪə/
menu (n)	/'menjuː/
message (n)	/'mesɪdʒ/
mobile phone (n)	/ˌməʊbaɪl 'fəʊn/
MP3 player (n)	/ˌem piː 'θriː ˌpleɪə/
must-have (adj)	/ˌmʌst 'hæv/

photocopier (n)	/'fəʊtəʊˌkɒpiə/
plug in (v)	/ˌplʌg 'ɪn/
press a button (v)	/ˌpres ə 'bʌtn/
put in (v)	/pʊt 'ɪn/
recognise (v)	/'rekəgnaɪz/
record (v)	/rɪ'kɔːd/
remote control (n)	/rɪˌməʊt kən'trəʊl/
safe (adj)	/seɪf/
select (v)	/sɪ'lekt/
set the time (v)	/ˌset ðə 'taɪm/
stationer (n)	/'steɪʃənə/
switch sth off (vb)	/ˌswɪtʃ sʌmθɪŋ 'ɒf/
switch sth on (v)	/ˌswɪtʃ sʌmθɪŋ 'ɒn/
turn sth down (v)	/ˌtɜːn sʌmθɪŋ 'daʊn/
turn sth up (v)	/ˌtɜːn sʌmθɪŋ 'ʌp/

Pages 70–71

annoying (adj)	/ə'nɔɪ-ɪŋ/
ban (v)	/bæn/
boring (adj)	/'bɔːrɪŋ/
break down (v)	/ˌbreɪk 'daʊn/
CD player (n)	/ˌsiː 'diː ˌpleɪə/
cheat (v)	/tʃiːt/
debate (n)	/dɪ'beɪt/
fall asleep (v)	/ˌfɔːl ə'sliːp/
film (v)	/fɪlm/
hide (v)	/haɪd/
hopefully (adv)	/'həʊpfəli/
incident (n)	/'ɪnsədənt/
laptop (computer) (n)	/'læptɒp/
policy (n)	/'pɒləsi/
realise (v)	/'rɪəlaɪz/
rude (adj)	/ruːd/
sensible (adj)	/'sensəbəl/
smell (v)	/smel/
text sb (v)	/'tekst ˌsʌmbədi/
throw sth away (v)	/ˌθrəʊ sʌmθɪŋ ə'weɪ/
valuable (adj)	/'væljəbəl/

Pages 72–73

add up (v)	/ˌæd 'ʌp/
average (adj)	/'ævərɪdʒ/
background noise (n)	/ˌbækgraʊnd 'nɔɪz/
chairman (n)	/'tʃeəmən/
chat (v)	/tʃæt/
consume (v)	/kən'sjuːm/
fixed (adj)	/fɪkst/
generation (n)	/ˌdʒenə'reɪʃən/
increase (v)	/ɪn'kriːs/
multi-tasking (n)	/ˌmʌlti 'tɑːskɪŋ/
pessimistic (adj)	/ˌpesə'mɪstɪk/
radio set (n)	/'reɪdiəʊ set/
search for sth (v)	/'sɜːtʃ fə ˌsʌmθɪŋ/
select (v)	/sə'lekt/
socialise (v)	/'səʊʃəlaɪz/
toy (n)	/tɔɪ/
traditional (adj)	/trə'dɪʃənəl/
TV channel (n)	/ˌtiː 'viː ˌtʃænl/
worldwide (adj)	/ˌwɜːld'waɪd/

Pages 74–75

camcorder (n)	/'kæmˌkɔːdə/
exactly (adv)	/ɪg'zæktli/
exchange sth (v)	/ɪks'tʃeɪndʒ ˌsʌmθɪŋ/
expect (v)	/ɪk'spekt/
headphones (n)	/'hedfəʊnz/

Word List

instruction book (n) /ɪnˈstrʌkʃən bʊk/
loud (adj) /laʊd/
manager (n) /ˈmænɪdʒə/
manufacturer (n) /ˌmænjəˈfæktʃərə/
nothing (pron) /ˈnʌθɪŋ/
printer (n) /ˈprɪntə/
properly (adv) /ˈprɒpəli/
receipt (n) /rɪˈsiːt/
recharge (v) /ˌriːˈtʃɑːdʒ/
refund (n) /ˈriːfʌnd/
scratched (adj) /skrætʃt/
stain (n) /steɪn/
wire (n) /waɪə/

Unit 10
Pages 76–77
break away (v) /ˌbreɪk əˈweɪ/
cliff (n) /klɪf/
coast (n) /kəʊst/
continent (n) /ˈkɒntɪnənt/
cool (adj) /kuːl/
crack (n) /kræk/
desert (n) /ˈdezət/
Earth (n) /ɜːθ/
extremely (adv) /ɪkˈstriːmli/
fair (n) /feə/
farm (v) /fɑːm/
field (n) /fiːld/
forest (n) /ˈfɒrəst/
freeze (v) /friːz/
frightened (adj) /ˈfraɪtnd/
island (n) /ˈaɪlənd/
jungle (n) /ˈdʒʌŋgəl/
lake (n) /leɪk/
mountain range (n) /ˈmaʊntən ˌreɪndʒ/
ocean (n) /ˈəʊʃən/
pavement (n) /ˈpeɪvmənt/
picnic (n) /ˈpɪknɪk/
river (n) /ˈrɪvə/
sandy (adj) /ˈsændi/
sea (n) /siː/
separate (adj) /ˈsepərət/
separate (v) /ˈsepəreɪt/
surface (n) /ˈsɜːfəs/
tiny (adj) /ˈtaɪni/
volcano (n) /vɒlˈkeɪnəʊ/
wave (n) /weɪv/

Pages 78–79
climate (n) /ˈklaɪmət/
damage (v) /ˈdæmɪdʒ/
decrease (v) /dɪˈkriːs/
drought (n) /draʊt/
extinct (adj) /ɪkˈstɪŋkt/
fear (n) /fɪə/
feed (v) /fiːd/
flood (n) /flʌd/
global warming (n) /ˌgləʊbəl ˈwɔːmɪŋ/
hurricane (n) /ˈhʌrɪkən/
ice (n) /aɪs/
insurance (n) /ɪnˈʃʊərəns/
malaria (n) /məˈleəriə/
melt (v) /melt/
melting (adj) /ˈmeltɪŋ/
polar bear (n) /ˌpəʊlə ˈbeə/
record temperature (n) /ˌrekɔːd ˈtemprətʃə/

refugee (n) /ˌrefjʊˈdʒiː/
return (v) /rɪˈtɜːn/
rise (v) /raɪz/
rising (adj) /ˈraɪzɪŋ/
salty (adj) /ˈsɔːlti/
sea level (n) /ˈsiː ˌlevəl/
sick (adj) /sɪk/
species (n) /ˈspiːʃiːz/
suffer (v) /ˈsʌfə/
typical (adj) /ˈtɪpɪkəl/
worrying (adj) /ˈwʌri-ɪŋ/

Pages 80–81
active (adj) /ˈæktɪv/
ash (n) /æʃ/
atomic bomb (n) /əˌtɒmɪk ˈbɒm/
bang (n) /bæŋ/
cloud (n) /klaʊd/
column (of smoke) (n) /ˈkɒləm/
crash (n) /kræʃ/
desk (n) /desk/
destroy (v) /dɪˈstrɔɪ/
destruction (n) /dɪˈstrʌkʃən/
diary extract (n) /ˈdaɪəri ˌekstrækt/
disappear (v) /ˌdɪsəˈpɪə/
disappearance (n) /ˌdɪsəˈpɪərəns/
dust (n) /dʌst/
enormous (adj) /ɪˈnɔːməs/
erupt (v) /ɪˈrʌpt/
explain (v) /ɪkˈspleɪn/
explanation (n) /ˌekspləˈneɪʃən/
explode (v) /ɪkˈspləʊd/
explosion (n) /ɪkˈspləʊʒən/
fear (n) /fɪə/
fortunately (adv) /ˈfɔːtʃənətli/
gunfire (n) /ˈgʌnfaɪə/
incredible (adj) /ɪnˈkredəbəl/
inspiration (n) /ˌɪnspəˈreɪʃən/
island (n) /ˈaɪlənd/
jump (v) /dʒʌmp/
loud (adj) /laʊd/
noise (n) /nɔɪz/
police officer (n) /pəˈliːs ˌɒfɪsə/
pour (v) /pɔː/
sail (v) /seɪl/
sailing ship (n) /ˈseɪlɪŋ ʃɪp/
scream (n) /skriːm/
seashore (n) /ˈsiːʃɔː/
shake (v) /ʃeɪk/
sign (n) /saɪn/
sky (n) /skaɪ/
smoke (n) /sməʊk/
suddenly (adv) /ˈsʌdnli/
turn (v) /tɜːn/
unfortunate (adj) /ʌnˈfɔːtʃənət/
uninhabited (adj) /ˌʌnɪnˈhæbɪtɪd/
volcanic eruption (n) /vɒlˌkænɪk ɪˈrʌpʃən/

Unit 11
Pages 84–85
actor (n) /ˈæktə/
add (v) /æd/
budget (n) /ˈbʌdʒɪt/
choose (v) /tʃuːz/
decide (v) /dɪˈsaɪd/
dialogue (n) /ˈdaɪəlɒg/

director (n)	/dəˈrektə/
dubbed (adj)	/dʌbd/
edit (v)	/ˈedɪt/
editing (n)	/ˈedɪtɪŋ/
editor (n)	/ˈedɪtə/
fantasy (n)	/ˈfæntəsi/
film (v)	/fɪlm/
film studio (n)	/ˈfɪlm ˌstjuːdiəʊ/
historical drama (n)	/hɪˌstɒrɪkəl ˈdrɑːmə/
horror movie (n)	/ˈhɒrə ˌmuːvi/
on location (n)	/ɒn ləʊˈkeɪʃən/
plan (v)	/plæn/
print (v)	/prɪnt/
producer (n)	/prəˈdjuːsə/
publicity (n)	/pʌˈblɪsəti/
romantic comedy (n)	/rəʊˌmæntɪk ˈkɒmədi/
scene (n)	/siːn/
science fiction (n)	/ˌsaɪəns ˈfɪkʃən/
script (n)	/skrɪpt/
special effect (n)	/ˌspeʃəl ɪˈfekt/
subtitled (adj)	/ˈsʌbˌtaɪtld/
thriller (n)	/ˈθrɪlə/

Pages 86–87

advert (n)	/ˈædvɜːt/
broadcast (n)	/ˈbrɔːdkɑːst/
cartoon (n)	/kɑːˈtuːn/
comedy series (n)	/ˈkɒmədi ˌsɪəriːz/
cookery programme (n)	/ˈkʊkəri ˌprəʊɡræm/
documentary (n)	/ˌdɒkjəˈmentəri/
episode (n)	/ˈepɪsəʊd/
ingredient (n)	/ɪnˈɡriːdiənt/
longest-running (adj)	/ˌlɒŋɡəst ˈrʌnɪŋ/
news (n)	/njuːz/
pepper (n)	/ˈpepə/
quiz show (n)	/ˈkwɪz ʃəʊ/
reality show (n)	/riˈæləti ʃəʊ/
soap opera (n)	/ˈsəʊp ˌɒpərə/
sports programme (n)	/ˈspɔːts ˌprəʊɡræm/
television series (n)	/ˈteləvɪʒən ˌsɪəriːz/
tuna (n)	/ˈtjuːnə/
version (n)	/ˈvɜːʃən/
viewer (n)	/ˈvjuːə/
weather forecast (n)	/ˈweðə ˌfɔːkɑːst/

Pages 88–89

attractive (adj)	/əˈtræktɪv/
be made into (a film) (v)	/bi ˈmeɪd ɪntʊ/
be released (v)	/bi rɪˈliːst/
be set in (v)	/bi ˈset ɪn/
be somebody's fault (v)	/bi ˌsʌmbədiz ˈfɔːlt/
bits (n)	/bɪts/
blanket (n)	/ˈblæŋkɪt/
by mistake (prep)	/baɪ mɪˈsteɪk/
character (n)	/ˈkærɪktə/
comic (n)	/ˈkɒmɪk/
duck (n)	/dʌk/
forgive (v)	/fəˈɡɪv/
guy (n)	/ɡaɪ/
have a bad influence on (v)	/hæv ə ˌbæd ˈɪnfluəns ɒn/
keep away from (v)	/ˌkiːp əˈweɪ frəm/
lie (n)	/laɪ/
magazine (n)	/ˌmæɡəˈziːn/
nervous (adj)	/ˈnɜːvəs/
newspaper (n)	/ˈnjuːsˌpeɪpə/
notice (v)	/ˈnəʊtɪs/

novel (n)	/ˈnɒvəl/
park-keeper (n)	/ˈpɑːk ˌkiːpə/
path (n)	/pɑːθ/
poetry (n)	/ˈpəʊətri/
(in the) present day (n)	/ɪn ðə ˌprezənt ˈdeɪ/
realistic (adj)	/ˌrɪəˈlɪstɪk/
responsibility (n)	/rɪˌspɒnsəˈbɪləti/
rubbish (n)	/ˈrʌbɪʃ/
short story (n)	/ˌʃɔːt ˈstɔːri/
single mother (n)	/ˌsɪŋɡəl ˈmʌðə/
sink (v)	/sɪŋk/
star (v)	/stɑː/
suggest (v)	/səˈdʒest/
sympathetic (adj)	/ˌsɪmpəˈθetɪk/
title (n)	/ˈtaɪtl/
upset (v)	/ʌpˈset/
weblog (n)	/ˈweblɒɡ/

Pages 90–91

abbreviation (n)	/əˌbriːviˈeɪʃən/
cafeteria (n)	/ˌkæfəˈtɪəriə/
call back (v)	/ˌkɔːl ˈbæk/
call (v)	/ˈkɔːl/
case (= small bag) (n)	/keɪs/
charge (v)	/tʃɑːdʒ/
concert (n)	/ˈkɒnsət/
excellent condition (n)	/ˌeksələnt kənˈdɪʃən/
experienced (adj)	/ɪkˈspɪəriənst/
notice (n)	/ˈnəʊtɪs/
notice board (n)	/ˈnəʊtɪs bɔːd/
recognise (v)	/ˈrekəɡnaɪz/
rock band (n)	/ˈrɒk bænd/
spotted (adj)	/ˈspɒtɪd/
tone (n)	/təʊn/

Unit 12
Pages 92–93

attack sb (v)	/əˈtæk ˌsʌmbədi/
break into (v)	/ˈbreɪk ɪntə/
burglary (n)	/ˈbɜːɡləri/
cheat (v)	/tʃiːt/
damage (v)	/ˈdæmɪdʒ/
download (v)	/ˌdaʊnˈləʊd/
drop (v)	/drɒp/
fake (adj)	/feɪk/
honest (adj)	/ˈɒnəst/
ID (identification) (n)	/ˌaɪ ˈdiː/
illegal (adj)	/ɪˈliːɡəl/
jewellery (n)	/ˈdʒuːəlri/
litter (n)	/ˈlɪtə/
play truant (v)	/ˌpleɪ ˈtruːənt/
risky (adj)	/ˈrɪski/
rob (v)	/rɒb/
robbery (n)	/ˈrɒbəri/
shoplifting (n)	/ˈʃɒpˌlɪftɪŋ/
speeding (n)	/ˈspiːdɪŋ/
steal (v)	/stiːl/
vandalism (n)	/ˈvændəlɪzəm/
wallet (n)	/ˈwɒlət/

Pages 94–95

accidentally (adv)	/ˌæksəˈdentli/
advise (v)	/ədˈvaɪz/
annoyed (adj)	/əˈnɔɪd/
annoying (adj)	/əˈnɔɪɪŋ/
arrest (v)	/əˈrest/

Word List

bored (adj)	/bɔːd/
boring (adj)	/ˈbɔːrɪŋ/
burgle (v)	/ˈbɜːgəl/
disappointed (adj)	/ˌdɪsəˈpɔɪntɪd/
disappointing (adj)	/ˌdɪsəˈpɔɪntɪŋ/
embarrassed (adj)	/ɪmˈbærəst/
embarrassing (adj)	/ɪmˈbærəsɪŋ/
fall over (v)	/ˌfɔːl ˈəʊvə/
frightened (adj)	/ˈfraɪtnd/
frightening (adj)	/ˈfraɪtn-ɪŋ/
frustrated (adj)	/frʌˈstreɪtɪd/
frustrating (adj)	/frʌˈstreɪtɪŋ/
grocery store (n)	/ˈgrəʊsəri stɔː/
hand over (v)	/ˌhænd ˈəʊvə/
interested (adj)	/ˈɪntrəstɪd/
interesting (adj)	/ˈɪntrəstɪŋ/
order (v)	/ˈɔːdə/
pleased (adj)	/pliːzd/
pleasing (adj)	/ˈpliːzɪŋ/
stab (v)	/stæb/
surprised (adj)	/səˈpraɪzd/
surprising (adj)	/səˈpraɪzɪŋ/
terrified (adj)	/ˈterəfaɪd/
terrifying (adj)	/ˈterəfaɪ-ɪŋ/
worried (adj)	/ˈwʌrid/
worrying (adj)	/ˈwʌri-ɪŋ/

Pages 96–97

ban (v)	/bæn/
be worth (v)	/bi ˈwɜːθ/
blame (v)	/bleɪm/
close sth (v)	/ˈkləʊz ˌsʌmθɪŋ/
commit a crime (v)	/kəˌmɪt ə ˈkraɪm/
cover sth (v)	/ˈkʌvə ˌsʌmθɪŋ/
equipment (n)	/ɪˈkwɪpmənt/
fear (n)	/fɪə/
get hurt (v)	/get ˈhɜːt/
hood (n)	/hʊd/
hoodie (n)	/ˈhʊdi/
increase (v)	/ɪnˈkriːs/
innocent (adj)	/ˈɪnəsənt/
iPod (n)	/ˈaɪpɒd/
judge (v)	/dʒʌdʒ/
leaflet (n)	/ˈliːflət/
likely (adj)	/ˈlaɪkli/
look around (v)	/ˌlʊk əˈraʊnd/
pensioner (n)	/ˈpenʃənə/
possession (n)	/pəˈzeʃən/
protect (v)	/prəˈtekt/
report (v)	/rɪˈpɔːt/
rights (n)	/raɪts/
rise (n)	/raɪz/
statistics (n)	/stəˈtɪstɪks/
threatening (adj)	/ˈθretn-ɪŋ/
valuable (adj)	/ˈvæljəbəl/
victim (n)	/ˈvɪktɪm/
violence (n)	/ˈvaɪələns/

Verb forms

Verbs + gerunds (-*ing*)

enjoy	I enjoy swimming.
finish	Have you finished eating your breakfast?
hate	I hate sitting at a desk all day.
like	I like having a snack late at night.
love	I love working with animals.
(don't) mind	I don't mind getting up early.
miss	I miss seeing my friends when I'm on holiday.
spend (time)	He spends hours texting his friends.
(can't) stand	I can't stand sitting in front of a computer all day.
***start**	She started playing volleyball when she was ten.
stop	Please stop looking at me.

Verbs + infinitive

agree to	We agreed to stay at home.
decide to	She decided to go to the cinema.
expect to	Do you expect to arrive early?
forget to	I forgot to email my mother.
hope to	We hope to go to Prague next year.
intend to	I intend to work on a farm next summer.
learn to	I'm learning to swim.
need to	I need to go home early today.
offer to	She offered to take me to the train station.
plan to	He's planning to travel to South America.
promise to	They promised to come to my birthday party.
remember to	Remember to take your gloves. It's cold this morning.
***start to**	She started to play volleyball when she was ten.
try to	I'm trying to start a new business.
want to	I want to buy a new car.
would like	I'd like to save more money this year.
would love	I'd love to visit Paris some day.

* **Start** can be used with both the gerund and the infinitive and has the same meaning.

Activities

Unit 3, page 21, exercises 10 and 12

Unit 12, page 93, exercise 9

How honest are you?

21–24 points: You are an extremely honest person but be careful you don't upset people with your opinions.

15–20 points: You are generally honest.

9–14 points: Maybe you are getting into bad habits?

0–8 pointes: Oh dear, honesty is not your strong point, is it?

Student B

Unit 2, page 13, exercise 7

Put the verbs in the correct forms. Use the irregular verb list on the back cover to help you.

Che Guevara

1 He _____ (be) a famous revolutionary in South America in the 1960s. After he _____ (die) his photograph _____ (become) famous all over the world.

2 He _____ (be) born in Rosario in Argentina on 14 June 1928.

3 He _____ (come) from a rich family and _____ (have) a happy childhood.

4 He _____ (go) to university and _____ (study) to be a doctor.

5 He _____ (get) married twice and _____ (have) five children.

6 The Bolivian army _____ (kill) him in 1967.

Unit 4, page 33, exercise 9

Martin

- eighteen years old
- very good English
- can't cook but wants to learn – sometimes helps his mother with the cleaning
- lots of experience with children (three younger brothers and often babysits for friends)
- enjoys football, basketball and tennis (he teaches children to play tennis)
- good sense of humour!

Mini Workbook, page 102, exercise 4

The sentences are about the American singer, Elvis Presley.